WRECKED

WRECKED

HOW THE AMERICAN AUTOMOBILE
INDUSTRY DESTROYED ITS
CAPACITY TO COMPETE

Joshua Murray and Michael Schwartz

Russell Sage Foundation NEW YORK

LIBRARY OF CONGRESS CATALOGING-IN-PUBLICATION DATA

Names: Murray, Joshua (Sociologist), author. | Schwartz, Michael, 1942– author.
Title: Wrecked : how the American automobile industry destroyed its capacity to compete / Joshua Murray and Michael Schwartz.
Description: New York : Russell Sage Foundation, [2019] | Includes bibliographical references and index.
Identifiers: LCCN 2018058890 (print) | LCCN 2019001438 (ebook) | ISBN 9781610448871 (ebook) | ISBN 9780871548207 (pbk. : alk. paper)
Subjects: LCSH: Automobile industry and trade—United States. | Automobile industry and trade—Japan. | Competition, International.
Classification: LCC HD9710.U52 (ebook) | LCC HD9710.U52 M79 2019 (print) | DDC 338.4/76292220973—dc23

LC record available at https://lccn.loc.gov/2018058890

Text design by Matthew T. Avery.

RUSSELL SAGE FOUNDATION
112 East 64th Street, New York, New York 10065
10 9 8 7 6 5 4 3 2 1

To my wife, N. Michelle Murray, without whose support I would never have finished this project, and to my kids, Sophia and John
—Joshua Murray

To my grandchildren, Mizel, Judah, Lila, Walter, Johanna, and Mathias
—Michael Schwartz

CONTENTS

LIST OF ILLUSTRATIONS

Figures

Tables

ABOUT THE AUTHORS

JOSHUA MURRAY is assistant professor in the Department of Sociology at Vanderbilt University.

MICHAEL SCHWARTZ is Distinguished Teaching Professor, Emeritus, State University of New York.

ACKNOWLEDGMENTS

This book and the larger project of which it is a part have a long and checkered history. Long, because the first stirrings of this research date back to the 1960s, when so many young people, and especially black students in the South, began excavating and reviving the history of struggle against all forms of oppression in order to challenge the injustices of the moment. Checkered, because that initial burst of hard-won analytic insight waited for other analytic and evidential threads to evolve into parallel or connected scholarship, with this book becoming the composed integration of these many threads and with debts owed to many clusters of scholars, activists, and scholar-activists who were separated by time, geography, and ideological distance. We therefore start by thanking that 1960s generation for proving that W. E. B. Du Bois was right in asserting that all social structures—even those most invulnerably oppressive—are constructed by people and therefore can be deconstructed by those on the wrong side of privilege. They inspired the cluster of pioneer social movement scholars who revived the Du Boisian tradition of undertaking research that would provide tools for the agents of social justice. We specifically thank, among many, many others, a few who wrote down some of what they had learned, including Steven Buechler, Stokely Carmichael, James Foreman, Alan Gilbert, Charles Hamilton, Sarah Mahler, Doug McAdam, Aldon Morris, Shuva Paul, Milagros Pena, Chester Rash, Naomi Rosenthal, Edward Royce, Charles Tilly, Kwame Ture, and Mayer Zald.

The 1960s also produced a new generation of labor activists, scholars, and activist-scholars who accessed the wisdom of the 1930s labor struggles and worked to understand how and when workers in factories were agents of economic development and social change. From that burst of activism, evidence, and insight, we realized how much we could learn by unpacking the dynamics of the Detroit social economy. We thank, among many others, Steven De Canio, Dan Clawson, Mary Ann Clawson, Sandor Fuchs, Arthur Goldberg, Jackie Goldberg, Michael Kogan, Wally Linder, Wanda Mallen, James Prickett, Margie Prickett, and Paula Shatkin.

Far from the centers of social protest, a motley crew of aspiring scholars had gathered around Harrison White, attempting to absorb, apply, and extend his insights into how networks were foundational to social systems, tying people into collectivities and organizations into social structures. Their thought and work provided the foundation for understanding the remarkable network structure that became the auto industry in Detroit. For this enduring contribution we thank, among many others, Edna Bonacich, Phil Bonacich, Peter Evans, Mark Granovetter, Rowan Ireland, Joel Levine, James Loewen, Bryan Sherman, Pat Steinhoff, Michael Weinstein, Barry Wellman, and Harrison White.

And when the new economic sociology used network analysis to understand the myriad ways that social networks altered and nullified the operations of economic markets, it pointed us toward understanding both the robust resilience of early Detroit and its ossified post–World War II structure. For this indelible contribution we thank, among many others, Mitchell Abolafia, James Bearden, Peter Brantley, Monique Centrone, Kevin Delaney, Rick Eckstein, Peter Freitag, Davita Silfen Glasberg, Robert Gogel, Carolyn Hendricks, Tom Koenig, Hyman Korman, Peter Mariolis, Patrick McGuire, Beth Mintz, Mark Mizruchi, Georgina Murray, Donald Palmer, David Roelfs, Frank Romo, Anna Sher, Linda Brewster Stearns, Takuyoshi Takada, and Brian Uzzi.

In the meantime, an army of scholars and activists took up the challenge of understanding that the global political economy conditioned both political and economic trajectories. This work insured that we would not lose track of the evolving trialectic among the auto industry, the U.S. government, and globalized capitalism. For alerting and educating us to these dynamics we thank Laura Anker, G. William Domhoff, Donna Di Donato, David Gersh, Jeffrey Goodwin, Richard

Lachmann, Prita Lal, Pablo Lapegna, Matthew Mahler, Michael Mc-Carthy, Jeffrey Paige, Richard Ratcliff, Peter Seybold, Michael Useem, J. Allen Whitt, and Maurice Zeitlin.

And, then again, when industrial decline became a national political-economic issue, a new generation of scholars and activists sought to apply the accumulated insights of the post–Civil Rights generations. Our work on the auto industry was built on the evidential and analytic foundations constructed by, among many others, Barry Bluestone, Peter Brantley, Caroline Childress, Hyman Korman, Jung-Kyu Lee, Ira Magaziner, Robert Reich, Frank Romo, Charlene Seifert, Glenn Yago, and Sen Yuan-Wu.

And finally, we owe thanks to a multitude of scholars, activists, friends, and families who have read, discussed, criticized, and contributed to this text in direct and indirect ways. We thank, among many, many others, Afife Idil Akin, Florencia Arancibia, Tarun Banerjee, Vivek Chibber, Carlos Encina, Louis Esparza, Gabriela Gonzalez-Vaillant, Emily Bartlett Hines, Carol Horwitz, Neica Michelle Murray, Kenneth Pierce, Fernanda Page Poma, Michael Restivo, Sasha Rodriguez, Hwaji Shin Tyson Smith, Marina Sitrin, Juhi Tyagi, and Kevin Young.

Lastly and mostly, this is our final shout-out to Suzanne Nichols, the irresistible force at Russell Sage. There were many times when she was the only person unwilling to give up on this book and this project, and she simply would not let it die. She has not only vetted every draft and innumerable fragments, but returned them with comments, directions, and inspiration. She simultaneously kept us moving along with encouragement and detailed instructions while also refusing to accept any text that did not live up to the project's promise.

INTRODUCTION

In November 2008, with their companies on the verge of bankruptcy, the CEOs of the Big Three U.S. automakers—General Motors (GM), Ford, and Chrysler—flew to Washington to ask the U.S. Congress for a $25 billion loan; in December, they were back again asking for more.[1] Ultimately, the federal government provided over $50 billion in funds to GM and Chrysler and helped restructure both companies through Chapter 11 bankruptcies.[2] GM's filing was the largest industrial bankruptcy in U.S. history.[3] The bankruptcy of two of the Big Three automakers and the need to have the entire U.S. auto manufacturing sector bailed out by the federal government marked a precipitous decline from the industry's peak in the 1950s and '60s.[4]

Just about a half-century before, in 1955, General Motors became the first corporation in history with profits that exceeded $1 billion, and the auto industry as a whole was the largest in the nation. As a direct outcome of auto success, cities dependent on the industry also flourished. For instance, in 1960, Detroit's 1.5 million residents had the highest per capita income among the country's big cities, and the 200,000 residents of Flint, Michigan, had the highest per capita income among the world's medium-size cities.[5] Mirroring the decline of their industries, these cities have now also nearly collapsed, losing most of their population and their wealth.[6]

So, what happened? How did the largest, most prosperous industry in the richest, most powerful country in human history crash and burn? In the December congressional hearing, GM CEO Richard Wagoner explained where he thought the blame for the Big Three's struggles lay: "What exposes us to failure now is not our product lineup,

Figure I.1 *Big Three Domestic Market Share, 1965–2015*

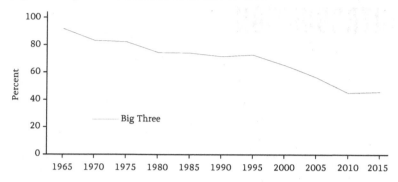

Source: Authors' calculations using WardsAuto data.

or our business plan, or our long-term strategy. What exposes us to failure now is the global financial crisis."[7]

On the one hand, the global financial crisis was obviously a key catalyst leading to the auto crisis. Widespread panic over bank failures led consumer credit markets to tighten, making it more difficult for people to get loans to buy vehicles. The result was an industry-wide crash and an almost thirty-year low for sales of new cars.[8] The impact of the crisis is illustrated well by General Motors: the company lost $82 billion between 2004 and 2008, over half of which was lost in 2007 and 2008.[9] On the other hand, the Big Three U.S. automakers had been steadily losing domestic market share over the past half-century. Figure I.1 shows the consistency of the decline: the three automakers controlled a collective 90 percent of the market in 1965, but only 45 percent by 2015.

In addition, there were major signs of dysfunction in the years preceding the economic crisis. For example, in 2005, GM lost $850 million in the first quarter alone, its stock dropped $4.71 in a single day, its earnings were 80 percent below projections for the fiscal year, and cash flow went from $2 billion to negative $2 billion.[10] In 2006, a feature story in *Fortune* titled "The Tragedy of General Motors" argued that the evidence pointed, with increasing certitude, to bankruptcy.[11] In other words, the economic crash in 2007–2008 may have poured gasoline on the fire, but the Big Three had been slowly burning for years, and their flammability was the result of factors that had been in place for decades.

The Received Wisdom

Aside from the Big Three leadership's self-serving explanation that left them blameless, analysts of the auto industry have posited three main explanations for the decline of the U.S. auto industry: (1) industrial maturity, (2) the culture of management at the Big Three, and (3) the "culture" of U.S. autoworkers, which is often a nice way of saying "greedy unions."[12]

PRODUCT LIFE CYCLE THEORY

Industrial maturity as an explanation for the decline of the U.S. auto industry is rooted in product life cycle theory, which sees the innovativeness of an industry, how producers compete, and the geographic location of production as natural consequences of the way market forces shape the development of a product over its life course.[13] That is, when a new product is introduced, the demand for that product is local, so production also remains local. As demand for the product grows, producers innovate to compete for a share of this growing demand. Eventually, paradigmatic technical innovations are exhausted, and the companies that had been most successful at innovating consolidate a sectoral oligopoly. At this point, the product is well known and in high demand, but companies are unable to increase profit rates through innovation, so they disperse production geographically to meet increased demand away from the place where the product was invented.[14] At this point, the product has reached maturity. Eventually, product expansion will reach its limit and the decline stage of the product life cycle will begin; at that stage, the only profit is in producing the standardized product cheaply. Since innovation in general is exhausted at this point in the life cycle, the only place to cut costs is labor. This is another place where market forces directly influence the product life cycle, as wages, and thus labor costs, are the result of the relative scarcity of labor (that is, the tightness of the labor market). Of course, the nature of the labor market is itself a result of the reciprocal relationship between government regulation and actions by unions and business. During this stage, production is relocated to areas with weak unions and lower government regulation, and thus cheaper labor. Often, foreign companies with the conditions for cheaper labor will make the product and export back to the country that invented it.

On the surface, product life cycle theory seems to perfectly explain the decline of the U.S. auto industry: from introduction of a new product made entirely in the southern Michigan region where it was invented, through the incredibly innovative growth stage ending right before the Great Depression, to postwar maturity with standardization of the auto manufacturing process and expansion across the United States and internationally, to the decline stage where the product was made by the Japanese in their U.S. transplants, using cheaper non-union labor, and sold to the United States. The seemingly perfect fit of theory to case led the Abernathy group at MIT to this conclusion: "So if in Detroit there is wringing of hands or gnashing of teeth, such lamentation is as useless as it is irrelevant. Neither in Lear's age nor our own has anyone discovered an effective remedy for the inexorable cycles of nature."[15]

The problem for the product life cycle narrative, however, is in the details. The theory is built on the claim that maturity comes when innovation is exhausted, which leads to geographic expansion and competition based on reduction of costs, which leads to production moving to countries where labor is cheaper. As we will demonstrate, however, Japanese automakers did not take market share from the United States primarily through labor cost advantage. Rather, their advantage lay in product and process innovation. In fact, Japanese automakers transplanted some production to the United States and used American workers. In addition, Japanese and European automakers have been in production for longer than the United States was before their industry reached maturity, yet the Japanese and European product is neither mature nor in decline, suggesting that neither is an inevitable part of a life cycle. As we will also demonstrate, in the United States the decline of innovation followed geographic expansion of production, not the other way around.

Although many of our challenges to product life cycle theory are not obvious and require significant evidence and explanation, all industry analysts have observed that the Japanese auto industry is highly innovative. Since this observation alone challenges the industrial-maturity orthodoxy, analysts have seen it as a puzzle to explain away. The dominant explanation focuses on cultural differences—between U.S. and Japanese management, and between U.S. and Japanese workers.

CULTURE: MANAGEMENT

The culture-of-management argument was first made in the 1970s and associated the virtues of the Japanese system with Japanese cultural practices. An exemplar of this type of analysis is Peter Drucker's 1971 piece in the *Harvard Business Review*. Drucker recommends that American management learn from Japanese management, but he also identifies the difference through culture, arguing that the Japanese apply "to the problems of an industrial society and economy the values and the habits developed far earlier by the retainers of the Japanese clan, by the Zen priests in their monasteries, and by the calligraphers and painters of the great 'schools' of Japanese art."[16] Today the culture-of-management argument focuses on American corporate culture instead of the uniqueness of Japanese culture. Yet, when analysts explain the decline of the U.S. auto industry as the result of a risk-averse management that prefers stability to change, or a management culture defined by arrogance and inattention to detail, the implication is that the Japanese are humble, innovative risk-takers who pay great attention to detail.[17] That is, in order for these cultural traits to explain the loss of market share by U.S. auto, they cannot be shared with Japanese management. Whatever factors are supposed to explain the loss of market share by the Big Three to the Japanese auto industry cannot be shared between the two groups. Hence, the modern cultural argument is not that different from the 1970s version—the innovativeness of Japanese auto is inevitable, as it is part of their culture, while the lack of innovation in the United States is equally inevitable and cultural.

The problem with the culture-of-management argument is that it implies that innovation is a choice and that the choice is informed by culture, assigning causal primacy to culture in explaining material reality. We will demonstrate that innovation is determined by the structural properties of the production system, and that the culture of management develops as a reaction to the material reality created by these structures. The smoking gun here is that the flexible production system that facilitates Japanese innovation was adapted from a similar production structure used in the United States before World War II. During the period when U.S. automakers used this system, their rates of innovation were extremely high and analysts described U.S. management culture as centrally valuing innovation and change.[18] Only once this production system was abandoned in the United States did the rates of innovation fall, and once innovation slowed, analysts began noting the "risk-averse" culture of U.S. auto management.

There is room in the model we present for the culture of management's focus on agency. The choice does not pertain directly, however, to innovation. Rather, management has agency over how to structure production, and this choice has consequences for innovation. That said, we do not see cultural differences as a primary explanatory factor in the differing decisions regarding production structure. We will demonstrate that both the U.S. and Japanese automakers' choices regarding production structure were the result of the interaction of class conflict, contingent events, and historical path dependency.

CULTURE: WORKERS

Company culture, however, is not the only factor used to explain the different rates of innovation in the modern Japanese and U.S. auto industries. Union culture in the United States is also targeted as a culprit hindering the competitiveness of U.S. industry. The basic narrative is that the culture of the United Auto Workers (UAW) and its rank-and-file members is shaped by conflict. Through union negotiations, autoworkers seek to do the bare minimum required by their contracts, demand higher and higher wages and benefits, and refuse to compromise on work rules. These factors all supposedly inhibit innovation.[19] As an explanation for the decline of the U.S. auto industry, the narrative of the greedy and lazy worker rests on the assumption that labor costs in Japan and Europe were dramatically lower than those in the United States, giving the imports a price advantage that allowed them to penetrate the U.S. market in the late 1960s and threaten the viability of the U.S. industry. In this narrative, the key moment becomes the UAW's successful insistence—when the imports started arriving—on maintaining its unsurpassed wage package. By the 1970s, this intransigence led, the narrative goes, to the forced migration of the industry to locations with cheaper labor costs—first the non-union American South, then across the border to Mexico.

Like product life cycle theory and the culture-of-management argument, worker culture as the cause of industrial decline falls apart upon close examination. First, the job migration supposedly triggered by foreign competitors using cheaper labor began in 1947, twenty years before the imports arrived. By 1962 (when imports were only 5 percent), 134,000 manufacturing jobs and 10 percent of the population had already been lost in Detroit.[20] Second, as we demonstrate later in the book, the competitive disadvantage of the U.S. auto industry derived mainly from the production inefficiency of the U.S. production system compared to Japan's, not from different wages and benefits. Finally, any claims that Japanese workers are more docile and willing to work harder than their American counterparts collapse as an explanation for the struggles of American auto when we examine instances such as Toyota's takeover in the 1980s of the Fremont factory, "one of GM's worst, a factory known for sex, drugs and defective vehicles. . . . [As] part of an historic joint venture, Toyota turned the plant into one of GM's best, practically overnight."[21]

If the drastic decline of the U.S. auto industry is not primarily the result of (1) the 2008 financial crisis, (2) the life cycle of products, (3) different management styles and labor work ethics rooted in national culture, or (4) decades of union activism greedily raising the costs of labor to restrictive levels, then what does explain the Big Three U.S. automakers' loss of half their domestic market and eventual bankruptcy? The immediate answer is that the Big Three produce lower-quality products, but must sell them at a higher cost than Japanese and some European automakers. This answer is not controversial, however, as most analysts agree this is the proximate cause of decline. Where we offer a drastically different story is in explaining why this is the current reality. In the next section, we offer a brief summary of our argument before laying out our strategy for explaining it in detail and providing empirical support for our argument throughout the rest of the book.

Summary of Our Argument

The Japanese automakers are able to produce higher-quality cars at a lower cost than the Big Three owing to the different structures of production used by U.S. and Japanese manufacturers.[22] The Japanese (and some Europeans) use a flexible production system characterized by geographic clustering, machine flexibility, long-term sole suppliers, and just-in-time delivery. This system facilitates continuous innovation in product and process, allowing the coordination of ongoing product improvement with constantly increasing worker productivity. The U.S. automakers use an ossified mass production system featuring geographic dispersal of production, parts and machine rigidity, and large stockpiles (what we refer to as a "dispersed parallel production system"). This system impedes the implementation of innovation.

The continued use by the Big Three of an ossified mass production system is the path-dependent result of choices made by management during the Great Depression, which led to the post–World War II abandonment of their own version of flexible production. Understanding the series of decisions that culminated in their abandonment of flexible production requires an examination of the pre–World War I U.S. auto industry.

Before World War I, Henry Ford invented the moving assembly line and began to develop a production system with features similar to what we now call "flexible production." Flexible production systems facilitate constant innovation that results in increased output using less labor. The system accomplishes this by horribly exploiting workers, inevitably leading to discontent and resistance. The production system's geographic concentration and just-in-time delivery of parts, however, also provides workers with maximal structural leverage (that is, the power derived from a party's structural role in keeping a system functioning). Thus, an epidemic of mass absenteeism and turnover at Ford Motor in 1914 crippled the company (despite the mass action being unorganized and without specific demands for redress). Henry Ford resolved this crisis by introducing the $5 day and establishing an "effort bargain" with his workers that traded very high wages and benefits for worker acquiescence to the physically oppressive production system. Shortly thereafter, General Motors and the rest of the U.S. auto industry adopted this effort bargain, and a moral economy developed in the auto industry where workers accepted the sacrifices required of attempts at innovation (including layoffs, furloughs, and wage rate cuts) in exchange for a share in the benefits of successful innovation (rehiring laid-off workers at wage rates higher than before the innovation). Essentially, the auto industry became governed by an ethos of shared sacrifice and shared reward (even if workers took on the larger share of sacrifice, while the company received a larger share of the reward).

This effort bargain and moral economy provide us with a context to understand the series of events during the Great Depression that led to the Great Flint Strike. At the start of the Depression, the Big Three engaged in massive layoffs and furloughs and slashed wages and benefits in order to avoid losing money when the economy crashed. This move, on its own, did not violate the moral economy of the industry. In 1936, however, when profits exceeded pre-Depression levels and wages were not returned to their previous levels, the effort bargain and moral economy were broken. By the end of the year, a few hundred workers had joined the United Auto Workers and engaged in a sit-down strike in a number of GM plants in and around Flint. This marked the first time autoworkers had successfully utilized their structural leverage in an organized fashion. As a result, a few hundred workers brought the largest corporation in America to its knees and within four years had unionized the entire auto industry.

Immediately after the Flint strike, General Motors began planning ways to disrupt workers' structural leverage. Its plans to reorganize production, however, were postponed by World War II. During the war, the power of the workers inherent in the system became obvious as thousands of "wildcat" strikes (strikes undertaken by local rank-and-file workers, unsanctioned by the national leadership of the union) won massive concessions from the Big Three. At the end of World War II, the captains of the auto industry could have chosen one of two paths. They could have accepted the demands of their now-unionized workers for an expanded—and explicit—version of the (previously implicit) effort bargain, in which workers would not only share in the profits of their labor but also gain a degree of control over the intensity of the production process. Or they could choose to undermine worker power by eliminating the workers' leverage. They chose the latter path. The automakers dispersed production away from Detroit to segregate new workers from the militant unionists and make strikes more difficult to organize; they eliminated single sourcing of all key components, so that work stoppages in one plant would not interrupt production elsewhere; and they maintained large stockpiles of inventory at every workstation so that upstream work stoppages would not (quickly) interrupt production. This massive restructuring of production did reduce workers' leverage, but it also had the unintended consequence of dramatically decreasing production efficiency and the rate of innovation.

While the Big Three and their suppliers invested vast sums of capital in creating this dispersed, ossified, and less efficient production structure, the resurgent auto companies in Japan implemented and elaborated the flexible system that Detroit had pioneered. Unlike the Big Three, they accepted the constraints of the system, rewarding their workers with very high wages, lifetime employment, and a degree of influence over production methodology. For fifteen or twenty years after the dismantling of flexible production—but before the arrival of foreign imports—the Big Three saw record profits. When the imports began arriving in the late 1960s, however, the U.S. auto industry spent far more money to produce a demonstrably inferior product. This advantage continued to amplify, because the Japanese could and did regularly introduce new features and more efficient production methods, an innovative dynamic that the rigid U.S. system could not match. Unable to compete in terms of efficiency, U.S. management chose to compete by lowering labor costs and expanded their strategic retreat from southern Michigan by relocating parts of production in low-wage areas inside and outside the United States.

The low labor cost strategy of competition has not regained any of their lost market share for the Big Three, largely because their Japanese competitors are able to also produce in areas with cheap labor. The difference is that the Japanese maintain geographic concentration by building entire complexes in cheap labor areas, whereas U.S. auto reinforces geographic dispersal by only moving parts of production. Thus, Japanese automakers continue using flexible production and maintain their advantage in terms of innovation, while limiting the U.S. ability to gain any cost-of-labor advantage. The major consequence of U.S. reliance on outsourcing parts of production, then, has been massive deindustrialization in former production centers like Detroit, while paving their own path toward decline by making a return to flexible production less likely.

The Organization of the Book

Having presented this summary of our argument without supporting evidence, we dedicate the rest of the book to detailing our argument with ample evidence to convince even the most skeptical reader. In addition, our argument raises a number of important associated questions to which we will provide in-depth answers, such as, if the Big Three were compelled to abandon the system in order to reduce worker power, why haven't Japanese companies also been forced by powerful workers to abandon flexible production?

In chapter 1, we establish two fundamental facts on which our analysis rests. First, we demonstrate that the bulk of the Japanese advantage in quality and price lies in product and process innovation. Second, we detail the features of flexible production, show that Japan utilizes the system while the United States does not, and fully explain the relationship of the structure of production to innovation. Thus, in this chapter we demonstrate that the root cause of the loss of domestic market share to Japanese automakers is lack of flexible production.

In chapter 2, we show that the pre–World War II U.S. auto industry developed a flexible production system and that the Japanese system was the result of mimetic isomorphism.[23] This chapter provides evidence that runs counter to the culture-of-management argument.

Chapter 3 is dedicated to answering why the United States abandoned flexible production. We first provide an in-depth discussion of the concept of structural leverage and elaborate how flexible production both maximizes leverage for workers and facilitates its activation. Then we give a detailed account of the series of events, starting with Henry Ford's establishment of the effort bargain in the industry, through the violation of the moral economy during the Depression, to the activation of structural leverage during the Great Flint Strike and the eventual shuttering of flexible production by the Big Three.

Thus, in this chapter we document the role of class conflict in moti-vating the Big Three to end their use of flexible production.[24]

Chapter 4 documents the relationship between abandoning flex-ible production and the decline of innovation in the U.S. auto indus-try. This link is the final piece of evidence in our dismissal of differing cultures as the primary explanation for the decline of the U.S. auto industry and the rise of the Japanese. Combined with chapter 2, it demonstrates that the Japanese advantage lies not in cultural differ-ence but in differing production structure.

Chapter 5 addresses the important lingering questions of why the Japanese were able to maintain their flexible production system in the face of worker structural leverage, and why the United States did not reinstitute flexible production when it became clear that it con-ferred a large efficiency advantage on Japanese automakers. In this chapter, we answer the first question by elaborating on the concept of deactivation of structural leverage through compromise, provid-ing two historical examples: Ford in 1914 and Toyota in 1953. We also analyze the divergent paths taken by Toyota and the Big Three after their initial deactivation of worker structural leverage. To answer the second question, we document how sunk costs established when the Big Three first abandoned flexible production, along with the broken trust with their workers that the Big Three continually reinforce through their actions, undermine efforts to reestablish flexible pro-duction.

We conclude with a discussion of two important lessons that stem from our analysis of the decline of auto. First, we discuss the way that structure guides human agency and shapes its consequences. That is, the decline of U.S. auto is the result of decisions made by Big Three management, but those decisions were guided by the structure in which they were embedded, and they led to decline because of how they interacted with economic and social structures. Finally, we pon-der what the lessons of our book suggest about the future of the post-crash domestic auto industry. Here we demonstrate that neither the Obama-era bailout nor Trump's recent policies fixed the underlying structural problems that caused industry decline. Thus, we expect further decline, plant closings, and loss of U.S. auto jobs.

THE JAPANESE ADVANTAGE: 1
FLEXIBLE PRODUCTION AND
INNOVATION

The foundation for our explanation of the decline of the American auto industry is twofold: first, that Japanese advantages in quality and cost are rooted in greater production efficiency stemming from constant product and process innovation; and second, that the differential rates of innovation and efficiency for Japanese compared to American automakers originate in the different structures of production they use. Specifically, the Japanese benefit from flexible production, which facilitates innovation.

In this chapter, we seek to empirically and theoretically establish this foundation. First, we identify the structural features of flexible production.[1] Next, we elaborate on the relationship between flexible production and innovation. Finally, we close the chapter by demonstrating that the vast majority of the Japanese cost advantage derives from innovation in product and process.

What Is Flexible Production?

The International Motor Vehicle Project at the Massachusetts Institute of Technology (MIT) provided one of the first descriptions of the Japanese system of flexible production (what these researchers, at the time, termed "lean production") by contrasting it with other systems of production:

> The craft producer uses highly skilled workers and simple but flexible tools to make exactly what the consumer asks for—one item at a time. Custom furniture, works of decorative art, and a few ex-

otic sports cars provide current-day examples. We all love the idea of craft production, but the problem with it is obvious: goods produced by the craft method—as automobiles once were exclusively—cost too much for most of us to afford. So mass production was developed at the beginning of the twentieth century as an alternative.

The mass producer uses narrowly skilled professionals to design products made by unskilled or semiskilled workers tending expensive, single-purpose machines. These churn out standardized products in very high volume. Because the machinery costs so much and is so intolerant of disruption, the mass producer adds many buffers—extra supplies, extra workers, and extra space—to assure smooth production. Because changing over to a new product costs even more, the mass producer keeps standard designs in production for as long as possible. The result: the consumer gets lower costs but at the expense of variety and by means of work methods that most employees find boring and dispiriting.

The lean producer, by contrast, combines the advantages of craft and mass production, while avoiding the high cost of the former and the rigidity of the latter. Toward this end, lean producers employ teams of multiskilled workers at all levels of the organization and use highly flexible, increasingly automated machines to produce volumes of products in enormous variety.[2]

Beginning in the late 1980s, a vast array of journalists, businesspeople, and scholars described and documented this stark contrast.[3] From these numerous analyses of the two systems, we identify four structural features that define flexible production as a distinct system: just-in-time delivery, machine flexibility, geographic clustering, and long-term sole supplier relationships.

JUST-IN-TIME DELIVERY

Scholars of the automobile industry generally agree that just-in-time delivery was a key element in Japanese ascendancy in the 1980s.[4] William Abernathy and his collaborators in Abernathy's last book, *Industrial Renaissance,* cogently express this view. They explain the 50 percent productivity increase at Toyo Kogyo (Mazda) between 1974 and 1977 in the following terms:

> Here, again, was the same structural problem that had confronted Henry Ford the better part of a century ago. And here, too, was an effort to solve the problem in a manner of which Ford would have heartily approved: make the production system correspond at all levels (even down to the individual metalworking operation) as closely as possible to the flow of water through a pipeline. In practice, of course, this meant synchronizing activities so as to eliminate bottlenecks and inventory floats wherever possible, an up-to-date application of Ford's notion of progressive production. In Toyo Kogyo's hands, it meant reliance on a "just-in-time" inventory system that transferred parts from one operation to the next precisely when they were needed and in the precise quantity needed.[5]

The just-in-time system diffused outward from the engine shop at Toyota City, where Taiichi Ono developed it in the late 1940s.[6] When Ono was promoted to plant manager, Toyota's sales were less than 100,000 vehicles per year, and intense domestic and foreign competition dictated that the firm manufacture small batches of several models of cars and trucks and improve them constantly. Ono initially sought to improve efficiency and reduce cost by removing the cumbersome stockpiles that had accumulated at many workstations. These stockpiles were the industrywide solution to the inevitable mismatches of production speed: some upstream operations could produce components more quickly than the downstream stations could use them. The standard policy in the late 1940s had been to accumulate one to two months' worth of product and then invest as much as three days to retooling the machine to produce a different item.

The stockpiles were very costly on several accounts. First, the vast space they consumed could be more profitably used for machinery and personnel. More efficient use of space enabled Toyota to accommodate expanded production without constructing a new engine plant. Second, the stockpiles were often not exhausted when one batch was completed and another begun. Thus, many stations had expensive-to-store stockpiles of parts for models that they would not use for several months. Finally, these leftover stockpiles were often rendered obsolete by design changes. In the rapidly changing market of the late 1940s, the losses from these lost stockpiles represented a substantial burden on Toyota's precarious bottom line.

Just-in-time delivery, by synchronizing upstream and downstream operations such that parts arrive exactly when they are needed, allows its adherents to rid themselves of stockpiles. Adopting a just-in-time approach has implications for the other aspects of the manufacturing process as well. The coordination of the entire production system requires that a number of structural conditions be met; taken together, these define flexible production. Before moving on to the other structural features of flexible production, it is important to briefly mention the importance of worker commitment to the entire flexible production system. The smooth functioning of just-in-time delivery is the most obvious place where worker commitment is key. With no stockpiles, and with downstream stations dependent on upstream suppliers, any delays can cripple production. Uncommitted workers can easily cause delays both intentionally (through tactics such as coordinated slowdowns or strikes) and unintentionally (through incompetence due to a lack of focus or even simple absenteeism). Although worker commitment is not a structural feature of flexible production, it is a prerequisite for the smooth functioning of the system. Later in the book, we demonstrate that the importance of worker commitment created by the structure of flexible production is a central part of the explanation for the decline of the U.S. auto industry.

MACHINE FLEXIBILITY

As previously mentioned, a common challenge in auto production is that component suppliers produce parts faster than assemblers can use them. The traditional response was to stockpile the extra parts. Under a just-in-time system, workstations that produced faster than their downstream customers could consume experienced periods of downtime. In response to this, Ono sought to modify or replace the machines so that they could move from one task to another much more quickly, and he rearranged the shop floor so that workers could work another station rather than remain with a temporarily idle machine. This feature of flexible production contrasted sharply with post–World War II mass production, which made use of single-purpose machines in multiyear production runs. During each run, workers followed a rigid routine established by production engineers. In contrast, machine flexibility not only allowed for better coordination of the delivery of needed components, but it could also increase the diversity of products offered. This is another place where worker commitment is important to the system. The rigid routines of single-purpose machines are easier for workers to become efficient with, while multipurpose machines can be mastered only with more effort, and thus buy-in, from workers. In addition, the benefit of flexibility is structurally dependent on multi-use parts to match the multi-use machines.

GEOGRAPHIC CONCENTRATION

Just-in-time delivery relies heavily on geographic concentration of suppliers and assemblers. In Japan, these are known as *supply keiretsu*.[7] These specialized groupings—exemplified by the production complexes that manufacture Toyota, Nissan, and Mazda automobiles—have three concentric circles. The core consists of the final assembly plants of the central manufacturer, which absorbs the various component parts of the automobile and fabricates them into a finished product ready for sale to consumers. The ring that surrounds the core is composed of first-tier suppliers. These are manufacturers—largely keiretsu members but also a few independents—who produce partially or fully fabricated components that are integrated into the finished vehicle. The third concentric circle comprises second-tier suppliers, who sell raw materials and subcomponents to the first tier.

Concentration of suppliers and manufacturers facilitates just-in-time delivery by increasing the ease of transport. At this juncture, we want to note that concentration is also key to the association between flexible production and innovation, as well as to the association between flexible production and worker power. That is, flexible production cannot function without geographic concentration, but geographic concentration also facilitates innovation and a powerful labor force. We discuss each of these relationships in depth later in the book, but for now we ask the reader to make a mental note of this point, for this is one of the key mechanisms that explains the decline of American auto.

Geographic concentration is also key to just-in-time delivery in enabling the shipping of partial products and needed components from their manufacturing source to the downstream facility that will incorporate them into the finished product. In compact concentrations of production facilities, transportation is part of the routine. When long distances separate suppliers from their customers, however, shipping can become a major expense, and the relationship is vulnerable to transportation breakdowns, with the attendant risk of disruptive and potentially disastrous interruptions in supply. These issues form the heart of the locational logic of classical industrial geographers.[8]

The importance of physical proximity to just-in-time delivery is well illustrated by the rise of Toyota.[9] In its early days, most of Toyota's suppliers were housed in or near Koroma, the suburb of Nagoya where the Toyota complex was located. But as the system matured and Toyota grew, the clutter of many factories created important centripetal forces, not only because of the expense of further concentration, but also because Toyota was tempted to use already established firms that were located elsewhere. Once Ono extended just-in-time to outside suppliers, however, transport distance became a central issue in the process of supply. This led to long-term cooperation with Koromo officials, who sought to facilitate the continued devotion of Toyota to their community. In 1955, they changed the name of the town to Toyota City and embarked upon a long-term plan to make it the home of every important production facility in the Toyota keiretsu. This policy included maintaining efficient public transportation, building specialized roads to accommodate particular transport needs among plants, and annexing nearby municipalities in order to capture existing plants or provide space for future ones. As a result of this focused and lavishly funded policy, Toyota City grew in proportion to the firm itself. Between 1950 and 1990, while auto-related employment increased to almost 86,472, overall population tripled (from 96,191 to 332,195) and city tax revenues increased 200-fold (from 506 million yen to 109 billion yen). In 1989, virtually the entire local economy was accounted for by the 461 automobile manufacturing firms within the city limits, and all of these firms had direct or indirect ties to Toyota's four major assembly plants. Moreover, these plants included nearly all of Toyota's 168 first-tier suppliers and, together with the large concentration in the surrounding Aichi prefecture, nearly half of the second-tier suppliers.

The concentration around the Nissan plants in Tokyo and the Mazda complex outside Hiroshima were not nearly as great.[10] Nissan, in fact, at first adopted a strategy reminiscent of the automation movement in the United States, relying more on computers and less on proximity to synchronize production and deliveries. By the early 1970s, however, the superiority of the Toyota strategy had been amply demonstrated, in large part because of a banal problem: traffic.

> Part stocks were again the major problem. They had become increasingly difficult to regulate due to the dispersal of Nissan's factories and suppliers, and the lack of strict controls on deliveries and buffer inventories. Even when managers tried to schedule deliveries at the last moment to keep stocks at the lowest possible levels, intermediate stations accumulated inventories as trucks got caught in traffic jams or, for other reasons, were unable to arrive on time.[11]

Nissan's executives therefore took steps to adopt those aspects of the Toyota system that they had not yet developed themselves, though they never achieved the levels of concentration found in Toyota City.

When journalists and scholars began analyzing the Japanese challenge to American auto hegemony, these concentrations became a part of the story, but not a central focus. As long as the Japanese challenge was primarily from imports, the structure of Japanese auto production was not the focus of American analyses. It was only in the early 1980s, when the Japanese transplants began appearing in North America, that spatial concentration moved closer to center stage.[12] Robert Perrucci, after a careful analysis of the first six such transplants, concluded that proximity to suppliers was the preeminent factor in determining the location of these plants and the complexes that grew up around them.[13] For example, Honda, the pioneer of North American assembly, chose to locate in Marysville, Ohio, for its location in the center of a vast concentration of auto parts manufacturers, but with enough room nearby to facilitate the relocation of Japanese suppliers as well. The other assemblers followed Honda's lead. Although none of the new production complexes replicated the extreme concentration of Toyota City, half of all suppliers and virtually all key suppliers were located within 150 miles of the assembly plants they serviced.[14]

By the early 1990s, the concentration of suppliers that serviced Japanese assembly plants had become one of the most publicized aspects of the transplant phenomenon in the United States. The issue of proximity became the subject of detailed analysis, particularly by Richard Florida and Martin Kenney, who documented the role of these concentrations in translating the just-in-time system to the United States.[15] They concluded that the creation of spatially concentrated complexes was the centerpiece of the successful establishment of Japanese manufacturing in North America:

> Instead of the decentralized branch plants of Fordist industry, Japanese firms transplant an entire level of the division of labor, grouping production activities and necessary inputs at specific sites to promote functional integration. They are now complementing this with localized product development and R&D. . . . One can envision a scenario wherein Japanese corporations develop localized and semiautonomous innovation-production centers that are responsible for design and production of cars for a specific regional market (e.g., Japan, United States, or Europe).[16]

Japanese transplants also took root in East Asia, originally in Korea, but later in Taiwan, Thailand, and Indonesia as well. This development led Richard Child Hill and his collaborators to reach a similar conclusion about automobile industries in these countries, though they found less independence from the corporate headquarters in East Asia than in North America: "Japanese operations in Southeast Asia depart from the hierarchical axial communication pattern associated with global Fordism and conform more closely to a polycentric system with many local development centers, each communicating with every other."[17]

It is not clear if Japanese automobile executives fully appreciated the importance of proximity to the overall efficiency of the just-in-time system. But they understood that long-distance supply lines were fraught with disruptive danger, and that production facilities should be clustered around the final assembly plants. As Kenney and Florida have documented, once transplants were constructed, care was taken to provide "the open space needed to develop broader just-in-time supplier complexes in the immediate vicinity": "While they certainly recognized that transferring just-in-time techniques to North America did not rest solely on geography, the Japanese firms saw locational decisions as among the crucial determinants of success in this regard."[18]

Nevertheless, there was at least a degree of ambivalence about moving the most complex operations overseas. This was most visibly expressed in the slow rise in local content of Japanese cars, even in the United States. In 1989, only Honda could claim more than 50 percent domestic content in the United States, and there were still no engines or transmissions constructed in the United States.[19] But by the early 1990s, all vehicles assembled in the United States had more than 50 percent domestic content, and all but two brands had over 60 percent. By 1993, Honda, Nissan, Toyota, and Mazda were all purchasing or producing transmissions or engines domestically. Apparently the commitment to proximity was strong enough to overcome the fear that overseas production would fail to replicate the precision of Japanese plants.[20]

LONG-TERM SOLE SUPPLIERS

The trust and interaction necessitated by the just-in-time system enhanced the value of long-term relationships with suppliers. The need to have suppliers concentrated around assemblers made long-term sole suppliers a virtual necessity. The development of flexible production at Toyota illustrates the utility of such long-term relationships.

In 1950, Toyota had adopted a corporate strategy of comprehensive outsourcing. As a consequence, between 1952 and 1957, as output increased by 500 percent, Toyota's internal employment increased by only 14 percent while supplier employment more than tripled. Nissan also adopted this strategy, and from 1960 onward parts suppliers accounted for over 60 percent of the employees and 50 percent of the value added in the industry.[21] For Ono, then, expansion of his system to outside suppliers was essential if he was to impact the overall cost of production.

Ono's changes began with the procurement departments of the individual Toyota plants, which received and stockpiled large shipments of parts and then distributed them as needed to the appropriate workstations. He eliminated the procurement departments altogether and forced suppliers to make daily deliveries directly to the station that would use their component. This innovation not only eliminated a whole layer of personnel (who were transferred elsewhere) but also freed up still more space for the now-ongoing expansion of the company. Even more significantly, it forced the suppliers to adopt flexible production within their own plants, since the delivery of small batches compelled them, too, to switch back and forth between different items—or else develop enormous stockpiles that were expensive to manage and might become obsolete before they were exhausted.[22]

One of the enduring consequences of this interaction was the dependence of Toyota on the engineering capability of its suppliers. This dependence rested on what Asanuma has called "design-approved" component development. Toyota applied this principle to most complex subassemblies. Only the general specifications of the component were developed in-house, and these general specifications were then shown to two or three potential suppliers during the earliest stages of model design. The potential suppliers submitted bids that included a detailed design developed by their own engineering departments. Once a particular supplier was selected, it was guaranteed a contract for the lifetime of the model, even though, because innovation was inherent to the system (a point we detail later), this lifetime would surely involve ongoing cost reductions and major modifications as the vehicle evolved. The other bidders might ultimately receive smaller contracts for the part, but more likely they would be selected to provide the same or similar part for other models or vehicles. The engineering dependence of Toyota was not, therefore, dependent on a particular supplier, but rather on a group of suppliers with whom Toyota retained long-term relationships.[23] Although intense informal interaction with supplier personnel had been a part of Japanese industrial groups for a long time, dating back to the prewar *zaibatsu*, the just-in-time inventory system placed it at the center of Toyota's operation. The dénouement of this evolution was that trust became an integral part of what were formally market relationships.

The intimacy and trust of Toyota's relationships with suppliers contrasted sharply with the supplier relations that emerged in the post–World War II period in the American automobile industry. Susan Helper succinctly describes that system:

> U.S. automakers created a fiercely competitive components industry. They did this by reducing barriers to entry through such mechanisms as taking complex functions like engineering and R&D almost completely in-house. They employed several (six to eight) competing suppliers for each part, offered only short-term (one year) contracts, and required suppliers to license major innovations. They also divided parts into small, easy-to-produce pieces, and hired managers to coordinate assembly of these parts centrally.[24]

The best indicator of the contrast between the two philosophies is that American assemblers generally maintained about ten times as many supplier relationships as the Japanese. In the mid-1980s, for example, Toyota had 177 first-tier suppliers while General Motors had about 1,500.

Once this system was consolidated, it created opportunities for the core assemblers or auto firms to drive down the price of each component by threatening to move their business to another firm. This competition increased assembler profits at the expense of the suppliers. Helper has summarized the functioning of the two systems by applying Albert Hirschman's exit-voice analysis to the contrast between them:

> Borrowing Hirschman's terminology, we can identify two types of responses to problems arising in customer-supplier relationship: (1) exit, where the customer firm's response to problems with a supplier is to find a new supplier, and (2) voice, where the customer's response is to work with the original supplier until the problem is corrected. Where the exit strategy secures compliance by use of the "stick" of threats to withdraw from the relationship, the

voice strategy relies on the "carrot" of increased profits for both parties due to improved products.

The key to the exit strategy is making credible the customer's threat to leave if its demands are not met. Therefore, the customer must have access to many interchangeable suppliers and/or the ability to tool up quickly for in-house production. In contrast, an extensive communications system is necessary to facilitate the rich flow of information needed for the "let's work things out" approach of the voice strategy. This information flow both requires and engenders a high degree of commitment to the relationship.[25]

In the system that evolved in the United States after World War II, if an assembler was discontented with the quality, price, or reliability of a particular supplier, the one-year contracts and the multitude of alternative suppliers made it a simple matter to shift that firm's share to one of the other sources already manufacturing the part. The threat of such a shift constituted the key device for ensuring quality work and constant attention to decreasing the cost of the part. Hence, the customer disciplined the supplier through the threat of *exiting* the relationship.

In the Japanese system, on the other hand, discontent could not be expressed by shifting the work to another supplier. The auto firm was dependent on its first-tier suppliers in the short run because there was often no alternative supplier available to manufacture the part for that model, and because the just-in-time inventory system meant that supplies of the part would be depleted almost immediately. Though alternative sources were technically available in the middle term, in practice they could not be made use of, since such a shift would undermine the credibility of the commitment to using a single supplier throughout the life of the model. Since the investment of huge resources in developing the part was predicated on this long-term commitment, such shifting would make it impossible in the long run for the assembler to undertake design-approved development. As a consequence, the cooperative relationships that evolved in the product development process became the vehicle for negotiating discontent: Toyota and other Japanese assemblers *voiced* their discontent and sought to resolve it, rather than *exiting* the relationship. This commitment on the part of the assembler to keeping the relationship engendered the trust necessary for suppliers to agree to modify their parts and machinery to accommodate just-in-time delivery.

How Does Flexible Production Facilitate Innovation?

JUST-IN-TIME DELIVERY

Just-in-time delivery facilitates two crucial factors necessary for innovation: the ability to engage in trial and error when working on an invention, and the ability to develop and implement new parts cost-effectively. First, successful innovation often requires trial-and-error learning. Once again, worker commitment is a key prerequisite to realizing this benefit of flexibility. The workers are the ones engaging in the trials and helping to tweak the process after the errors. When workers are committed to figuring out how to implement innovative ideas, the just-in-time delivery system facilitates the process. For instance, in a just-in-time system, suppliers who are prepared to quickly alter their product and deliver it at a moment's notice make it possible to overcome errors and embark on new trials. In a rigid production system where the supplier mass-produces parts and assemblers stockpile them, an error in a new design is a costly disaster, since months' worth of parts containing the error will be produced. This cost discourages the trial-and-error process, reducing the odds of successful innovation.

Second, even after workers successfully get through the trial-and-error process and figure out the best way to implement an innovation, the result is a need for new components that are compatible with the innovation. In a production system with large stockpiles of inventory, this requirement leaves companies with two equally unattractive options. The first is waiting for the stockpile of old parts to be exhausted, thus losing time and money. In addition, because the innovation is likely to involve change at multiple stations, companies must also wait for stockpiles of multiple types of parts to be used up. The second option is to implement the innovation immediately with the new parts, thus rendering the entire stockpiled (and already purchased) inventory obsolete. These costs can be prohibitive enough to discourage implementation.

The history of the disc brake provides an example of the costs associated with inventory serving as a barrier to implementing innovation.[26] Disc brakes have many advantages over the drum brakes that were the dominant design up until the early 1960s. Disc brakes last longer, are more consistent, and do not slip or grab when water or grease enters the braking system. Yet, despite these clear technical advantages, disc brakes did not become standard on American cars until 1973. According to Abernathy, U.S. manufacturers were reluctant to scrap drum-brake manufacturing equipment and invest in disc-brake equipment. They reasoned that disc brakes were not suited to use as parking brakes, and that under normal conditions the drum brake performed adequately. It is telling, however, that American companies implemented disc brakes in their European subsidiaries well before adopting them on cars produced in the United States. In fact, according to Abernathy's timeline, English Ford, in 1960, was the first company to apply disc brakes to a mass-produced automobile; shortly after, disc brakes became standard on European cars. The key difference between English Ford and American Ford was the large inventory stockpiles carried by the Americans. Changing to disc brakes would have been extremely costly in the United States because all the stockpiled parts required for drum brakes would have had to be discarded. Just-in-time delivery, by eliminating stockpiles, removes the cost of obsolete parts from consideration when implementing an innovation. The stockpiles, however, were not the only barrier to implementing disc brakes. Each of the other features of the system, such as machine flexibility, geographic concentration, and long-term sole suppliers, makes a unique contribution to innovation and played a role in slowing down U.S. implementation of disc brakes. In the interest of clarity, we discuss in this section only the role that just-in-time delivery played. In the subsequent sections, we detail how the other features function to facilitate innovation.

MACHINE FLEXIBILITY

Just as inventory stockpiles make implementing new ideas more costly, the use of single-purpose machines is also a barrier to innovation. If a company's machines are all designed to produce a certain component or model, then changing the product through innovation makes all that machinery obsolete. The company must eat the costs sunk in the machinery, while simultaneously paying for new equipment (which may also become obsolete in the near future). Machine flexibility played a role in the shift from drum brakes to disc brakes, but it played a crucial role in the delays to the Big Three's implementation of aluminum engines.

Mercedes-Benz used the first aluminum engines in the early 1900s, but it took until the 1950s for them to be widely used as a more efficient alternative to the cast-iron engines that dominated the industry. As with the previous example, aluminum engines were adopted in Europe by American-owned subsidiaries well before they were used in the United States.[27] In fact, the aluminum engine was pretty much standard on cars in Europe by the late 1950s, yet by 1978 it was present in fewer than 10 percent of all American cars.[28] Abernathy points out that the major advantage of aluminum engines over cast-iron is their lighter weight and thus greater fuel efficiency. He cites a concern in Europe with fuel economy as the reason for the wide adoption of this innovation there. American buyers were less motivated by fuel efficiency, and American companies began attempts to implement aluminum engines only once the more fuel-efficient European cars hit the market. Despite these efforts, adoption was delayed even after fuel-efficient cars were in demand in the United States, which Abernathy explains as the result of U.S. manufacturers' already heavy investment in the machinery needed to produce cast-iron engines. That is, because the machinery being used to produce the old engines was single-purpose machinery, American automakers would absorb major losses when that machinery was made obsolete by the transition to aluminum.

As with disc brakes, other factors related to a nonflexible production system played a role, such as large stockpiles. Here we focus on flexible machinery to illustrate its unique contribution to innovation. The use of multipurpose machinery solves the problem of throwing away expensive machinery. A multipurpose machine can usually be fine-tuned to allow for production of a new product without discarding the machine. When it cannot be used to make the new part, it can still be employed for one of its numerous other purposes. Thus, even if new machinery is needed for a drastic change in product or process, the old flexible machinery retains some value, lowering the cost of innovation.

GEOGRAPHIC CONCENTRATION

Successful innovation often relies on long-term, face-to-face interaction among the principal actors.[29] The presence of a planner on the assembly line, the attendance of a production engineer at planning meetings, or the oversight of a responsible individual from a parts supplier when a component is first used in final assembly are all important ingredients in the management of ongoing innovation.

The disruption caused by product innovation frequently extends beyond the confines of a particular establishment; that is, the implementation of the new design requires that several sets of production facilities be consolidated or reconfigured. In concentrated geographical areas, an ongoing readjustment of production facilities can take place. Functions can be shifted to more appropriate settings without the vast disruption created by moving immense amounts of machinery and people (both semiskilled labor and high-skilled experts) long distances. Even vast reorganizations can be undertaken in the trial-and-error manner that offers the best possibility for arriving at a maximally efficient solution. In a spatially dispersed setting, such recombination is always expensive, often overwhelmingly complex, and rarely susceptible to experimentation.

As products change and production processes evolve, the issues involved in transporting partially or fully assembled components from one step in the production stream to another also change. Long-distance transport of a manageable amount of a certain product may evolve into the inefficient transfer of huge amounts of bulky, fragile, partially assembled items. The huge increase in the use of glass that came with the rise of the enclosed body forcefully illustrates this pattern.[30]

Up until the late 1950s, the dominant method used by U.S. producers to construct the body of an automobile was body-on-chassis design. When foreign companies, which used unit body construction, began to import their smaller cars in greater numbers in the late 1950s, U.S. producers were forced to attempt unit body construction. Unit body allowed for a larger seating capacity for a given weight than body-on-chassis design did. Thus, producers using unit body were able to make smaller, more fuel-efficient cars. By 1961, 45 percent of American cars produced were made with unit body design. However, GM and Ford gradually shifted back to the body-on-chassis design, citing the cost of both style changes and production in general as mitigating factors. The body-on-chassis design allowed for the dispersed feeder plants to produce components and parts and then ship them to the final assembly plant, where the chassis was located. By contrast, the use of unit body design required either that the entire assembly process take place in a concentrated geographic area or that the entire car body be shipped from plant to plant as each specialized part was constructed. Shipping an entire car body from plant to plant was unrealistic, both because it created immense transportation costs and because it introduced great risk. At any point in the body's journey, it could be lost or damaged and the entire process would need to begin again. On the other hand, geographic concentration was also not a realistic option because of the immense sunk costs the Big Three had in the dispersed plants. We discuss in chapter 5 the sunk costs of a dispersed system as a barrier to the geographic concentration necessary for flexible production. For now, it suffices to say that the unit body example illustrates the relationship between innovation and the proximity of supplier and assembler.

LONG-TERM SOLE SUPPLIERS

As we have already documented, just-in-time delivery (and thus, flexible production) requires ongoing and intense interaction between an assembler and its first-tier suppliers. This type of interaction is also integral to innovation because it facilitates trial-and-error design and implementation. There are two requirements, however, for intense face-to-face interaction with suppliers: first, suppliers must be in physical proximity to the manufacturers (the importance of geographic concentration), and second, there must be trust between the suppliers and the manufacturers. This trust is built on the foundation of long-term sole supplier relationships.

The importance of these aspects of the supplier-manufacturer relationship was proven in Japan in the 1950s, when car design was changing rapidly. Every part of an automobile had to be under constant scrutiny for redesign, and the alterations had to be implemented very quickly. Each supplier was forced to monitor changes taking place at Toyota to make sure its component fit into the reconfigured vehicles, and Toyota demanded a declining cost curve among suppliers that paralleled its own.[31] The suppliers were therefore forced to maintain active engineering departments that constantly scrutinized their own product design and manufacturing methodology, as well as the changes taking place at the Toyota plants. Each first-tier supplier became dependent, in turn, on the ongoing interaction of its engineers with design and production personnel at Toyota and on the reciprocal interaction of Toyota engineers with its production personnel. Though the legacy of the prewar zaibatsu made these sorts of cooperative relationships familiar, under Ono's stewardship Toyota's involvement in the operations of its first-tier suppliers became more comprehensive than anything that had preceded it. The company was consciously organized to manage ongoing product innovation and continuous methodological improvement.

Toyota ultimately constructed a formal system to achieve this goal, creating design teams populated by personnel from key keiretsu members as well as the major plants within Toyota. These teams were established during the earliest design stage for a car model and remained intact well into the production run. They became the heart of new projects, and they consolidated the cooperation that began with the just-in-time delivery system. Once in place, these teams also led to the atrophy of Toyota's own in-house engineering in areas for which Toyota did not have manufacturing responsibility. Because of the close cooperation with component suppliers, the assembler could restrict its own expertise to those components that were manufactured in-house and access other expertise through the mediation of the design groups.

The maintenance of keiretsu arrangements depended on informal but nevertheless binding commitments between the assemblers and their suppliers. Toyota and others regularly promised contracts to design-approved suppliers for entire model runs, but such promises rarely had any official status and could have been reneged upon with no legal consequences. Yet there were apparently no instances, at Toyota or any other automobile keiretsu, of the agreement being abrogated. One explanation lies in the personal relationships developed by employees of the supplier and assembler (for instance, when workers participated in planning groups or spent time on the line in factories beyond their own), which strengthened the ties between the organizations. More significantly, the ongoing operation of the system simply required that Toyota honor these commitments. Even when Japanese suppliers moved to the United States to service transplant assembly facilities, while there was rarely any formal agreement that the move would be rewarded by supply contracts, here again the promises were nevertheless fulfilled.

Finally, we have discussed how long-term relationships with suppliers were governed by a voice system rather than an exit system. The voice system also contributes to innovation. In her discussion of the distinct advantages of each system, Helper details the mechanisms through which voice facilitates innovation:

> The exit strategy gives the customer a great deal of bargaining power because it has little commitment to any one supplier. Conversely, the voice strategy reduces the customer's bargaining power by increasing its cost of switching between suppliers. On the other hand, where significant investment is required either to communicate the existence of a technical problem or to implement a solution to that problem, voice is likely to be superior. The reason is that without the detailed information and long-term commitment characteristic of a voice relationship, a supplier's innovation may well be inapplicable to the customer's needs. . . . The exit strategy maximizes customer bargaining power, the voice strategy maximizes most types of technical change.[32]

Though bargaining power yields lower supply costs in the short term, ongoing innovation will eventually overcome these advantages through improved product design and more efficient production strategies.

The Japanese Advantage

In the introduction to this book, we laid out our central explanation for the loss of domestic market share by U.S. firms to Japanese: that

Japanese automakers are able to produce higher-quality cars at a lower cost than the Big Three owing to the high rates of innovation yielded by their production system compared to American systems. Having fully demonstrated the ways in which flexible production enables innovation, it would seem that our argument is on solid ground so far. Yet it is possible that the Japanese get only a small advantage from innovation, while the rest of their advantage stems from other sources. If so, our story would not be totally accurate. In fact, many analysts do identify a source of Japanese cost advantage other than product and process innovation: labor costs.

One of the dominant strategies to explain the Japanese advantage in quality and cost has been to blame the UAW. The "greedy union" narrative has been put forth with the thinnest veneer of evidence.[33] A typical instance occurred during the 2008 auto industry financial crisis. *New York Times* reporter Bill Vlasic falsely asserted that a massive wage and benefits differential between unionized workers in Detroit ($74) and non-union Toyota workers in Tennessee ($45) prevented the Big Three from matching "the cost structure of nonunion plants operated by foreign automakers in the United States."[34] These figures are extremely misleading because, while Toyota paid much of its workforce very close to the reported hourly wage of $45, the Big Three do not pay most of their employees the reported wage and benefits of $74 per hour. That is, approximately half of the employees of U.S. automakers are located outside the United States (mostly in Mexico), where they are paid around one-tenth of the reported package—less than $10 per hour.[35] Hence, although the U.S. assemblers paid a select few very high wages, the fact that the vast majority made much less brought the U.S. cost of labor down.

It is true, however, that before the Big Three moved much of production to low-wage areas, U.S. auto paid substantially higher wages than their Japanese counterparts. Even when the United States did pay more for labor, however, these costs did not account for a majority of the Japanese advantage. In fact, labor costs accounted for only a small fraction of that advantage. The competitive disadvantage of the U.S. auto industry derived mainly from production inefficiency.[36] This deficit was first documented in a series of longitudinal studies by William Abernathy's research group at MIT.[37] Table 1.1 reproduces key evidence from their 1981 measurement, focusing on the GM-Mazda comparison.

Table 1.1 *Comparative Costs and Labor Productivity in Selected U.S. and Japanese Automobile Companies, 1981*

	GM	Mazda (U.S. Plants)	Dollar Differential	Percentage Manufacturing Differential
Manufacturing costs				
Labor cost per hour	$22	$11.70	$546	26%
Employee hours per small car	83	53	660	31
Total labor costs	$1,826	$620	1,206	57
Purchased components and materials	$3,405	$2,858	547	26
Other manufacturing costs	$730	$350	380	18
Total manufacturing costs	$5,961	$3,828	2,133	100
Nonmanufacturing costs (shipping, tariffs, and the like)	$325	$1,100	−775	
Total costs	$6,286	$4,928	1,358	

Source: Dollar and percentage differentials calculated by authors in Murray and Schwartz 2017a. Adapted from Abernathy, Clark, and Kantrow 1983, 61.

Only one-quarter ($546) of the massive $2,133 cost-of-production differential derived from lower wages in 1981. Almost three-quarters ($1,687) derived from three aspects of flexible production, including:

- A $660 (31 percent) savings for Mazda because GM required thirty extra hours of labor (fifty-three versus eighty-three) to assemble a comparable automobile. This differential derived from Japanese production innovations during the twenty-five years after U.S. automakers abandoned flexible production.

- A $547 (26 percent) advantage for Mazda in the cost of components, deriving from the geographical proximity of suppliers, sole sourcing, and the participation of Mazda's suppliers in improvements deriving from flexible production.

- A $380 (18 percent) advantage deriving from Mazda's "diligent control of the whole system of production"—that is, the tightly coupled character of flexible production, including, for example, the savings in delivery expenses due to the extremely low storage costs incurred through low inventories and just-in-time deliveries.

Thanks to flexible production, the Japanese auto manufacturers were producing better cars for less than two-thirds the cost of the Big Three. For example, a Mazda car comparable to a GM car priced at $5,961 cost $3,828 to assemble. Despite the substantial costs of U.S. tariffs and transpacific shipping ($775)—which more than offset the lower wages in Japan—Japanese manufacturers were still able to sell a superior product in the United States for more than $1,000 less than a U.S.-manufactured car.

These findings should definitively disprove the "greedy union" narrative. Even paying the same wages as the Japanese, U.S. auto manufacturers in the early 1980s would have been at a serious cost disadvantage. And though U.S. firms have cut into the labor-hours-per-car advantage over time—Toyota had only about a six-hour advantage in 2005—the difference in labor costs in the United States has also been cut.[38] In addition, as we have already discussed, if we take into account the U.S. global workforce, labor costs are even lower for U.S. manufacturers.

Our analysis also challenges the product life cycle theory as an explanation for American decline—namely, the argument that the industry reached maturity after innovations were exhausted. It was innovation in product and process that led to the greater efficiencies documented here. The Abernathy data, however, are far from the only evidence that the vast majority of the Japanese advantage sprang from the innovativeness of the flexible production system. For example, taking advantage of a unique data set with detailed information on twenty-nine new models brought to market between 1980 and 1987 by American, Japanese, and European manufacturers, Kim Clark used regression analysis to measure the impact of the Japanese supply system on two key components of product development.[39] First, the Japanese used less than one-third the number of engineering hours during the development process—1,155,000 hours as compared to 3,478,000 hours in American firms. Second, the Japanese needed much less time to bring a new model to market—only 42.6 months compared to 61.9 for the Americans.[40] Clark's analysis attributed a substantial portion of these remarkable differences to the supplier system:

> It appears that supplier involvement (and strong supplier relationships) accounts for about one-third of the man-hours advantage

[of Japanese producers] and contributes four to five months of the lead time advantage. Even these numbers understate the role of suppliers, since a strong network of suppliers allows many of the Japanese firms to use more unique parts in their designs, thus improving the performance of the product.[41]

Translated into dollars, the four months of lead time saved by the Japanese represented several hundred million dollars in *profits* (over $1 million a day), and the nearly 800 fewer engineering hours added another $100 million to the bottom line.

The rate of turnover for parts was also a factor, as Michael Cusumano emphasizes: After five to ten years of active inventory reduction, American firms still had stockpiles three times as large as those in the Japanese plants.[42] Largely as a consequence of these smaller stockpiles, the average Japanese plant was 20 to 40 percent smaller than an American plant of comparable capacity. Richard Child Hill and Yong Joo Lee point to the role of flexible production in maximizing space: the rapid retooling and flexible machinery that just-in-time methods had inspired allowed Japanese firms to produce eighty models in 1991, while the Big Three produced fifty-three models in many more plants.[43] Alan Altshuler and his colleagues at the MIT Automobile Group tabulated patents as a measure of the firms' ability to adapt to the vast changes in the American operating environment.[44] During the decade between 1970 and 1980, the Japanese share of new patents filed in the United States increased from 16 percent to 56 percent, while the American share dropped from 54 percent to 24 percent. And perhaps most significantly, the MIT Group calculated a productivity advantage of 34 percent in 1989 (25.1 hours per car for the Big Three compared to 16.8 hours per car for the Japanese), which they attributed largely to the reverberations of just-in-time through the entire production system.[45]

Defect rates have been particularly important in these comparisons, in part because they were widely publicized to consumers in the 1980s (through surveys by *Consumer Reports* and J.D. Power and Associates) and thus became a key element of the purchase decision. Beyond this market concern, however, lay a historic dilemma that had confronted manufacturers since the creation of the moving assembly line. If defects were to be caught and corrected in process, the tight linkages in the assembly process would lead to the idling of a substantial portion of the workforce in nearby stations. If, on the other hand, the line was kept moving, the defect could become buried in the guts of the vehicle and either render itself invisible or substantially escalate the cost of repair. After World War II, American firms used the large stockpiles at each workstation to replace defective parts without stopping the line, and they sought to identify and fix any undiscovered problems after assembly. This yielded high productivity and a high defect ratio, since workers had the parts to replace defects but not the time needed to identify where they were needed. Nevertheless, for two decades this process was tolerable, since no manufacturer could do any better.

The flexible production system did not permit this compromise on defects, since there were no stockpiles from which to replace defective parts. The dilemma turned into a long-term virtue, however, since "the absence of buffer stocks made it essential to avoid bad parts" altogether.[46] Machinery was modified to automatically signal important defects, and Japanese producers required individual workers to stop the line and address them immediately. Though this created profound disruption in the short run, the stoppages were used to develop production modifications that eliminated the source of the problem. Eventually, the Japanese system came to embody the best of both worlds: infinitesimal defect rates and only occasional (and brief) line stoppages.[47]

This low defect rate became a key element in the rise of Japanese imports in the American market. In the late 1970s and early 1980s, the defect differential between American and Japanese cars was sometimes as large as ten-to-one.[48] Such differences were visible to the naked eye of the retail consumer, who could drive a Japanese automobile off the lot with reasonable assurance of avoiding the several return trips that American manufacturers had established as the norm for new cars. Nevertheless, in 1989, after a decade of concerted effort to reduce the Japanese advantage in this realm, the Big Three defect rate remained 37 percent above that of the Japanese imports— eighty-two per American vehicle compared to sixty for the Japanese.[49]

The contrast between the keiretsu system and the supplier relationships maintained by the American Big Three automobile manufacturers in the 1970s and 1980s was so striking that it led most observers to assume that the just-in-time system was a dramatic departure from all previous production arrangements. Yasuhiro Monden, one of the first English-language scholars of the system, expressed the view of most when he concluded that it "would probably not be overstating our case if we said that this is another revolutionary management system."[50] These assumptions are definitively undermined by a close look at the American system of the 1920s and 1930s. Although there are many contrasts between that system and Japanese flexible production, the similarities are too striking to ignore, particularly if we focus on the relationships between suppliers and assemblers. In fact, the American system of supply of the 1920s resembled the Japanese keiretsu more than it resembled the arrangements that developed in North America after World War II.

INNOVATION AND THE STRUCTURE OF PRODUCTION IN THE EARLY U.S. AUTO INDUSTRY

In the previous chapter, we demonstrated that the constant innovation facilitated by flexible production is the fundamental cause of the Big Three's loss of domestic market share over the last fifty years. Although this fact may be foundational to our argument, it is not, on its own, dramatically different from the observations of many other analysts of the automobile industry. Most analysts agree that the Japanese automakers are more innovative than their U.S. counterparts. There is also a general recognition in the literature that the flexible production system utilized by Japanese automakers produces higher-quality automobiles than the current U.S. system. We have made a contribution by directly linking flexible production to innovation, but this does not dramatically change the existing narrative. That is, Japanese innovativeness has long been attributed to their culture. Our shift to the structure of production does not necessitate a shift away from a cultural explanation, because flexible production is viewed as a Japanese innovation. So, if the quick adoption by Japanese automakers of innovations like unit body construction and aluminum engines is attributable to the structure of their production system, their use of that system is still explainable as the result of their uniqueness as a culture.

Where our argument seriously changes the narrative is in our position that flexible production was *not* a Japanese innovation. In fact, it was not a new production system when it came to the United States in the 1970s. Rather, it was created and practiced first in the United States, prior to World War II, and later copied (and improved upon) by Japanese automakers (and eventually European automakers). Thus, cultural differences between the United States and Japan cannot explain the differences in the production system utilized, and consequently they cannot explain the different rates of innovation. To understand the root of U.S. decline, then, we must answer the following three questions: Why did the United States abandon flexible production after World War II? Why have the Japanese not similarly abandoned it? And why has the United States not readopted flexible production?

We engage these questions in the chapters that follow, but first we seek to establish that the early U.S. auto industry did indeed use a form of flexible production before World War II, that the system facilitated remarkable innovation, and that the Japanese did indeed learn the system from the Big Three before implementing it in Japan.

Characteristics of Early U.S. Auto Production: Flexibility and Innovation

The hallmarks of the early American system were continuous innovation in the design and performance of the automobile, which necessitated the continuous evolution of an assembly line system that allowed for the production of ever more complicated vehicles at ever lower prices.[1]

The Ford Motor Company emerged from World War I as the hegemonic auto assembler. By 1920, it was producing just under one million Model T cars per year at about one-third their original 1908 price. This sales figure made up just over half (55 percent) of all automobiles sold that year. With General Motors contributing nearly 400,000 vehicles, the Big Two accounted for almost 75 percent of the market.

This moment in the history of U.S. auto production serves as another piece of counterevidence to product life cycle theory. That is, it could well have marked the beginning of product and process stabilization, since the industry was exhibiting many of the "tell-tale signs of maturity," just as it did twenty years later.[2] Why it did not reach maturity, despite the telltale signs, can help us understand why it had not actually reached maturity during the postwar period. Several signs of maturity were evident in the 1920s. The market share controlled by Ford and GM was already far higher than the usual standard for maturity. And the number of smaller competitors was declining rapidly, from two hundred in 1909, before the rise of Ford, to under one hundred in 1920, on its way to twenty-three in 1929. The basic parameters of design—a gasoline-powered, longitudinal, four-cylinder engine and a rear wheel drive serviced by a torque tube taken from the front-mounted engine—became universal in the industry once the Model T established itself as the dominant force in the American market. No important challenges to this design were on the horizon.

The standard production methodology had been created during the legendary period between 1908 and 1915 at the Ford Highland Park plant, when the moving assembly line was first successfully implemented. Since the process was not based on complex or proprietary technology, it was quickly copied by local competitors, who could hire Ford-trained production supervisors. Nevertheless, the moving assembly line revolutionized production. In one assembly plant studied by the *Monthly Labor Review*, the construction of a single automobile took 4,664 hours in 1912, before the firm began copying Ford's methods. This was reduced to 4,119 hours in 1914 by the simple expedient of creating specialized work teams. It was reduced another 20 percent, to 3,241 hours, when the first primitive conveyers were installed in 1915. In the next eight years, as the firm refined its conveyer system and adjusted the work process to the new arrangement, it cut production time a further 66 percent—to 813 hours.[3] These gains were so massive—and so simple to execute in the Detroit region—that in the three years after Ford built its first moving assembly line in 1913, almost all of the big producers in southern Michigan had successfully adopted it.[4] By the end of World War I, moving assembly lines were standard practice.

Beyond these basic prerequisites for maturity lay a set of less visible developments that could well have indicated that the period of rapid innovation was coming to an end and that standardization—even ossification—was well under way. The centerpiece of this standardization was the image of the "unchanging" Model T. The production run of the Model T, the "car for the ages," was projected to continue indefinitely.

This intended permanence was etched into Ford's strategy in purchasing machinery for the assembly line. The production tools were so specialized that they admitted no variation whatsoever, in terms either of producing several models simultaneously or of easily adapting to an evolving design. Contemporary observers saw this as one of the hallmarks of Ford's accomplishment:

> Here was an organization whose every machine tool and fixture was fitted for the production of a single product whose every part had been standardized to the minutest detail. Any change in any part of that product involved radical changes in production methods and equipment all the way back, in many cases, to the raw material from which that part was produced.[5]

This standardization of manufacturing tools was part of a broader standardization of manufacturing processes. The tools themselves represented a major expense, and the production system built around them was an even larger investment. The whole system was indubitably inflexible, and it therefore introduced significant rigidity into the entire system of design and production. One contemporary observer stated that before any new design was put into production, it was "turned over to the manufacturing expert to see that it is adaptable to high-speed production methods and tools."[6] Often it was not. The boxy body of the Model T, for example, was maintained long after the technology was available for a more streamlined design because the metal stamping machines that were installed in the Ford plants could not create curved panels. More generally, the cost of replacing machinery was a key factor in the Ford Motor Company's determination to freeze the design of the Model T, since any substantial changes would entail eliminating large stockpiles of inventory, discarding and replacing huge numbers of machines, and redesigning the assembly process.[7] This is an early example of a feature we document more thoroughly in this chapter: how the structure of production can either facilitate or impede the implementation of innovations. Unlike the post–flexible production industry we document in chapter 5, in the early U.S. industry these structural impediments eventually led to changes in production designed to ease innovation.

River Rouge is an example of eventual changes in the structure of production that facilitated innovation. These changes did not, however, occur immediately. The very conception of the massive River Rouge complex in Dearborn—which gradually replaced the original Highland Park plant during the 1920s—embodied the principles of maturity and mass production, not innovation and flexible production. It sought not only to exploit economies of scale to a degree never before attempted but also to carry division of labor to new extremes. Despite the subdivision of tasks that had been the hallmark of the original assembly lines, production at Highland Park had relied on a large quantum of skilled labor, including a cadre of craftsmen and foremen whose expertise had been critical to effective production. The transfer to River Rouge thus created a division between the skilled workers, who were left behind in the doomed Highland Park plant, and the unskilled workers who were hired to populate the various assembly lines at the Rouge.[8]

In addition to eliminating taxing dependencies on skilled workers and production foremen, Ford sought to eliminate its equally costly reliance on outside suppliers. The Rouge complex was intended to be the ultimate in vertical integration, a place where "raw materials come in one side, a finished motorcar comes out the other."[9] The self-contained nature of the complex held the promise of allowing Ford to fully standardize the entire process from beginning to end, eliminating virtually all dependence on the vagaries of the automobile parts market and freeing Ford from the problematic relationships that the Japanese keiretsu system so effectively managed.

Paradoxically, this massive centralization was accompanied by an equally drastic decentralization of final assembly. When Model T sales exploded before World War I, Ford discovered that the huge costs of transporting bulky cars in awkwardly designed rail carriages could be drastically reduced by shipping the more compact components separately and then assembling them within driving distance of the dealerships. This strategy was also an essential marketing tool, since it provided owners with reliable repair services "at the factory" in an era when problems were plentiful and automotive expertise was scarce. Contemporary observers saw this combination of concentrated basic production and dispersed final assembly as a virtue to which every large firm should aspire: "Few institutions . . . could have taken equal advantage of a policy whereby the manufacturing was done near the source of supply and the assembly near the point of distribution. This policy is of course followed by other manufacturers, but nowhere else on such a large or efficient scale."[10]

By 1920, there were twenty-seven branch assembly plants sprinkled around the country and a growing number in foreign countries. The existence of this far-flung network became a strong motive for standardization, since any change in production methodology or alteration in vehicle design required systematically changing the final assembly operation in all the plants.[11]

Ford had an additional, but crucially important, incentive for product stability. By 1920, the Model T was viewed by the public as a fixed part of the social landscape. As a consequence, any visible alteration "created a peculiar marketing problem for Ford Motor Company. The company could not use change or 'improvements' as a selling point."[12] There was thus no apparent reason to resist the cost-based imperative to keep design features the same.

The final prerequisite for maturity—and the slowed pace of innovation that flows from it—was the oligopolization of the auto market in the early postwar years. Ford's hegemony was derived from the Model T's domination of the low-cost car market. General Motors controlled well over half of the remaining production, even before the Sloan transformation of GM to flexible production in the 1920s.[13] This virtual monopoly should have allowed for the market control necessary to accomplish maturity. That is, it would have been no surprise if competition had migrated away from product and process innovation and become focused on "styling, dealer service, and economies of scale in production."[14]

Despite these prerequisites, maturity did not occur. Instead, the first half of the 1920s was a period of almost constant improvement in vehicle design and of successful assault on production bottlenecks. The primary force that drove this continuing innovation was General Motors, which refused to concede the low-price niche to Ford. Beginning in 1920, GM mounted an all-out assault on the Model T under the direction of William Knudsen, a former Ford production executive who was installed as the head of the struggling Chevrolet division. In the next five years, Knudsen exploited the full range of new ideas and products percolating in the Detroit production culture to create a vastly superior car priced only $90 above the Model T.[15]

Even more significantly, GM introduced the yearly model change in all its product lines. Unlike the model changes of the 1950s and 1960s, when production had stabilized and the major innovations in American automobile manufacturing had been completed, these model changes were occasions for the introduction of major advances, including such new features as synchromesh gears, inflatable tires, and electric starters. Like the Japanese auto assemblers in the 1970s and 1980s, General Motors spared no effort to develop and exploit price and product advantages designed to steal market share from Ford.

GM's successful implementation of these changes rested on a new round of innovations on the shop floor. The moving assembly line system that might have become standardized was revolutionized once again, this time by the introduction of multipurpose machines. In place of dedicated tools designed to produce a single standardized product, Chevrolet pioneered the creation and use of multipurpose machine tools that could adapt to changing product design or manufacture several different designs on the same assembly line. These changes positioned GM to sustain a rapid pace of change for the foreseeable future and definitively undermined the incipient maturity that Ford had cultivated.

The brutality of this competition can be seen in the following simple chronology. In 1920, when the Model T reigned supreme, Ford had a 55 percent share of the American automobile market, and the Model T accounted for over 80 percent of the low-cost market. In 1926, after six years of fierce General Motors competition featuring yearly model changes, declining prices, and major technical innovations, Ford's share had dwindled to just over 30 percent, and the Model T had just 50 percent of the low-cost market.[16] The loss of 25 percent market share by a single company was a much more precipitous drop than the decline caused by the Japanese invasion sixty years later, which saw GM's market share decrease from 48 percent to 33 percent in twice as many years.

Despite the image of the unchanging Model T, Ford responded to this assault with a range of styling changes and a number of improvements in the guts of the Tin Lizzie. These included a new engine design, which necessitated major changes in the assembly line; an electric starter, which forced the redesign of the cylinder block and timing gears; and the all-metal body, which was so disruptive to the manufacturing process that it took three years to implement.[17]

There were also ongoing improvements in the assembly line, the consequence of the constant push to increase production and improve productivity. These improvements included an elaborate information system that allowed engineers to search for inefficiencies within the Highland Park and River Rouge production complexes and to compare internal Ford production with comparable companies outside the firm. It became an ongoing routine for the machine tools to be redesigned or replaced, for the power supply to be redirected or enhanced, and for conveyor belts to be rearranged.[18] Hounshell concludes that product and process innovation "was accommodated through a bureaucratic routine that worked so well that, for the most part, change was not noticed outside the company."[19]

Despite the many significant changes implemented at Ford, by 1926 the Model T was outmoded. Its braking system had been declared unsafe in several states, and these safety concerns had led to a ban on its import into Germany; its ignition, transmission, and suspension systems were all inferior to the Chevy's; and it lacked certain features that had become standard equipment by then on other cars. These included synchronized transmissions, shock absorbers, and a choice of colors in the final finish.[20] Moreover, it even experienced competition from higher-priced GM models: "For less than the price for a new Model T one might buy a not-so-elderly secondhand car like a Buick and have such conveniences as a self-starter, demountable rims and a smoother ride on the road."[21]

Ford responded by shutting down its two assembly lines on May 26, 1927, and introducing the Model A on October 27, 1927. To produce a new model in five months was astounding: today it typically takes four to five years. The fact that the new model was a state-of-the-art low-priced vehicle that, by 1929, had recaptured most of the company's lost market share, claiming 45 percent of the market, makes the story of the Model A worth focusing on. It highlights the capability of the early flexible system, since the changeover explicitly involved the transformation of a single-product process into the more flexible system developed by General Motors:

> More than fifty percent of all the production machinery had to be either replaced, re-designed, or supplemented by additional equipment. As an illustration of what a mere change in gear design involved, one hundred and sixty-six gear generating machines were completely rebuilt, at a cost per unit of $3,000, to

produce two gears included in the rear axle assembly. The purchase of 4,500 new machine tools, and the alteration of 15,000 existing ones involved an expenditure of $10,000,000.[22]

Not only was flexible machinery built, but outside supplier relationships were developed, a just-in-time delivery system was utilized, and—most important of all to the changeover—the workers were committed to the trial and error necessary to the endeavor. Hounshell describes the formalization of relationships with outside suppliers:

> Despite Charles Sorensen's compulsion to maintain the Rouge as an industrial colossus, in mid-1928 he and A. M. Wibel moved toward a strategy—which departed significantly from "high Rouge" strategy—whereby Ford came to depend increasingly upon outside suppliers as much as it had once done. General Motors and Chrysler, of course, had been consciously following such a strategy for a long time with obvious success. As Sorensen informed Edsel Ford: "This week we are working on stimulating the outside buying sources, so that we can make further jumps in production by getting as much help as we can from the outside and at the same time make the minimum expenditure for tools, etc., in our own plants." Wibel subsequently pursued this strategy with great vigor, and it became even more prevalent at Ford Motor Company when the Depression struck. Ford went to outside suppliers more and more during the early years of the Depression. This strategy may well have played a major role in reducing the time and the cost of the changeover to the V-8.[23]

The sort of cooperation cultivated during this period was exemplified by the troubles that Ford experienced in the gas tank of the Model A. Henry Ford had developed a radical new design, and its apparently straightforward assembly turned into a production nightmare: the seams could not be adequately sealed, even with the most advanced seam-welder available on the market. The Gibb Company, which manufactured the welder, responded to the crisis by sending its technicians to the Rouge to collaborate with Ford engineers and production personnel. The ad hoc team worked together in the Ford factory, redesigning the fuel tank, the welding machines, and the assembly process simultaneously. When assembly began on the Model A, the group continued to work on the shop floor until, after six months of collaborative effort, production reached the targeted 450 tanks per shift.[24]

The changeover to the Model A involved a multitude of these sorts of problems, resolved either at Ford or at the suppliers' shops. Sorensen ultimately established a routinized procedure for dealing with them:

> Each day Ed Martin and I would meet with these division heads and pass on tools and equipment. Since time was the essence on these projects, we had prepared charts showing bottlenecks, and follow-up crews were put on these spots. Men in outside tool- and machine-manufacturing plants gave us daily progress reports on the items that were behind on promises. All this meant an organization that could coordinate. Discord would show up and spoil effort. That was where I came in—looking for the weak spots, and I would live with them night and day until they cleared up.[25]

The important cooperation with outside suppliers would be moot, however, had workers not been committed to the process of innovation. In fact, the methodology employed in developing the Model A reflects—in an exaggerated and therefore very useful way—the integral role of production workers in developing new production techniques. When the line was reopened in January 1928, most of the myriad problems with the radical new design had not yet been resolved. The strategy for resolving these many problems was an exaggerated version of the famous Toyota methodology of speeding up the line and having workers stop it when they discover bottlenecks or sources of defective assembly. In this case, the entire process was kept in motion, often with handwork substituting for what would later be machine work. Each location was scrutinized and the production methodology to be used at that site was developed, as it were, from the ground up. Very frequently, informal teams of engineers, machine tool vendors, and line workers labored together for several months, collectively developing and refining the strategy for a particular station or process. Much of this was done with trial and error, with line workers serving as the ultimate arbiters of effectiveness.

To successfully change over from the Model T to the Model A, Ford had constructed a flexible production system staffed with committed workers. With all the necessary elements in place for rapid innovation, product and process change continued long past the changeover. When the business reporter Fay Faurote visited River Rouge during 1927, one engineer told him, "By the time you get this material in type and into the readers' hands, it will be out of date in the Ford factories."[26]

The fact that Ford could accomplish this transformation in less than a year contrasts dramatically with the decades-long incapacity of the American producers to respond to the Japanese challenge fifty years later. Moreover, despite a drastic reduction in demand for autos, innovation continued through the onset of the Great Depression. In 1931, Chrysler implemented a host of new innovations on the Plymouth; among the new features was a novel suspension that smoothed the ride and drastically reduced vibration, a feature unavailable even on much higher-priced cars.

With the entry of Plymouth, the intensity of competition was ratcheted up still another notch, and Ford's market share began dropping again. This time the free fall reached a new low of 25 percent in 1933, just before the introduction of Ford's legendary V-8 engine. This engine did more than establish a new standard in performance: it was manufactured on a radically redesigned assembly line that involved unit casting, pouring iron into a moving mold, using harder steel in the cutting tools, and simultaneously assembling four- and eight-cylinder engines on the same line. The resulting production efficiencies allowed the V-8 Ford to make a dramatic entrance into the low-priced market, and it restored the company to financial viability. It did not, however, recapture the mantle of industry leadership from General Motors, which GM would retain until the multiple debacles of the 1980s.[27]

The innovative resourcefulness of the early U.S. auto industry rested, as the discussion in this chapter has hinted, on production system features that are cornerstones of the flexible production process, such as just-in-time delivery, flexible machinery, geographic concentration, and long-term supplier relations. Later in the chapter, we detail how each of these components of flexible production was present in the early industry and contributed to the innovative climate.

At this juncture, we want to pause and emphasize the important role of worker commitment to innovation. Worker commitment is not a feature of flexible production, but rather a necessary condition for flexible production to function smoothly and facilitate innovation. This distinction is important to our overall story, because it was an inability of the Big Three to generate sufficient worker commitment that led them to dismantle their flexible production system. Later, we detail when and why worker commitment declined, what would have been needed to regenerate it, and why the U.S. automakers chose instead to abandon flexibility (and as a consequence innovativeness). For now, we focus on the importance of generating worker commitment if flexible production is to facilitate innovation and on the reasons for that. We begin by detailing the relationship between worker commitment and innovation.

WORKER COMMITMENT AND INNOVATION

The Model A changeover, discussed earlier, demonstrates the thin margin between the rote work of mass production and the creative work of innovation. If innovation is to be implemented and perfected on the shop floor—as in Old Detroit and in post–World War II Japan—then ordinary line workers must offer positive energy to the process. Without their commitment, the calibration of the work pace cannot be perfected, many errors will not be detected, and many corrections will not be effectively enacted.

Once this role is acknowledged and embraced, line workers become a part of the engineering team, contributing in an integral way to the process of change. Consider, for example, the introduction in the early 1930s of a new rustproofing machine in the Ford Flat Rock plant, where head and tail lamp assemblies were constructed. The new methodology was first developed by an outside supplier and then subjected to the routine Ford procedure of on-line testing by production workers. This led to the discovery of a potentially fatal flaw in the process: "the deterioration of the steel surface by acid action before the deposition of the rustproofing agent." Astute line workers discovered, however, that a coat of low-grade gasoline on the affected surfaces removed the problem. Ultimately, the manufacturer of the machine modified it to automatically apply the gasoline.[28]

This incident reveals two elements of the innovation process that characterized both Old Detroit and later Japanese production. One is the savvy of line workers, who understood the coating process well enough to suggest the non-intuitive device of gasoline coating. This reflected their ongoing involvement in these processes and their awareness of underlying chemical and production principles about which post–World War II American automobile workers had little interest and little knowledge.

But even more significant is the routinized way in which workers were expected to be involved in the introduction of new methodologies. The trial of the rustproofing machine "on the line" was seen as the only effective way to test out and modify new ideas. As Barclay commented in his detailed discussion of early Depression-era production:

> Ford production methods have long been famous, but not everyone is familiar with the details of the vast plan of research and experimentation that goes hand in hand with production at every stage of manufacture in the Rouge plant.
>
> Although all designs for Ford and Lincoln cars originate in the Ford Engineering Laboratory, there is no single large building devoted exclusively to research. Much of it may originate in one of the fourteen laboratories scattered throughout the Rouge plant, and it rightfully belongs as near as possible to the production of the work under consideration.[29]

This pattern was replicated throughout Detroit: at Chevrolet, where Knudsen walked the line and developed the flow technique for painting by talking over his ideas with production workers; at Buick, where engineers contemplating a change in the size of cylinders discussed its implications with the tool operators who would be machining the new product; and at every supplier that found itself talking to its own workers and those of the assemblers as new innovations were developed.[30]

In the following sections, we detail how the specific features of flexible production in Old Detroit facilitated innovation. In each instance, however, worker commitment permeated the entire process and was necessary for the system to work.

JUST-IN-TIME DELIVERY

When the Olds Motor Works plant in Detroit burned down in 1901, it quickly returned to production by moving to Lansing and contracting out all component parts from nearby suppliers.[31] One of the key issues that the Olds management had to address in their new production system was the issue of inventory. Inventories were a multiplex problem: the small rented space in the new assembly plant was one aspect of this problem, but there were many others. Owing to the financial strain of the fire, Olds did not have large amounts of money to invest in stockpiles; the pace of change in the industry made such stockpiles dangerous (since they might not be exhausted before specifications changed); and the uncertainty of the market made it inadvisable to commit to long production runs.

It was a relatively easy matter for Olds to resolve these problems by using what become known as "hand-to-mouth inventories." This slightly derogatory term captured the essence of the method: to offer each production station only enough of its needed components to get it through a short production run. In those days, Detroit was still a small town, and all of the needed suppliers were within striking distance of the Olds assembly plant. Even without telephones, Olds could place orders in the morning and expect delivery by the afternoon. Since the parts were the same as those used by other assemblers, no special production was needed, and therefore existing stockpiles at the component producers could act as inventory for Olds's production.

In an economy where most car producers were struggling with small capital and rapidly shifting markets, the hand-to-mouth system, like so many other innovations in Detroit, spread quickly to the other assemblers and became an assumed part of the Detroit production culture. As a backdrop against which parts suppliers did their business, the system influenced many of the later developments. Certainly it added to the compulsion for proximity, since hand-to-mouth deliveries required presence in Detroit—not only because of the difficulty of long-distance shipment, but also because of the likelihood that a less-than-perfectly organized assembler would suddenly discover the need for more parts. It also added drive to the standardization movement, since such rapid response required that the supplier be able to use the same part for many different customers.

But the hand-to-mouth system was never elevated into an icon of Detroit production. Unlike its Japanese cousin, it was not hailed when it was developed, nor does it appear in history books as a key to the rise of Detroit—or even as a central feature of the developing production system. Instead, the moving assembly line took that role; in doing so, it pushed many of the other innovations from view—including hand-to-mouth inventories.

In fact, Ford's moving assembly line substantially undermined hand-to-mouth inventory arrangements, particularly during the period just after the assembly line was mechanized in 1913. The massive disruption that led to 400 percent turnover that year and the many bottlenecks that appeared as part of perfecting the line made large stockpiles at individual stations a virtual necessity, and the huge dimensions of the Highland Park plant left ample room to accommodate them. Moreover, Ford, with its immense retained earnings and huge market, had no problem investing its capital in such stockpiles. And finally, the commitment to an unchanging Model T removed the danger that such stockpiles might become obsolete before they were exhausted.

Though it remained a viable strategy for the smaller and less secure assemblers, the hand-to-mouth system thus fell into disuse among large assemblers after World War I, not only at Ford but also at GM, Packard, Essex, Hudson, and other firms that had large and stable markets. Like the rise of the system, its decline passed unremarked and unsaluted. Hand-to-mouth inventories were simply not a big deal.

In the early 1920s, however, the hand-to-mouth system enjoyed a more acclaimed revival, and it became one of a number of policies saluted as hallmarks of the efficiency of the assembly line system. At Ford, the return of such inventories was motivated by financial considerations. During the terrible recession of 1921—when automobile sales declined by 22 percent in one year—Ford faced a major cash flow crisis, particularly when Henry Ford Sr. decided that the solution to reduced sales was a $200 reduction in the selling price of the Model T. To finance this strategy, Ford searched for ways to free up capital for cost-reducing innovations, and all eyes soon became focused on the $60 million in parts inventory sprinkled around the Highland Park and River Rouge plants. Henry Ford, in his typically peremptory manner, ordered an immediate return to the hand-to-mouth system within the plant and between the plant and its outside suppliers. He described the logic of the shift in his first book, *My Life and Work:*

> We found out how to use less money in our business by speeding up the turnover. . . . [and] reducing the cycle of manufacture from twenty-two to fourteen days. That is, raw material could be bought, manufactured and the finished product put into the hands of the distributor in (roughly) 33 percent less time than before. We had been carrying an inventory of around $60,000,000 to insure uninterrupted production. Cutting down the time one-third released $20,000,000.[32]

At General Motors, the same recession triggered a return to hand-to-mouth, but through a somewhat different causal chain, one that more closely resembled Toyota's logic. The initial impetus also came from a desire to reduce inventories during the 1921 recession, but this was soon supplemented by other motives. Sloan had hired William Knudsen to remake Chevrolet into a worthy competitor for the Model T, and Knudsen implemented a policy of ongoing innovation that soon evolved into the annual model change. This strategy put enormous pressure on each production station, particularly in the early years when changes could be introduced at any time. Large stockpiles were counterproductive in exactly the same way that they became counterproductive thirty-five years later in Taiichi Ono's engine plant. They would have to be cleared away when a new version of an old part was introduced, there might have to be several stockpiles available to accommodate several different versions of the car, and they might have to be shifted from one station to another as the production system evolved.

Here again, it was a relatively easy matter to switch back to hand-to-mouth inventories. The suppliers were accustomed to such deliveries with their other customers, they were virtually all located nearby, and they had large stockpiles, since they sold similar or identical parts to other assemblers.

The new system yielded impressive immediate gains for General

Motors. During the period between 1923 and 1925, when Chevrolet was making its move into the low-priced market, production at GM increased from 450,000 to 850,000 vehicles. At the same time, inventory decreased by 5 percent, from $117 million to $112 million.

The revived hand-to-mouth system gained momentum in the mid-1920s, not only in the automobile industry but also in many other industrial and commercial sectors.[33] This expansion was energized largely by the rapid pace of innovation in both product design and production methodology. The constant product change made large stockpiles dangerous, since they might have to be discarded if they became passé. And the production improvements led to a downward spiral in component prices, thereby rewarding low stockpiles with lower cost. At the same time, the transportation system in and around Detroit was made more effective—in large part in response to the rise of hand-to-mouth inventories. This allowed for even lower inventories and even greater savings.[34]

By the late 1920s, therefore, both Ford and GM had become strongly committed to the new system and had built its assumptions into the design of their factories and their relationships with their suppliers, both internal and external. As the system settled in, it took its place as one of the main constituent elements in the Detroit production culture, attracting the attention of business journalists and scholars and becoming a point of pride for automobile executives to write about.[35]

Ford's system was developed by Ernest Kanzler, a personal protégé of Edsel Ford. The logic he followed was strikingly similar to Taiichi Ono's process of rediscovery fifty years later. He initiated the hand-to-mouth system internally at the Fordson tractor plant and then extended it to outside suppliers as well. By 1924, he had developed it to a fine art: "So exact were his schedules that radiators, castings, etc. were utilized a few hours after their arrival to dispatch completed tractors."[36] Edsel then asked Kanzler to implement the system at the automobile plant as well; by 1926, the system was fully functioning at River Rouge.[37]

In keeping with the tradition of rapid diffusion in Detroit, the tight linkages developed at Ford were also implemented at GM. In fact, it is difficult to discern which firm copied the other, or whether it was a case of specific ideas traveling back and forth between them.

In any case, at General Motors the most spectacular hand-to-mouth achievements were found in the Buick division, which, like Toyota, sought to reduce inventories to the barest minimum and then adjust the manufacturing process accordingly. By 1927, C. B. Durham, one of the executives in charge of Buick production, wrote a long article for the *Magazine of Business* extolling GM's recent gains in productivity and highlighting the inventory system as a key element in this success.[38] His description of the finished system makes it sound like a clone of Ono's later methodology:

> Nowhere in our plant is there space for a day's supply of any finished part except frames. . . . Deliveries [are] carefully specified so that no excess material or part will be stored up. On purchased parts, one day's supply comes in some time during the day before it will be used. Raw material stock comes in much the same way. . . . Incoming materials or parts . . . are unloaded from the freight-car and handled directly to the point where they will be used; this saves the customary handling from stock to machine.

Durham provides spectacular details of the superiority of the system, once again evoking images of the enthusiastic descriptions of the Japanese system. He describes, for example, the reduced time from delivery to inclusion in finished products: "It used to take 18 days from the time a wheel entered the wheel paint-shop until it was ready to use. Now, within 4 hours of the time a wheel enters the paint-shop it is on the automobile." He also speaks about the space-saving due to the reduction of stockpiles: "It would take a new set of buildings if we undertook to keep [more than one day's supply]. In fact, it is beyond the mind's capacity to figure out, except by painstaking paper work, even an approximation of the increased floor space we should have to have." And he explains the subjection of internal transfers to an even more extreme version of the same system: "Our production showing is due entirely to putting the stuff through faster, using conveyors and automatic machinery, scheduling it so exactly that we eliminate storage. Not over 10% of the floor space in all of our factory buildings is used for storage of any sort."

Durham attributed the largest part of a 40 percent decline in Buick prices to the operation of the hand-to-mouth system. In short, at Buick the just-in-time inventory system was implemented with the same spirit and yielded the same results as would be seen thirty years later at Toyota.

It is an interesting exercise to compare the efficiency of the hand-to-mouth system with the just-in-time methods of the Japanese, as well as with the later efforts of the Americans to emulate the just-in-time system. As we noted earlier, Cusumano offers useful evidence in terms of inventory turnover.[39] In 1983, Toyota achieved a turnover ratio of thirty-six, compared to eleven or twelve for the American firms. Put more simply, American stockpiles were over three times as large as those in the Toyota plants. We do not have strictly comparable figures for the 1920s and 1930s, since measurement of inventories is very difficult, the system kept changing, and automobile executives during the period did not view them as a key variable in assessing corporate performance. Nevertheless, the rough figures available suggest that the hand-to-mouth system was capable of operating with inventories as small as or even smaller than the just-in-time system. In the mid-1920s, for example, Ford limited all stockpiles to less than thirty days' supply (except for iron ore during the winter), and the average department inventory was less than ten days. This translates into a turnover ratio between thirty-five and forty—exactly comparable to Toyota's legendary achievement sixty years later.[40]

MACHINE FLEXIBILITY

At Chevrolet, GM implemented flexible machinery themselves, aided by the personnel transfer that was a feature of the concentrated Detroit production culture. William Knudsen, one of Sorensen's top assistants in constructing the moving assembly line, was the key designer of the new manufacturing system.[41] After Knudsen left Ford because of friction with Henry Ford, Alfred Sloan hired him, and by 1922 Sloan had placed him at the helm of Chevrolet with the explicit mandate to transform the crisis-ridden division into effective competition for the Model T.

At the helm of Chevrolet, Knudsen embraced and implemented what had been a slow evolution toward machine flexibility because of the imperatives created by his campaign to challenge Ford's domination of the low-priced market. Two factors drove his increasing commitment to machine flexibility: (1) the continuous innovation in the early 1920s, which required assembly lines to be redesigned to simultaneously produce many different products and to accommodate ongoing change without substantial disruption of production; and (2) the tendency of the reduced inventories associated with the hand-to-mouth system to yield idle machines.

When Knudsen moved to Chevrolet, he completely revamped the assembly line there with the intention of creating a much more flexible system that could produce several different models simultaneously and change models frequently. The linchpin of this new system was the purchase of new machines more suitable for flexible production. In Knudsen's own account of the new system, he emphasized these new machines as his main contribution: "The machine equipment was first tackled, with the result that gradually all old machines were discarded, new heavy type standard machines (not single purpose) were installed, and fixtures strengthened so as to withstand the spring," which he cited as "the greater factor than wear" in causing inaccurately machined parts.[42] Hounshell describes Knudsen's revolution:

> This new direction at Chevrolet allowed limits of precision to be lowered, resulting in the reduction of scrapped material. . . . It is important to emphasize that the entire Chevrolet production system, though led by a former Ford production expert, was based on standard or general-purpose, not single-purpose, machine tools. For this reason, Chevrolet could accommodate change far more easily than could the Ford Motor Company.[43]

This system had been fully implemented by the mid-1920s, and it enabled Chevrolet not only to offer a vast variety of features to its customers but also to absorb new innovations without major disruptions in production. Flexible machinery was quickly extended to other GM production facilities. In 1941, Alfred Sloan himself would comment that visitors to GM assembly plants were "bewildered as they observed eleven kinds of chassis taking final shape as Oldsmobiles, Pontiacs, and Buicks. And all this happens on the same assembly line."[44]

The use of flexible machines at Chevrolet, coupled with the industrywide need for flexible machines to avoid idling as a result of low inventory, would lead one to expect Ford and GM to implement flexible machinery in all of their plants, as Toyota later would. Unlike in Japan, however, suppliers of the early U.S. auto industry had implemented flexible machinery in their production processes even before Chevrolet did. This provided GM and Ford with the option to take advantage of preexisting flexible machinery by increasing outsourcing.

This option derived from the combination of the constantly expanding used-car market and the breakdown of the standardization movement, which had forced the component suppliers to embrace flexible production as a way of life. Bendix, for example, needed to produce replacement brakes for several versions of the Model T, including those with and without the new pressed brakes that had been developed in the early 1920s. They also needed to accommodate all the different years of GM's many different models and to simultaneously keep up with Chrysler's burgeoning line. As an original equipment supplier to both GM and Chrysler, Bendix was responsible for delivering huge amounts of the appropriate types of brakes in some months and relatively few in other months, as demand fluctuated with the seasons and with the vagaries of competition. Many of these fluctuations were predictable, but others were not, and Bendix was often forced to accommodate sudden orders, sometimes on one or two days' notice.

As if these problems were not enough, Bendix and other component suppliers also faced the enormous pressure of ongoing innovation. They had to be prepared each year to quickly develop an altered design of each type of brake they produced to accommodate any changes in the design of the GM and Chrysler cars for which they were original parts suppliers. And beyond this, they had to be searching for new innovations and developing more effective and efficient ways to produce their existing products, lest they lose market share to the three other major brake suppliers in Detroit.

One way to manage these multiplex demands was to maintain huge stockpiles of every type of brake, and many component suppliers adopted this strategy as a way of managing the system, just as many of Toyota's suppliers would do three decades later.[45] This was an expensive proposition in the short run, since it required buying large numbers of multiple items long before they would be used. But it also involved huge waste whenever annual model changes or design improvements made current models passé, since they might have to wait years before the stockpile could be sold as replacement parts. In brakes, for example, it usually took two years before there were substantial replacement sales.

The more effective reaction was the development and proliferation of flexible machinery. Insofar as component suppliers could move seamlessly from one type of item to another, they could maintain small inventories of the many products they supplied and quickly shift their production to accommodate sudden increases or decreases in demand. When new designs were implemented, they could quickly retool their machinery to accommodate these changes and therefore avoid wasteful stockpiles of parts that could not be sold until the replacement market kicked in.

GEOGRAPHIC CONCENTRATION

The geographic concentration of auto production in the United States was not intentionally developed in service of either just-in-time delivery or innovation. Rather, auto production became geographically concentrated owing to the particular needs of a nascent industry.[46] When automobile production began on a car-by-car basis at the beginning of the twentieth century, no single firm could manufacture even a substantial portion of the finished product. Automakers therefore relied on suppliers of the various components to provide them with the bulk of the constituent parts. These dependencies yielded a loose territorial imperative as the early car industry arose near concentrations of already established industries that supplied needed parts to the fledgling manufacturers. For the most part, this imperative implied proximity to machine shops, carriage makers, bicycle producers, or any type of engine manufacturing. Two areas of concentration eventually emerged: the broad area between Chicago and southern Michigan, which housed important concentrations of machine shops, carriage makers, and the struggling gasoline engine industry; and an even broader area stretching from Rochester and Buffalo in New York southeastward through New Jersey and into Connecticut, which housed major centers of bicycle and electric engine production, as well as the machine tool firms that supplied these industries.[47]

In light of what emerged later, the East would have been a much better location for the auto industry. First, since European immigrants were the chief source of noncraft labor, Detroit was a poor choice for an industry that, by the mid-1920s, would require approximately 600,000 additional unskilled workers.[48] The East had the best access to this resource, since about 90 percent of the new immigrants entered the country through New York or Boston. Detroit was not even particularly close to Chicago—the nearest secondary destination of immigrants.

Second, existing large-scale industrial production was largely concentrated in the East. The mid-Atlantic region housed such staples of mass production as armaments, sewing machines, and bicycles, and the skills in labor supervision were therefore concentrated there.[49] Here again, Chicago was a secondary center, but one too far away to be of immediate use. In a very real sense, Ford had to reinvent these skills and then train a cadre of production supervisors, a process that generated enormous turnover and disruption until the institution of the Five Dollar Day in 1914.[50]

Finally, Detroit lenders had no experience with large-scale industrial enterprise, and owners like Ford had to acquire this experience as the industry developed. Wall Street, on the other hand, had played a crucial role in nurturing (or even constraining) Eastern industries.

Beyond these initial inadequacies of Detroit, the evolution of the automobile that was triggered by mass production further undermined the Detroit area's suitability as a center of production. The carriage industry—a principal factor in the concentration of early production there—rested largely on woodworking and was located in the area because of Michigan's proximity to forests. As auto production expanded, the exhaustion of the supply of nearby lumber contributed to the evolution of all-metal bodies. (Eventually even the wood steering wheels were replaced.) Proximity to lumber was consequently no longer significant.[51] The industry would have been better served if it had been proximate to the steel industry.

Similarly, the increased speed of autos soon led to the invention of inflatable rubber tires and thus to dependence on the rubber industry. The development of fully enclosed bodies led to dependency on the glass industry. Self-starting engines and night driving led to dependence on electrical components. None of these inputs were initially available in or around Detroit. And the transportation system into and out of Detroit was at best underdeveloped; it could not handle the vast quantities of incoming raw materials and outgoing automobiles required by the huge expansion of production. Southern Michigan's resources thus made it a reasonable choice for an industry that produced hand-crafted automobiles for a small market, but an unfortunate choice for large-scale assembly line production.

This mismatch did not, however, play a significant role in limiting the development of the industry there, because the Detroit area possessed one overwhelming advantage. It housed the production culture that created (and was created by) the methodology that we associate with the assembly line. It was therefore the only location that could develop this new system to its full potential. This advantage was intuitively grasped by all concerned parties: the local entrepreneurs who sought to emulate Ford; the local banks that invested in these experiments; Eastern automakers who did not attempt to mass-produce automobiles; Wall Street bankers who did not encourage Eastern emulation of Ford's methods (but instead began investing in Detroit); the new feeder industries that arose in nearby production centers like Akron, Dayton, and Anderson, Ohio; and the huge numbers of workers who flooded into southern Michigan to populate the new factories.

Michael Storper and Richard Walker argue that "industries produce regions," and the rise of southern Michigan as the center of automobile production exemplifies this process: "Industry location patterns are created through the process of growth rather than through a process of efficient allocation of plants across a static economic landscape. That is, industries produce economic space rather than being hostage to the pre-existing spatial distribution of suppliers and buyers."[52]

The Concentration of Production at Ford

Henry Ford Sr. very early sought to fully integrate the entire production process into a single facility. Even before the River Rouge plant was constructed with this idea in mind, the Highland Park plant grew to sixty thousand employees as Ford absorbed suppliers or constructed new facilities to displace them. By the mid-1920s, the High-land Park complex manufactured its own tires, constructed its own batteries, and processed its own textiles for interior upholstery.[53]

Charles Sorensen offered a succinct summary of the logic that un-derlay Ford's construction of River Rouge:

> Its immensity and completeness are now so much a matter of course as to cease being a wonderment. What is overlooked, how-ever, is its basic simplicity: raw materials come in at one side, a complete motorcar comes out at the other. Also frequently over-looked is the essential philosophy behind its building and opera-tion.[54]

Later, he explained the rationale for this philosophy in describing the inclusion of a steel mill in the complex:

> Between 1919 and 1929 the demand exceeded the supply. We were tearing our hair. Purchasing steel and following up orders and de-liveries produced headaches in many of our manufacturing divi-sions. Shortages meant holdups and layoffs in production. The profit motive seemed to interest steelmakers more than increasing facilities. Somewhere there had to be an increase in steel output. An increasing demand was apparent to anyone—all-steel auto bodies, furniture, refrigerators, stoves, freight cars, home utensils; someone had to cut loose and put up more steel mills. If others would not provide enough steel for our needs, then we would. It was just as simple as that.[55]

It wasn't that simple. Even if Ford had succeeded in its ambition to stabilize automobile design around the Model T template, it could never have manufactured every constituent component, even in its huge plants. Once GM imposed ongoing innovations on the industry, auto production became even more complicated, since rapid evolu-tion required new parts and sometimes different proportions of raw materials each year.

The changes wrought by the rapid pace of expansion and innova-tion thus created a strong counterforce to centralization throughout the 1920s and 1930s. As the automobile evolved and production runs increased, Ford was forced to rely on local or distant outside suppli-ers. In the early 1920s, for example, the exponential rise in the number of cars sold exhausted the supply of leather and forced Ford to purchase synthetic upholstery from a variety of sources. These synthetics were cheaper to produce than leather, thus rendering Ford's tanning facilities obsolete.[56] These same expanded markets, combined with the ascendancy of closed bodies, vastly increased the use of glass. Hence, despite its internal glass-making facility, Ford was forced into outside sourcing of finished windows, and this led to purchases from a variety of suppliers around the country.[57] At about the same time, the proliferation of inflatable tires altered the type and quantity of rubber needed by the industry, consolidating Akron as the geographical center for rubber production. Ford, like the other assemblers, began to purchase tires from Akron companies.[58]

In 1927, after GM's emphasis on elegant body styling contributed to the demise of the Model T, Ford decided to offer the Model A with a variety of difficult-to-manufacture body types. Because the existing facilities could not simultaneously construct several body types, and because even the huge River Rouge complex could not (at least at first) physically accommodate the complex production process, more than half of the Model A bodies were purchased from Briggs Manufacturing. As Ford later became caught up in the V-8 and in continuous model changes, its dependence on outsiders for bodies extended through the Depression.[59]

These and other developments created ongoing and increasing violations of Ford's philosophy of centralized production and might have yielded a substantial geographical decentralization of Ford's production as early as the mid-1920s. Two factors worked against decentralization, at least in the case of Ford: the concentration of most of its suppliers in the southern Michigan complex, and an ongoing process of recentralization stimulated by the same disruptions in supply that had motivated the original concentration.

Briggs Bodies, located near Ford's Highland Park complex, illustrates the process that created a clustering of parts suppliers in the Detroit area. Walter Briggs, the firm's founder, was a longtime auto man who had worked in many local firms before going into business for himself. Howard Bonbright, the firm's treasurer, was a local venture capitalist and a personal friend of Edsel Ford's.[60] Like the vast majority of component suppliers that depended on auto for the bulk of their business, Briggs Bodies thus had its origins in southern

Michigan and had every personal and business incentive to remain there.

For the most part, therefore, when Ford sought outside suppliers, it found them in the immediate area among the vast number of ongoing ventures or new firms, virtually all of them operated by entrepreneurs who were integrated into the local production culture.

There were important exceptions to this pattern, however, exemplified by rubber and glass. Rubber, though it grew up largely as a consequence of the auto industry, had vast numbers of other uses, and its location in Akron, Ohio, reflected this dual nature. It was close enough to Detroit to be considered within the southern Michigan production complex, but sufficiently separated to allow for the development of a rubber-based production complex around Akron. Glass, on the other hand, historically preceded the auto industry and was never highly dependent on it. It therefore developed its own production centers in New York and Pennsylvania before the rise of Detroit. Rubber for tires and glass for windows were two components that were therefore not initially available in southern Michigan, and once Ford's modest production capacity was exhausted, the company found its supplies outside the local area.

Unlike the Japanese sixty years later, the distance did not, by itself, violate Ford's production principles. But the company found itself facing the same sort of supply disruptions that motivated the original "one-big-plant" strategy, and these set in motion an oscillating process of recentralization and re-decentralization. At the same time, these oscillations introduced the evolving automobile production methodology into these other industries, where it motivated a new round of innovation.

In the case of rubber, Ford had originally created a small facility in its Highland Park plant but had discontinued production once inflatable tires made it obsolete. Nevertheless, as Henry Ford commented in 1926,

> If those who sell to us will not manufacture at the prices which, upon investigation, we believe to be right, then we make the article ourselves. In many cases, we manufacture just enough of a product to get thoroughly familiar with it, so that in an emergency we may make it ourselves. . . . We have made rubber tires, although we have no present intention of going into the tire business. [But]

the price of rubber may be forced inordinately high. In any event, we have to be prepared. It would never do to have to shut down our production for lack of tires.[61]

The emergency that triggered recentralization was the rise of the union movement, which would later engulf the auto assemblers during the Flint sit-down strike. Sorensen explained that "shutdowns, sit-downs, and slowdowns made it impossible for such tiremakers as Firestone, Goodrich, and Goodyear, our chief suppliers, to deliver regularly enough to meet our demands. We were sitting on a powder keg—sitting, looking, waiting, and hoping for a solution of that problem."[62] Ford's solution was to construct a modern plant at River Rouge to handle 50 percent of its tire needs. Firestone sent its top engineers to help design the plant after Sorensen assured Harvey Firestone that, "when we get the plant running, if it is a success, you can take over. We don't want to make tires. All we want is assurance of a continuous supply."[63]

The new facility, by combining Akron's rubber expertise with Detroit's assembly line production methods, substantially increased production efficiency. According to Sorensen:

I suggested [to Harvey Firestone that] he lend us a good man who knew all operations, time, and cost. I wanted him in the Rouge plant to lay out plans, then stay with us and erect and operate the plant. . . .

The Firestone people sent us E. F. Wait, one of their experts. We brought in the United Engineering Company and with their engineers laid out a new progressive plant. Every operation was mechanized, with the units feeding into a final tire assembly—a typical Ford assembly line.

Shortly before Christmas, 1937, the plant began operations and did exactly what had been predicted. It lightened the heavy, laborious work and turned out more tires per man. We could train men for each operation. We had variable wage rates and no piecework, which was the real problem on labor relations in Akron. With this installation our worries about the tire supply vanished.[64]

It is important to note that geographic concentration was not an explicit part of Ford's corporate strategy. Though this account by Sorensen contains a clear pride—almost conceit—that the incorporation of rubber into the Rouge complex yielded significant improvements in both product quality and production methodology, Sorensen appeared to believe that the creative virtues of concentration were temporary. Once the new innovations were complete, they could be exported to distant locales without loss of efficiency. This sentiment is partially captured in his account of the closure of Ford's rubber plant once the United Rubber Workers had unionized the industry, putting an end to the labor crisis and providing the worker commitment necessary for the new methodology to diffuse into the industry: "Within a couple of years things changed, Akron got over her early labor problems, and we finally stopped making tires. Thus we made good on our promise to Mr. Firestone that we would get out of the tire business as soon as we felt suppliers could handle our requirements safely."[65]

This attitude—and the oscillation between geographic concentration and deconcentration to which it contributed—was vividly expressed by Ford's experience in glass production.[66] When the automobile changed "from an open summer vehicle to a closed year-round means of transportation," demand for glass simply outstripped supply.[67] At first, Ford sought to meet its needs by purchasing the Allegheny Glass Company in Glassmere, Pennsylvania, but this facility never had sufficient capacity. So the top executives applied their ongoing centralization strategy:

> We decided we must have our own plate glass as soon as possible and install a new modern plant at the Rouge. It was scheduled for 10,000,000 square feet. This revolutionized plate-glass manufacturing. A smelting furnace with mechanical charging of the silica sand so that it could produce a continuous ribbon of the glass was built.
>
> Plate glass was cast in an endless unbroken strip, something the experts of the glass industry declared impossible. Then grinding and polishing was done on a continuous process. We designed and built this machinery. It was an immediate success. Instead of costing from 30 cents to $1.50, our glass was made for 20 cents a square foot.[68]

Once this very considerable set of innovations had been consolidated, Ford executives saw no ongoing virtue in sustaining geographical concentration. When increasing demand outstripped the capacity of the River Rouge glass plant, no effort was made to expand locally. Instead, Ford applied classic comparative cost principles by building a new facility (which incorporated the new innovations) in St. Paul, Minnesota, "where we had both water power and silica sand in the same site."[69] Ironically, the process went through another cycle when safety glass was introduced in the late 1920s. Since Ford's internal facilities could not supply this new product, the firm once again came to rely on outsiders, in this case Pittsburgh Plate Glass and Libbey-Owens-Ford. Since both of these firms maintained large facilities in southern Michigan, this shift to outside suppliers resulted in a return to local sourcing.

The attitude that pervades Sorensen's accounts of oscillating geographic concentration and deconcentration illuminates the process that determined the ultimate shape and content of the southern Michigan production complex. Suppliers who serviced only the automobile industry, like those that built auto bodies, grew up in the region or became more or less permanently concentrated there. Suppliers that served multiple markets, like the glass and rubber industries, developed their own complexes, but were nevertheless drawn to Detroit and established facilities there. Though the impetus for this attraction was largely the interruption of supplies due to production shortages, transportation problems, or labor stoppages, the concentration process yielded significant product improvements and production innovations, of which Sorensen and other Ford executives were fully aware.

They did not, however, believe that future innovation depended on continued concentration of production. To Sorensen and Ford, there was a once-and-for-all aspect to the changes that took place at the central factory. Once the assembly line system was applied to the production of a certain commodity, the major work was finished. Further modifications could take place in the hinterlands without the surrounding support system of the central facilities. The only enduring justification for the huge Highland Park and River Rouge plants were transportation bottlenecks: "A big factory sometimes pays. Our Fordson [River Rouge] plant pays because it brings raw materials together economically. Our finished product . . . goes out with a minimum transportation charge. But if Fordson did not deal in heavy, bulky raw materials it would not pay. It pays because it combines quick transportation both inward and outward."[70]

This philosophy was the underlying force in the creation of Ford's ill-fated branch assembly plant system, which symbolized the glorious rise of the Model T and then fell into disarray with its decline. Its history allows us to glimpse the contrary quality of the territorial imperative—that is, the strong incentives for geographical dispersion and the incompatibility between such dispersion and ongoing innovation.

Ford's branch assembly plant system was one of the key developments during the firm's early dominance in the industry. When demand for the Model T began increasing exponentially after 1909, Ford became the first automobile maker to face the multiple problems and opportunities of a national market.[71] Like many firms before and since, it discovered that the cost and difficulty of shipping bulky finished products to distant markets could be partially resolved by shipping unfinished components and assembling them locally. According to Henry Ford, the firm followed classic locational theory in establishing its branch plant system: "Really big business cannot concentrate in one place, for the reason that transportation charges, aside from all other factors, discourage it. A great business has to have far-flung markets, and in these days it does not pay to transport heavy products, raw or finished, over long distances."[72]

Within this logic, the attractiveness of branch plants was enhanced by two less universal features of the early auto industry. The first was the odd shape of assembled autos, which did not allow them to fit comfortably onto existing freight cars. Only four Model Ts could be loaded onto a single flatbed, and the cost of shipping the finished automobile was therefore twice the cost of shipping tightly packed components separately.[73] The second factor—which was particularly compelling in the early years—had to do with the lack of consumer confidence in the primitive repair and parts distribution system before World War I:

> The assembly plant system was designed to give every purchaser of a car immediate or very quick supplies in case of broken parts. It gave a miniature factory at a strategic location to serve that location or neighborhood, which stimulated sales because of the

investment in that particular plant in that immediate locality, assuring purchasers that they would have their troubles and complaints well looked after.[74]

The first branch plant was established in Kansas City in 1913. When it proved successful, Ford launched a massive expansion that continued until 1916 and yielded twenty-nine assembly plants.[75] Despite their undoubted success in reducing transportation costs, the branch plants did not settle the locational issues they were meant to address. Instead, they created a new set of problems in the ongoing dialectic of centralization and decentralization. Efficient operation of the dispersed assembly plants depended on the timely arrival of each and every component. The absence of even a small part could shut down the line. Such interruptions were difficult to avoid when shipping to distant destinations, and Ford now faced the sometimes unmanageable job of coordinating transport to twenty-nine different locations.

The initial resolution to this problem was a stockpiling system, in which large amounts of each component were shipped to the branch plants during slow sales periods in the fall and winter and then used when sales increased in the spring and summer. This methodology had the serendipitous virtue of allowing the Highland Park and (later) River Rouge plants to operate steadily throughout the year, instead of responding directly to seasonal sales fluctuation.[76] But it also created a vast storage problem at the branch sites, since huge facilities were needed to hold the large inventories that accumulated during the winter months. The problem was especially acute for auto bodies, since their bulk made them particularly difficult to stockpile in large numbers.[77]

These stockpiling and transportation problems were part of a nexus of provocations that triggered ongoing evolution in the branch assembly plant system. Most significantly, they created a new incentive for further decentralization, which was expressed in the shift of body assembly to some of the branch plants: "Only a few years ago, seven touring car bodies made a full load for a standard thirty-six-foot freight car. Now the bodies are shipped knocked-down to be assembled and finished in the branches, and we ship 130 touring car bodies in the same sized car—that is, we use one freight car where we should formerly have used eighteen."[78]

The branch plants also began to follow distinct evolutionary paths. Like the Model T itself, Ford had expected them to be standardized as to capacity and manufacturing technique, but this expectation did not take into account increasing production runs and the many changes in the Model T, even before the changeover to the Model A in 1927.[79] Eighteen months after the development of the moving assembly line was completed at Highland Park in 1915, it was installed in virtually all the branch plants, with little formal coordination to allow for future innovations. This led each plant to develop its own distinct style, with only informal attempts at sustaining uniformity or diffusing the most effective new innovations to all the plants. The manager of one branch plant described the dynamics as competition rather than coordination:

> There was quite a contest between the different branches. . . . It was actually a competitive situation. If one branch made a better production performance than another there would be an exchange through the grapevine to see how the better method was handled. Detroit manufacturing would let you know anytime they picked up a better, quicker way of doing anything from some other branch.[80]

In a surprisingly short period, some of the branch plants began to absorb various aspects of the production process. By 1920, the St. Paul facility had become a secondary center for manufacturing mechanical components and had even begun shipping parts to other assembly sites. By 1924, the Los Angeles plant had become a secondary hub as well, replete with local suppliers: "At Los Angeles, the branch plant makes bodies and as many parts as can be made more cheaply there than at St. Paul or Detroit. For cushions, the plant consumes cotton from the Imperial Valley and from Arizona."[81]

This evolution created vast problems for Ford in the mid-1920s, when it responded to the GM challenge by altering the Model T. Though many changes could be absorbed with relatively few alterations in assembly techniques, many others required major overhaul in one or several parts of the process.[82] As a consequence, the unique features in each plant became a source of difficulty, since no general template could be developed and the engineers in Michigan had little knowledge of the specifics of the branch plants.

These difficulties—as well as the huge market fluctuations during this period—led to a very high death rate among the branch plants. By the mid-1920s, six of the original twenty-nine plants had closed and been replaced by new ones, and virtually all the others had been remodeled at least once. The changeover to the Model A yielded two more deaths and another remodeling for the remainder. In this upheaval, the St. Paul and Los Angeles facilities lost the bulk of their manufacturing functions. Subsequent changes in the Model A yielded five more replacements by 1932, when depressed sales led to eleven closings. By that year, only three of the original twenty-nine plants were still operating.[83]

James Rubenstein succinctly summarized the fundamental dynamics of this breathless and costly evolution: "The short life-span of the first-generation assembly plants reflected the rapid changes in motor vehicle production."[84]

This comment points to the incompatibility between the sort of geographical dispersion that Ford practiced and the ongoing process of innovation, both in the product design and in production methodology. The problems of coordinating change at twenty-nine separate plants would have been daunting if they had all been identical in structure. Their separate evolution made the process even more unmanageable, and this difficulty was exacerbated still further by the lack of efficient coordination between the designers in Michigan and the branch managers.[85] Without intense interaction, new ideas in the surrounding area had to depend on the grapevine to be diffused to other branch plants, and they rarely entered the consciousness and planning of Sorensen and his crew in Michigan.

The closings and remodelings of branch plants were expensive and disruptive, and it is not possible to determine with precision whether they were offset by the benefits Ford derived from reduced shipping costs and enhanced customer satisfaction.[86] It is this balance of costs and benefits that illuminates the very powerful contradiction between ongoing innovation and maximizing profits in national (or international) markets.

Though it was never articulated in this way, Ford thus had an implicit choice of several less than perfect alternatives in managing the branch assembly system. The first choice was the policy Ford pursued, with local autonomy that permitted independent evolution and yielded many short-term efficiencies. In the long run, however, the firm absorbed huge added costs, since each plant developed independent solutions to specific production problems and absorbed a different mix of manufacturing functions. This led to expensive remodeling of the plants when large changes were made in auto design, and in many cases entire plants had to be discarded.

The second choice would have preserved local autonomy but augmented it with a well-organized monitoring system that evaluated each local change and sought to diffuse effective innovations to the system as a whole. In this scenario, local decision-making would still have yielded significant differences based on local preferences and conditions, but the central administration could have become an active partner in managing alterations and thus reduced (without eliminating) the disruption of adapting the many different plants to the changes in auto design.

The final option would have involved the imposition of uniformity on the branch plants. Local changes would have been approved by the central administration only if they could be adopted everywhere or were deemed nondisruptive to ongoing innovation. Such a program would have removed the bulk of the disruption during model changes, since central designers could develop changeover plans that would have been applied at each site. The firm would then have had to forgo the virtues of local innovation, which created substantial cost efficiencies based on the creativity of local managers and workers and the idiosyncratic structure and environment of specific plants. Moreover, such centralized control would have been difficult to develop and maintain; a vast data gathering and processing system would have been required, as well as an elaborate national administrative apparatus populated by skilled central executives and cooperative local managers.[87]

This dilemma did not become an active issue for Ford's leadership. When the branch system was initially developed, they expected the Model T to be a standard product with few changes that could disrupt local assembly. If this expectation had been fulfilled, they would have avoided the enormous costs of replacement and remodeling, and the branch system—replete with local autonomy and innovation—might have been an unmitigated success. In a sense, therefore, dispersed assembly was premised on product standardization, as

Henry Ford implicitly acknowledged in describing the 1925 modifications in the Model T:

> The advantages of standardization are apparent in production. The disadvantage is the expense incurred when changing from the standard. . . .
> Last year we made certain changes to the end of turning out somewhat better cars. The engine we did not touch—that is, the heart of the car.
> In all, eighty-one changes, major and minor, were involved. None of these changes was made lightly. The new designs were thoroughly tried out all over the country in actual service for many months.
> All of this sounds simple enough, but here is what is meant to make only eighty-one changes. We had to design 4,759 punch and dies and 4,243 jigs and fixtures. We had to build 5,622 punch and dies and 6,990 jigs and fixtures. The labour cost of this amounted to $5,682,387, while the material ran to $1,395,596. Installing enamel ovens in thirteen branches cost $371,000, and changing the equipment in twenty-nine branches cost $145,650. That is to say, these changes cost us upward of eight million dollars, not estimating time lost from production.[88]

This immense cost of change created an ongoing incentive for standardization within the Ford system beyond the original commitment to the unchanging Model T. Ford, though reluctant to publicly admit that his firm would respond to such incentives, nevertheless implicitly acknowledged their force when he declared that "the cost of such changes is usually more than compensated by the improvements which a change gives the opportunity to make."[89]

At Ford, the contrary tendencies for spatial centralization and decentralization remained unresolved.[90] On the one hand, the firm responded to the pressure of GM's challenge to seek out new innovations that would keep their automobiles competitive with a greater tendency to concentrate production in the Highland Park and River Rouge complexes or access state-of-the-art suppliers within the southern Michigan production culture. On the other hand, the cost of transport created strong incentives to disperse assembly plants to local markets. The pressure to innovate, however, led many of the dispersed assembly plants to follow in the footsteps of the Los Angeles plant and use many local suppliers, which created concentrated production geographies (at least in the early auto industry, before the events of the Depression and World War II, which we discuss in chapters 3 and 4).

Concentration of Production at General Motors

General Motors, as the driving force for ongoing innovation in the auto industry, would appear to be the likely locale for a creative response to the contradictory impulses for dispersion and concentration. Unlike the Japanese, however, GM's leadership never articulated the connection between geography and innovation, and it therefore could not be integrated into explicit decision-making. Like Ford, General Motors significantly contributed to the concentration of the industry in southern Michigan, but it also contributed to the unsystematic and haphazard pattern that eventually emerged.

The origins of General Motors prevented it from entertaining Ford's one-big-plant strategy. William Durant, in his two periods as president, absorbed a broad array of assemblers and component manufacturers into the company in a fashion that many observers have characterized as haphazard at best.[91] By the time the board of directors removed him in 1921, General Motors—with seventy-five factories in forty cities—reflected the geography of the industry as a whole. The majority of these plants were located in the Detroit area, and the bulk of the rest were distributed in the northern parts of Indiana, where they could partake of the southern Michigan production culture. Nevertheless, a substantial minority of the plants were in the automotive hinterland, including at least five very important establishments in the old Eastern production centers.[92]

Billy Durant's lack of geographical consciousness underscores the significance of his tendency to move plants from the hinterlands to southern Michigan. As early as 1906, when Durant was president of Buick and had not yet created General Motors, he "set out to woo Westin-Mott from Utica to Flint" because the firm's axles "were not arriving in Flint in a timely manner."[93] Four years after the move, General Motors acquired the company. This example was repeated in many different variations, all of them consistent with increased concentration in Detroit. Some companies, like Westin-Mott, moved to Michigan before General Motors absorbed them into the parent firm. Others, like AC Spark Plugs, were acquired first and then moved.[94] Still other acquisitions, like Fisher Body, grew up in southern Michigan. Finally, a few subsidiaries and suppliers, like Hyatt Roller Bearings, were not moved to southern Michigan because the disruptions that motivated such moves were not severe enough to force the migration. At the time of Durant's departure, therefore, there were still ten component plants in New York, Pennsylvania, New Jersey, and Connecticut.[95]

Since these early patterns could be seen as the peculiar dynamics of a young industry or as a reflection of Durant's restlessness, it is important to note that this process of geographical concentration continued long after Durant's departure. It extended through the boom period of the 1920s and well into the 1930s—when demand for automobiles contracted by 50 percent. For the most part, therefore, General Motors increasingly concentrated all aspects of production in southern Michigan, including top executives, manufacturing facilities, and the research and design centers.

At the same time, however, GM embraced the contrary tendency toward decentralization: it constructed a network of dispersed Chevrolet assembly plants; it nurtured separate production complexes for non-automotive parts and electrical components in Dayton, Ohio, and Anderson, Indiana; and it created stand-alone production complexes in Canada, England, and Germany.[96]

The various documents and public pronouncements of General Motors executives contain no official statement that the firm had decided to sustain or enhance the already existing concentration in southern Michigan or in Flint, the ultimate center of the General Motors production network.[97] Nevertheless, Sloan himself observed this pattern and—without endorsing it as a policy—attributed it to the uncertainty of supplying needed components from long distances: "A dependable supply of parts might well make the difference between success and failure. Distance added uncertainty. It was natural, therefore, for the industry to correlate all its manufacturing within a rather narrow geographical area. It was a practical urge, but underneath it was a very definite economic justification."[98] Sloan's observations are remarkably un-astute for an individual of his insight and vision. If the concentration process had reflected only the uncertainty of delivering supplies, it would not have included the systematic centralization of design and planning in the Detroit area as well. During the 1920s, General Motors itself was the most important contributor to this trend.

When the Sloan team was installed in 1920, GM had already established the General Motors Research Laboratory, which would soon become the fountainhead of GM innovation and a source of technical advance for the industry as a whole.[99] The laboratory was located in Dayton, Ohio, because Charles Kettering, its director and guiding force, was associated with Delco, a major electrical component subsidiary located there. Four years later, after the laboratory had proven its worth with such developments as a knockless gasoline and the Duco lacquer finish, the by-then huge operation was moved to Detroit, a relocation that facilitated cooperation between Kettering and the production executives who implemented his innovations.

The impetus for this shift in location was provided by a bitter dispute between Kettering and various production executives over the ultimately failed attempt to produce a cost-effective air-cooled engine. This innovation, which promotional materials called the "Copper-cooled Engine" because it used high-conductivity copper wings to draw heat off, had been developed after World War I by Kettering's team in Dayton. Pierre DuPont, the GM board chairman in the first years after Durant's departure, strongly supported its implementation, and this set in motion a four-year process that led to not only the relocation of the laboratory but also an affirmation of the rights of division presidents to veto most design changes in the automobiles they produced.

In early 1921, the GM board—after an inspection trip to Dayton—was satisfied with Kettering's experimental engines and ordered the development of both four- and six-cylinder production models. Despite the strong opposition of division managers, the air-cooled models were to replace the water-cooled engines in the Chevrolet and Oakland divisions. According to Sloan:

> This was the first time, to my knowledge, in the history of General Motors that intimate cooperation was called for between the Research Corporations and the divisions, and no established means

existed by which this cooperation was to function. Since the initial production as well as the creation of the design was assigned to Mr. Kettering's research group in Dayton, and the actual mass production was assigned to the divisions, the responsibilities were blurred.[100]

The initial resolution of this dilemma was the establishment of a small production facility in Dayton that would work out the manufacturing problems and then hand over the completed project to the Chevrolet and Oakland assembly plants for mass production. During 1921, GM executives at the Oakland brand served as advisers to the development process and made occasional trips to Dayton to monitor progress and help Kettering's team with emergent production bottlenecks.

The first Dayton-produced test models arrived at the Oakland plant in Detroit in late 1921, and the first mass-produced copper-cooled Oaklands were scheduled to be introduced at the New York auto show in January 1922. This highly publicized timetable became a huge embarrassment for GM when Kettering's test car "failed its tests at the Oakland division."[101] Moreover, the Oakland engineering team could not resolve the technical and production problems revealed by the test, and GM ultimately canceled the new model altogether.

Undeterred, GM's leadership turned to the four-cylinder Chevrolet, intending to introduce it in late 1922. This time two Chevrolet engineers were sent to Dayton to ensure the inclusion of practical expertise during the development process. This strategy yielded adequate test cars, and the copper-cooled Chevrolet 490 was "the sensation of the New York Automobile Show in January 1923."[102]

Nevertheless, the project foundered on production and maintenance problems. Despite the attempts at early coordination, the translation into mass production was unwieldy at best. A huge number of new technical issues arose as the Kettering production process was translated to a full-scale assembly line, and only about one thousand of the projected ten thousand Chevrolet 490s were produced during the first months of 1923. When the handful that had been produced began to develop a variety of troubles, William Knudsen at Chevrolet lost confidence in the project. According to his biographer, he confronted Kettering directly: "This car isn't any good. . . . You and the people you have working on it down in Dayton . . . aren't automobile people. This car isn't strong enough, the rear axle isn't any good, and even if you get these things worked out so they are good, the car will cost too much for Chevrolet to make."[103] After several other false starts, the project was canceled altogether in late 1923, and General Motors waited until the Corvair was introduced in the 1960s to finally complete its development of an operational air-cooled engine.

These events created such bitterness that Kettering tendered his resignation, which he only withdrew after Herculean feather-smoothing efforts by Sloan. Throughout his subsequent career, which extended into the 1950s, he never altered his conviction that the project had been sabotaged by shortsighted production executives who had not sought to solve what he considered to be relatively minor problems. Sloan, who during this episode replaced DuPont as the all-powerful leader of GM, tended to agree with Kettering, but differed with him over how to handle such resistance:

> Management involves more than technical problems. . . . It was not my policy then or at any time afterward to force on the divisions a thing of this kind against their judgment. On this question there had unfortunately opened a wide gap in the corporation, with Mr. Kettering, his laboratories and Mr. DuPont on one side, and myself and the divisions on the other. [Now that I was chairman] I was anxious to close it.[104]

This incident consolidated the autonomy of the operating divisions, and they retained their newly acquired veto power over any new innovation until after World War II. It also led to a policy that the implementation of new innovations would be managed by the divisions themselves, thus removing the awkward (and ultimately unsuccessful) transfer of a completed and therefore difficult-to-modify product from the laboratory to the assembly line.

But this shift also altered the physical relationship of the laboratory to the divisions: instead of production divisions sending representatives to Dayton to participate in the translation from experimental to production models, the laboratory was required to send its designers to southern Michigan. Since ongoing innovation created an almost continuous demand for laboratory personnel to be simultaneously present in Dayton and southern Michigan, this arrangement was inefficient at best and unmanageable at worst.

Though the significance of the failed copper-cooled engine from the point of view of production geography largely eluded Sloan, spatial dynamics did figure in the ultimate resolution of the conflict. Since the production executives had never won him over to their opinion that the engine was simply a lemon, he ultimately analyzed the failure as an organizational problem. Although the largest part of the problem was resolved by granting division executives a veto over new ideas, a secondary issue was the hostility and distrust that remained between Kettering's shop and the various production personnel with whom it would have to coordinate for future innovations to be adopted. The resolution of this issue lay in establishing spatial proximity to allow for constructive day-to-day interaction. In 1924, despite the already huge investment that had been made in the Dayton facilities, the laboratory was moved to Detroit. This is an example of the process of innovation demanding proximity. Moving the laboratory allowed designers physical presence in production facilities, which put them in contact with the line workers implementing the designs on a trial-and-error basis.

Sloan applied this principle of locating design and development personnel in the Detroit area with considerable rigor for the next fifteen years. The new orientation was already apparent in 1925, when GM's leadership team, after discovering the designer Harley Earl in a Los Angeles customizing shop that created ostentatious specialty cars for Hollywood stars, brought him to Detroit to design their new luxury line, the LaSalle.[105] When industry consensus credited the success of the new model to Earl's radical design ideas, Sloan created a new administrative unit, the Art and Styling Section, and hired Earl to head it. Despite the presence of a rich design culture in Los Angeles that had nurtured Earl's creative development and would have contributed substantially to his efforts, there was never any consideration given to locating the new unit on the West Coast. After the copper engine fiasco, Sloan and his team would not risk any arrangement that did not involve ongoing interpersonal contact between development and those tasked with producing Earl's new creations.

Earl's first assignment after the successful launch of the LaSalle was to improve the appearance of the Cadillac as part of an effort to overtake Packard, the longtime industry leader in the luxury category. But this relatively narrow project soon diffused into other divisions, resulting in a growing Art and Styling Section that designed the elaborate and ostentatious bodies that came to characterize first General Motors and then all American automobiles, and after World War II became the principal form of competition among the Big Three.

These and other less significant institutional accretions to the southern Michigan production culture were clearly not an expression of supply issues, but rather a reflection of the emergent necessity for physical proximity as a component of ongoing creativity and change.[106] Although Sloan may not have appreciated these dynamics, they were nonetheless visible to those who analyzed his administration. Arthur Kuhn, for example, after a comprehensive analysis of Sloan's leadership during this period, concluded that "close proximity" was essential to the process of ensuring that "auto divisions were using the best methods isolated by the Advisory staff."[107] In the broader context of the industry as a whole, James Rubenstein concluded after a comprehensive geographical analysis of the Big Three, the "most successful pioneers either grew up in the area or migrated there."[108]

Sloan's myopia about the role of concentration in facilitating ongoing innovation does not invalidate his observation that supply issues were an equally compelling force for geographic concentration. These supply issues were most visible in the almost unadorned increase in the concentration of GM production facilities in and around Flint. During the 1920s, when production expanded enormously, General Motors built at least four new engine plants and five new drivetrain plants, all in southern Michigan.

These choices were made despite a number of significant incentives to locate elsewhere. First, workers were expensive and scarce in the Detroit area. Wages for the semiskilled labor that populated the auto assembly lines were the highest in the country, driven up by Henry Ford's Five Dollar Day policy, and this by itself should have been a large incentive for migration. It was further confounded by ongoing labor shortages throughout the 1920s, brought on by the rapid expansion of the industry during this period and by Detroit's distance from the ports of entry for immigrant labor.[109]

Second, the legacy of Durant's acquisition policy gave General Motors important production outposts in other cities. Throughout the 1920s, GM operated engine and drivetrain plants in Buffalo and Syracuse, New York, Harrison, New Jersey, Bristol and Meridian, Connecticut, and a variety of locations in Ohio, Indiana, and Wisconsin. These plants might have been expanded, or they could have become the center of small production complexes that did not suffer from the disadvantages of southern Michigan. Though many of these plants were continuously modernized during this period, General Motors chose to expand only in the Dayton, Ohio, and Anderson, Indiana, outposts. For the most part, plants continued to be moved into the Detroit area, though at a slower pace than in the earlier period.

A particularly illuminating instance of such migration involved the Pennsylvania-based Fleetwood Metal Body Company.[110] Fleetwood had established itself as a significant supplier of luxury bodies early in the century, when many of its customers were Eastern and European assemblers. After Detroit became the dominant force in luxury cars in the 1920s, the body maker was pulled into the General Motors orbit and was eventually acquired by Fisher Body in 1925.

GM did not at first move Fleetwood to southern Michigan. In the late 1920s, however, the demands on Fleetwood escalated as Harley Earl's high styling became the centerpiece of model changes for the Cadillac and LaSalle nameplates supplied by Fleetwood. Earl's innovations created significant manufacturing challenges for the body maker, since sloping fast backs, cowl ventilators, and sculptured fenders could not be mass-produced with existing methodology.

Eventually, special steel was developed that was simultaneously "flexible enough and strong enough to endure the tremendous strain" of the newly developed molding processes required by Earl's smooth design lines. Earl was placed in charge of producing complete body designs for the luxury models.[111] The back-and-forth process between designers and body makers became increasingly cumbersome, and then the Depression forced General Motors to lower the price of its luxury cars. This created added pressure to develop low-cost production methods. In 1931, the accumulated weight of all these factors led GM to move the entire Fleetwood operation to Michigan, thus establishing the tight coordination among designers, suppliers, and line workers at the body makers that was necessary to ensure cost-effective solutions to these ongoing challenges.[112]

General Motors moved other plants to Michigan during this period as well. Many of these moves were made in the first years of the Depression, when lower consumer incomes forced a decrease in car prices and compelled manufacturers to develop less expensive production methodologies. Brown-Lipe-Chapin, for example, was a pioneer manufacturer of differential gears that had been acquired by General Motors in 1923. GM had repeatedly modernized the subsidiary's Syracuse, New York, plant, and by 1930, the facility contained state-of-the-art equipment, much of it designed and constructed by company employees. Nevertheless, when the Depression drastically reduced automotive demand, GM chose to shutter the Syracuse factory and move the advanced machinery to Michigan locations rather than close less modern plants already located near Detroit.[113] This move, and many others like it, reflected the practical experience of the industry: that both transportation costs and efficient coordination outweighed the temporary chaos of relocations.

SUPPLIER RELATIONSHIPS

At first glance, the propensity of Ford and General Motors to absorb their trading partners—rather than cultivate long-term cooperative relationships—seems to violate an important aspect of flexible production. Viewed from this perspective, the structure would appear to create substantial rigidity, since such absorption could and should lead to ongoing patronage of inefficient subsidiaries who could not compete with innovative outside suppliers. In carefully analyzing these dangers in the context of the ossification of the American automobile industry after World War II, Helper points to two interconnected pathologies.[114] First, the core assembly company could, in the interests of immediate profits, allocate the bare minimum to *inside* suppliers, which would starve them of the funds necessary to pursue promising innovations or production methodologies and thus deprive itself (and possibly the industry) of new developments. Second, the assembler could refuse to implement any improvements developed by *outside* companies, in an effort to protect inefficient internal subsidiaries.[115]

But in the context of the 1920s and '30s, the consolidation of internal subsidiaries had a very different impact, both practically and symbolically. Rather than creating rigidity and inhibiting innovation, the practice of absorbing suppliers was designed to maintain the flexibility essential for innovation.

The need to absorb suppliers stemmed from the manner in which the early American automobile industry developed. First, it yielded a comprehensive network of component suppliers that, collectively, could supply all elements of a completed vehicle.[116] Henry Ford, in fact, constructed his first automobile completely from purchased parts, undertaking only the assembly process. This supplier network more than quadrupled in size between 1909 and 1920 as automobile production increased from 128,000 to 1,905,000. As many as one hundred assemblers began business during the World War I period, either entering the market in the manner of Ford, with no production facilities, or emulating the Dodge brothers, who integrated downstream from their position as the manufacturer of key components for Ford and other assemblers.[117] And even after Ford and GM rose to dominance, the supply network remained intact and independent of the assemblers. Chrysler entered the market in the early 1920s with the most sophisticated drivetrain in the industry, but the firm itself was responsible only for the design—the vehicle was assembled in a rented facility using commissioned parts. In short, the Detroit automobile industry evolved out of a structure that bore a strong resemblance to the nonhierarchical production networks found in the textile regions of Italy and in Silicon Valley.[118]

Second, Detroit component suppliers had significant ties among themselves, even while they maintained competitive relationships. These began with the personal relationships among the pioneers, but they matured into an active production culture involving the exchange of production techniques and collective development efforts. They also involved extensive personnel transfers, with entrepreneurs and employees shifting from one firm to another and therefore diffusing new ideas rapidly across corporate boundaries. By World War I, these informal ties had developed into significant formal relationships, including trade groups, political lobbying efforts, and a patent-sharing agreement that made all new innovations immediately available to the community as a whole.[119] The rapid spread of the assembly line just before World War I was the most striking symptom of this structure.

The successful effort to establish size and quality standards for automotive parts illustrates how these factors interacted to motivate assemblers to absorb their suppliers.[120] As early as 1903, the newly formed Association of Licensed Automobile Manufacturers, dominated by Detroit-area component producers, sought to establish standards for such items as screw threads, wheel rims, and spark plugs. By 1921, these standards had matured into an extensive set of guidelines enforced by a successor group, the Society of Automotive Engineers (SAE), still centered in Detroit and still dominated by the component manufacturers.

The impact of the standards was dramatic. Size standards or recommended material content were developed for 224 different parts, thus eliminating a bewildering number of competing products that had served the same purpose and establishing consistent content (and therefore consistent strength and machineability) for key components. Among the most noteworthy accomplishments in size standardization were the reduction of 300 lock washer designs to 35 and the reduction of 1,100 varieties of steel tubing to 150. The most noteworthy victory in materials content was the imposition of quality measures for iron and steel alloys after a long struggle with foundries and mills. By the mid-1920s, virtually all aspects of automotive production had been brought under the rubric of the SAE standards.[121]

These new standards were a key aspect of cost reduction in the World War I period, particularly among the firms that supplied the fifty or so independent assemblers. Since most parts manufacturers supplied components to several assemblers, standardization allowed for "mass production economies, even though individual orders remained small."[122] In many cases, the cost reductions were quite substantial; for example, costs were reduced 30 percent in the manufacture of ball bearings. While precise figures of their overall impact are unavailable, one analyst estimated that they yielded a $750 million savings—about 15 percent of the value of motor vehicles in the early 1920s.[123]

But none of the five largest assemblers endorsed the new standards. Their complaint derived from the rigidity that the standards imposed on innovation, since "a product or part once standardized among many companies was not easily altered for a more advanced design."[124] The SAE acknowledged this problem by avoiding certain areas that were undergoing rapid development, notably piston and cylinder design. The assemblers were nevertheless discontented with the standards for items whose design had apparently stabilized; very frequently, new production processes or new product embellishments could be most efficiently implemented by altering the design of a mundane item like a lock washer or steel tubing. The discipline of the SAE made it difficult to purchase such parts from suppliers whose manufacturing operations were geared to mass production of standardized items. Problems of this sort led to a two-year conflict, starting in 1920, over the design of axles for trucks, and the rancor created by this struggle did not subside for several years. By the mid-1920s, GM—by then the largest assembler—had begun publishing its own set of standards, which it changed when its designs changed.[125]

For the largest assemblers, particularly Ford and General Motors, the solution was to acquire parts suppliers. George V. Thompson, the principal historian of the standardization movement, expressed the logic of acquisition quite simply: "The task of changing a detailed part standard within a single firm was infinitely easier than that of getting many companies within the industry to agree upon any single change."[126] After the struggle over truck axles, the assemblers who could obtain the resources for acquisitions or new construction applied this logic relentlessly, and the proportion of internally manufactured parts rose from 45 percent in 1922 to 74 percent in 1926.[127]

To be sure, this transformative change was not caused solely by the constraints of standardization. A large component of the motivation for internalization was the desire to guarantee the supply of critical items in a rapidly expanding market where shortages were endemic. But this had been a problem throughout the previous fifteen years, without producing the same magnitude of vertical integration.

At Ford, this rationale for absorption was elevated to the level of explicit ideology, iterated and reiterated by Ford himself in his three published books and by Sorensen and other executives who also spoke directly to the Ford philosophy.[128] The internalization of steelmaking, glassmaking, tire-making, sawmills, a cement factory, and a host of other functions were all deemed necessary to a coordinated assembly process and to ongoing innovation.[129] Most of these functions would have been performed by Tier I suppliers in the Japanese keiretsu, and some (such as the sawmill and cement factory) would probably have been found among Tier II suppliers.

The internalization of steelmaking at the River Rouge facility provides an instructive illustration of the ways in which the behemoth Ford complex could achieve the same results as the keiretsu arrangements cultivated by the Japanese. The internalization process was motivated by the vast industrial expansion in the early 1920s, which created an undercapacity in the steel industry that threatened to limit automobile production. As Sorensen had written, shortages in steel production slowed auto production upstream and reverberated downstream, causing the need for layoffs.[130]

The shortages faced by Ford, then the dominant firm in the industry, demonstrate the weakness of its ties to the steel industry and therefore reveal the absence of keiretsu-like relationships. Toyota, Nissan, and Mazda all had privileged relationships with steelmakers, which would respond to shortages either by giving them first access to limited supplies or by investing the capital necessary to serve their primary customer. In the American context, these commitments were not forthcoming, and the steel industry had many other customers with equal or greater claim on its output. As a consequence, the internalization of steelmaking was cost-effective for Ford, which had vast amounts of investment capital and access to all the inputs and expertise necessary to produce its own steel.

It wasn't long before Ford discovered the innovative potential of this incorporation. From the middle 1920s until World War II, Ford became a fountainhead of innovation in specialty steel for automotive applications. One example was the single-block V-8 engine. Ford's premier engineering achievement during the Depression era, the V-8 engine was cast from a moving forge. This methodology could not have been developed without internal steelmaking facilities, nor could it have been so easily extended into other realms. By the mid-1930s, for example, Ford was producing a cast-steel crankshaft, "a feat which many foundry men have regarded as impossible." The new crankshaft had superior performance characteristics, lasted longer, weighed ten pounds less than its predecessor, and was less expensive to produce.[131]

A second important innovation was Ford's development of a sheet steel cold-finishing mill in the mid-1930s, one of many cost-saving new facilities constructed during the Depression.[132] This mill, which Barclay characterized as "the most revolutionary and far-reaching improvement in steel mill practice in the last two decades," reduced the cost of production by 60 percent compared to previous methods, while improving the performance characteristics of the sheets.[133] Much of the savings was achieved by extending the conveyor system to make the movement of the product almost completely automatic and continuous, a novel application of Ford's assembly line techniques. Another was improving the efficiency of coke ovens, thus servicing the gas needs of the entire River Rouge facility while reducing coal consumption by 20 percent.

It is unlikely that these innovations could have been effectively implemented in cooperation with external steel suppliers. The struggle over specialty steel standards in the early 1920s reflected the strained relationships between steel and automobile, and not much changed during the ensuing decade. Unlike the Japanese context, in which long-standing zaibatsu relationships facilitated a cooperation without formal ownership linkages, the American steelmakers were not particularly proximate to Detroit, nor did they have the facility to work in a flexible way with the rapidly changing automobile industry. To attain the sort of innovative dynamics that the Japanese attained within keiretsus, Ford needed internalization. In some sense, then, the internalization of steelmaking because of the steel shortage in the early 1920s was a fortunate accident: it created the conditions for significant advances in steelmaking for automotive applications.

At General Motors, Durant's original conglomeration of the company was not motivated by a vision of ongoing internal cooperation, but it nevertheless laid the foundation for such a structure. By 1920, General Motors had absorbed at least fifteen key suppliers, including Westin-Mott, Northway Motors, and Jaxon Steel Products, all manufacturers of drivetrain elements that even Japanese manufacturers might produce in-house.[134] GM's acquisitions also included AC Spark

Plug, Harrison Radiator, Klaxon, and the companies in the Delco-Remy complex—firms that manufactured spark plugs, radiators, horns, and electrical components that the Japanese keiretsu system would have allocated to Tier I suppliers.

This laid the foundation for Alfred Sloan—who arrived at GM as part of the acquisition of Hyatt Roller Bearings—to create symbiotic and intermeshed relationships among the various internal subsidiaries. It was this system of internal coordination that would produce the prototypical multidivisional company and fuel General Motors' drive to industry dominance.[135] Many of these arrangements were based on specific experiences that forced Sloan and his executive team to rearrange parts of the system because they did not function efficiently as they stood. This process best reveals the functionality of vertical integration.

The example of Fisher Body is particularly useful in illustrating the many instances in which only internalization could accomplish the sort of coordination that was achieved by Japanese in keiretsu relationships. Fisher Body had been founded in 1908 by Fred and Charles Fisher, who had learned the craft of building carriage bodies from their father and grandfather.[136] They were soon joined by their four brothers, and by 1916 the company was the largest body manufacturer in the industry, selling to several automobile assemblers, including General Motors.

During World War I, large hydraulic presses that could form compound curves in auto bodies were developed, and Fisher began working with the Hudson Company to apply these to closed-body construction. Until that time, closed bodies were only available at cost premiums of 25 percent or more, but by 1918 the joint efforts yielded a low-cost closed body that was incorporated into the midpriced Essex with a selling price about 10 percent above the price of comparable open-body cars.

This success convinced the Fishers that the closed body was the wave of the future and the key to making the automobile into the dominant means of transportation.[137] They developed a plan to integrate downstream into assembly to overcome the lack of vigor with which the assemblers were pursuing this option. They must have been encouraged in this endeavor by the spectacular entrance of the Dodge, which had transformed itself from a key Ford supplier into a major producer in 1914.[138] The rise of Dodge, which substantially disrupted Ford production when the firm stopped supplying Model T parts, must also have impressed General Motors, since Durant quickly made the brothers a lucrative offer to purchase a 60 percent share of Fisher Body.

This transaction served both parties, but it was particularly enticing for the Fishers. Besides consolidating their personal fortune and giving them a substantial stake in the future of General Motors, the acquisition agreement guaranteed Fisher Body all of GM's business while allowing them to sell to other assemblers, and it assured the brothers of ongoing managerial autonomy by giving them a majority of the voting stock. For GM, the agreement guaranteed the continued flow of Fisher Bodies and kept a potentially formidable competitor out of the assembly business.

This arrangement continued through the boom years of the early 1920s, with the arm's-length relationship working in much the same way that partial ownership within keiretsu operated. (The 40 percent stake of Toyota in its largest supplier, Nippondenso, comes to mind as a good parallel.) However, unlike analogous keiretsu relationships, in which the equity share of the assembler tends to be reduced over time as the relationship becomes consolidated and the supplier becomes financially viable, in 1926 GM acquired the remaining Fisher Body stock and absorbed it completely. The main impetus for this move was the inability of GM to achieve keiretsu-level coordination without such absorption.[139]

These two issues—the sharing of reduced production costs and physical proximity—were regularly confronted by Japanese assemblers, and their positive resolutions are among the notable achievements of keiretsu organization. Asanuma, for example, discusses at length the elaborate (but informal) rules through which cost reductions by suppliers were shared with assemblers, and he argues that this arrangement was necessary to sustain keiretsu relationships over the long term.[140] We have already discussed physical proximity at length, but it is useful to recall that many Japanese suppliers migrated to North American and Asian complexes without formal contracts, moves that attest to the power of keiretsu discipline.

In Detroit, however, the strong ties among suppliers and Fisher's multiplex ties to other assemblers—including the personal ties among the pioneers of the industry—allowed it to resist pressure from General Motors in both of these realms, even with GM holding a 60 percent share of its stock.[141] In fact, the nub of the locational dispute was a proposed sixty-mile move of the Detroit Fisher Body plant to a site in Flint opposite the main Chevrolet assembly facility.[142] The struggle over this apparently short move was symptomatic of these deeper issues. Fisher preferred remaining in Detroit to better coordinate with its other customers—notably the upstart Chrysler Company—and GM wanted the Fisher plant moved to guarantee coordination with the rapid design changes energized by the rise of the closed body, the onset of the annual model change, and Chevrolet's drive to industry dominance.[143] Because such crosscutting ties were precluded both by the structure of the keiretsu and by the geographical separation of the three distinct Japanese automobile production cultures, these sorts of issues simply did not arise in the Japanese context.[144]

The differing contexts faced by Japanese and American assemblers therefore led to different arrangements that accomplished similar results. In Japan, keiretsu relationships were capable of achieving the level of coordination needed to proceed with rapid innovation and cost reductions; in Detroit, internalization was often needed to achieve the same result. But what is important is the degree to which the two systems found resolutions that allowed for substantial coordination and—with that coordination—the facility to simultaneously sustain ongoing innovation and production cost reductions.

For both Ford and General Motors, sustaining the creative tension with internal parts suppliers relied on the existence of viable alternative outside suppliers. The logic behind this was enunciated by the leadership of GM: "Unless a truly competitive situation is preserved as to [parts] prices, there is no basis upon which the performance of the divisions can be measured."[145] This conclusion led to a policy of allowing the heads of the five motorcar divisions to use outside suppliers if such outsourcing was cost-effective. This principle was succinctly enunciated in 1927 by John J. Raskob, the chairman of GM's Finance Committee:

Each [parts plant] is operated upon the basis of maximum efficiency so that the price of the output will be such as to induce the heads of the car divisions to purchase from G.M.C. accessories divisions instead of buying outside. They are free to do so, however, if they find it advantageous. Hence, it is the aim of each G.M.C. accessories division to outstrip competition both in quality and price. The Saginaw foundry, for example, aims to produce gray and malleable iron castings, which shall meet the specifications of the different car divisions at a price which they could not be bought in any other foundry.[146]

The Ford solution, though different, reflected and enacted the same concerns:

The engineering department . . . often drew graphs consisting of two curves, one of Ford Motor Company's manufacturing cost for a particular part or assembly (for example, the body), the other for prices paid to outside suppliers. . . . The company constantly sought prices on components from outside suppliers as a means of checking the company's own production costs. In the process, despite the increasing integration of the Rouge, Wibel and his lieutenants came to realize that "going outside" could be profitable.[147]

Both firms also encouraged their internal subsidiaries to supply other firms with key parts, particularly when substantial profits could be made in such transactions. This allowed for direct market pricing of these components, and it created an ongoing barometer of that subsidiary's competitive standing. The internal and external sourcing structure, as well as the sale of internally produced items to other manufacturers, became rooted in the structure of both organizations and eventually came to be known among scholars and industry personnel as "tapered integration."[148]

This set of relationships through which Ford and General Motors sought outside suppliers for internally produced parts and allowed their internal subsidiaries to sell to the remainder of the industry created a set of constructive tensions within each organization. This dynamic allowed for the replication of the fruitful relationships that were celebrated in the Japanese keiretsu. These relationships could sustain the innovative process that was ongoing during this period, and yet they also allowed either the supplier or the automotive division to look elsewhere in the many circumstances when such alternatives were necessary. The ongoing friction created within the organization by these conflicting interests is a sign of this creative tension.

The foundation of the two automakers' tapered integration—a network of outside suppliers that themselves used flexible production and thus could interact with inside suppliers and assemblers to sustain innovation—was laid in the 1920s. For instance, the annual model change doomed the thriving independent market (that is, autos *not* produced by the Big Three) by escalating the cost of competition, but it also created a huge used-car market that relied on replacement parts. This secondary market offered parts suppliers the opportunity to sell Ford and GM parts in large quantity, since used-car dealers and auto mechanics constituted a sophisticated clientele for cheaper or better components that could be inserted into Ford and GM models. This market also placed a premium on innovation, since superior quality, greater durability, or cheaper prices were the chief devices available to the parts suppliers in their attempts to outcompete the Big Two for their own after-market. By 1926, parts suppliers sold almost $1 billion in replacement parts, which constituted almost half of their sales.[149]

To outcompete the Big Two for their own parts business, the successful component manufacturers necessarily developed flexible production.[150] Most fundamentally, they needed to routinely produce several different versions of an item in order to fill the demand for several different models and years for each of several different companies in the replacement market. At the same time, they needed multiple versions of that item for each model they supplied in the new-car market. Beyond this, they needed to quickly implement modifications in their products to conform to new designs by customers, and still further, they had to be prepared to absorb a drop in demand when a client was forced to reduce production, as well as to increase output drastically when a new customer came on board with an emergency order.

Once the assemblers exhibited renewed willingness to purchase innovations from outsiders (without subsequently reinternalizing the function), resourceful entrepreneurs began tackling long-term problems that the assemblers had been unable to address, even when there was no substantial used-car market for the new products. One notable example was stiffness in clutches, a problem that discouraged many people, particularly women, from driving on a regular basis. This problem escalated for the industry as a whole in the 1920s when the more powerful engines developed then exacerbated it. It was resolved by the perfection of single-plate clutches and the development of manufacturing techniques that allowed them to be profitably included in low-priced vehicles. Most of these developments took place in independent firms, which, by the early 1930s, had captured 75 percent of the new-car market in clutches.[151]

Finally, component manufacturers began developing entirely new products for which there was no secondary market and selling them to Ford, GM, and the other assemblers for inclusion on new cars. Ultimately, outside suppliers even invaded the hallowed ground of engine production. One notable instance was a pump that took oil from the top of the sump, where the oil was cleanest, instead of the bottom, where sludge accumulated. Because this substantially extended engine life, assemblers began including these new pumps in the mid-1920s, and by the 1930s they were standard in the industry.

To be sure, these relationships cultivated by Ford and General Motors were not identical to the carefully constructed and formally instituted keiretsu relationships. In the mature Japanese system, formal research and development teams worked together in an orderly way on product development, and all parties understood the general guidelines for pricing new components or tools. In Detroit, the situation was more feral. Each new collaboration was newly negotiated; there were no formal teams that worked collectively on new models, and the pricing relationships were negotiated and renegotiated on a regular basis.

But as Helper and others have demonstrated, these differences are not the crucial measure of the efficacy of collaborative relationships. The key is the existence of trust that informal agreements will be honored, and the collateral use of "voice" rather than "exit" as a way of navigating through difficulties. By this measure, Detroit achieved the same sort of community as the keiretsus.

Like the keiretsu—and unlike the later pattern in Detroit—Ford and General Motors cultivated deep dependence on crucial suppliers, and these suppliers were willing to place the fate of their firms in the hands of the major assemblers.[152] GM, for example, obtained more than half of its brakes from Bendix, and this constituted more than half of Bendix's brake production.[153] After the sale of National Plate Glass, GM relied on two outside suppliers for windshields, with Libbey-Owens-Ford garnering more than two-thirds of GM's market. Beyond its tight relations with Firestone Rubber, Ford was dependent on Kelsey-Hayes for wheels and brake shoes, Alcoa for aluminum, Diamond Manufacturing for radiators, and Briggs Body for assembled bodies.

In these cases and myriad others, the assemblers and suppliers cultivated a dependence that made both vulnerable to the vagaries of the other's business. In the 1930s, when strikes at key component suppliers became a major issue for assemblers, they also became the occasion for spectacular expressions of the use of voice to manage interfirm difficulties. Ford was particularly active in this regard. In one instance, Ford became actively involved in settling a strike at Kelsey-Hayes in order to restore the flow of brakes and wheels into River Rouge. Union negotiators involved in the dispute referred "to the one vacant chair in the conference room" occupied by "the despotic spirit of the elder Ford." And despite its ferocious opposition to unions, Ford prevailed on Kelsey-Hayes to grant an enormous wage increase that brought its workers to $6 per day, a settlement that one labor leader called "epoch-making."[154] In the case of a series of strikes at Briggs Body, Harry Bennett, Ford's personnel director and a notorious union buster, surveyed the Briggs operation and attributed the troubles to Briggs' "labor management." He called for major changes in the manufacturing system aimed at reducing layoffs, as well as an end to the practice of docking workers when the assembly line was idle for any reason. Even Henry Ford became involved, talking to striking workers and then sending Sorensen into the plant to investigate their complaints. The negotiations between the two companies ultimately involved every important executive on both sides.[155] In short, Detroit in the 1920s and 1930s utilized a voice system of problem resolution. The exit methodology, so amply documented by Helper and others, developed after World War II.

The Origin of Japanese Flexible Production

The fact that Ford and GM used a production system between the two world wars with all the features of Toyota's flexible production—including its associated high rates of innovation—is a serious strike against a cultural explanation for the differing trajectories of U.S. and Japanese auto. We could salvage the explanation, however, if Toyota had independently come up with its version of flexible production. The Japanese system and the early U.S. system were not identical. If Toyotism had been developed independently in Japan, we might be able to argue that the differences between U.S. and Japanese flexible production resulted from cultural differences.[156] This would then open the door to claiming that these differences (cultural in nature) are the key to the Japanese system's greater longevity and its ability to reverse maturity.

Unfortunately for the cultural explanation, Toyotism and Japanese flexible production were not developed independently of the U.S. system. In fact, Eiji Toyoda, who coauthored Toyotism with Tai-ichi Ono, learned its key features and structures from observing the U.S. auto industry. Eiji Toyoda told Ford CEO Phillip Caldwell during a 1982 dinner, "There is no secret to how we learned to do what we do. We learned it at the Rouge."[157] This trip, and Toyota's subsequent construction of an auto complex modeled after the River Rouge plant, has been enshrined in official Toyota history as the beginning of modern auto production in Japan.[158] Toyoda himself, however, pointed out that it was only one of many trips to Detroit by Toyota executives. In his view, the 1950 trip only updated and confirmed information that the Toyoda family had previously obtained and was preparing to use:

> When Toyota began making cars before [World War II], it had taken a good look at what automakers were doing in America. I'd arrived in Detroit with some background knowledge, and what I saw while I was there convinced me that, because little progress had been made [by Toyota] during the war, the information that I had remained for the most part valid.
>
> After my return to Japan, I was often asked: "How many years before we catch up with Ford?" To tell the truth, there was no way of knowing. I felt that I was being honest in saying: "Ford's not doing anything we don't already know.'" But at the same time I was certainly not presumptuously downplaying Ford's tremendous lead.[159]

Thus, the Japanese version of flexible production was the result of what Paul DiMaggio and Walter Powell call "mimetic isomorphism," which is the tendency of organizations to imitate the structure of other more successful organizations.[160] The development of the Toyota system through emulation is important, not just for ruling out the cultural explanation for the decline of U.S. industry, but also for understanding the different trajectories of U.S. and Japanese flexible production—namely, why one was abandoned, while the other is still in use today. Because Toyoda explicitly emulated the system, Toyota's management grasped the importance of just-in-time and the other elements of flexibility as essential to both ongoing production efficiency and ongoing innovation. In Detroit, on the other hand, the system developed through trial and error, leading to a less explicit understanding of the elements of flexible production. Detroit executives viewed their organizational structure and the functioning of the broader production culture as a series of developments flowing from the challenges and inefficiencies that derived from the moving assembly line. In Detroit, therefore, they stood ready to abandon the system if it appeared to be outliving its usefulness or if other factors made its short-term cost advantages less attractive.

In addition, the emulation of the American system by Toyota was only a starting point for a long evolution.[161] There were minor differences between the two systems as a result of that evolution—for instance, the Japanese sole reliance on outside suppliers compared to the U.S. mix of outside and inside, and the geographically separated keiretsu organized around different automakers compared to the concentration of all auto production in southern Michigan. Nevertheless, they largely ended up functioning similarly in terms of cost reduction and facilitation of innovation. These differences did have one consequence that is important to our understanding of the different trajectories of flexible production in the United States and Japan—the rate of industrywide diffusion of innovation.

In the U.S. industry, the geographic concentration of Ford, GM, Chrysler, and all of the suppliers in the southern Michigan region facilitated the transfer of personnel and ideas between companies, as our previous discussion of different innovations in the early U.S. industry illustrates. The spatial separation of the Toyota, Nissan, and Mazda keiretsu, on the other hand, created a semipermeable barrier to diffusion of innovation. This inhibited emulation much more successfully than was possible in the fully permeable Detroit network, and there was often a measurable time lag between the introduction of new ideas at, say, Toyota and their diffusion to Nissan or Mazda.

The different rates of diffusion become an important piece to the puzzle of why the Americans would abandon flexible production, given its benefits. As long as the primary dynamic of the automobile industry was the expansion of existing markets, new ideas and new production methodologies increased the sales of the industry as a whole and therefore rewarded the original innovator, even if competitors rapidly acquired the new innovations. But once the market stabilized or shrank, as it did in the 1930s, innovations were only profitable if they yielded increased market share—that is, if the innovator could claim proprietary rights on the product, either through exclusion of other producers or through customer loyalty.[162]

In short, there arose rather large incentives for General Motors to inhibit innovation, since the potential gains were so drastically deflated, while the costs of failure remained high. These incentives were not, however, sufficient to change the firm's strategy, since the dynamics of the industry as a whole carried General Motors with it; it could not choose to abandon innovation unless the rest of the system did as well. And this was unthinkable in the context of the Detroit production culture of the 1930s. Soon, however, the lack of appreciation of the innovative nature of flexible production, along with the decreasing benefits of innovation, would take on a new significance. Within a contingent moment in history—the rash of sit-down strikes and later wildcat strikes in the decade preceding the end of World War II—these factors would create a context where abandoning flexible production was logical to the Big Three automakers.

CLASS CONFLICT AND THE IMPETUS TO ABANDON FLEXIBLE PRODUCTION

3

In the previous chapters, we elaborated on the following pillars of our explanation for the decline of the U.S. auto industry: (1) the Japanese cost and quality advantage is rooted in greater production efficiency, leading to higher rates of product and process innovation; (2) those high rates of innovation are facilitated by the structure of production used by the Japanese, namely, flexible production; and (3) between the world wars, the U.S. industry utilized a version of flexible production and also had high rates of innovation.[1] These three points are the foundation of the first part of our argument. They establish that the United States has lost domestic market share to Japanese automakers owing to different rates of innovation, resulting from different production structures, rather than to greedy unions, cultural differences, or industry maturity.

We refer to these three points as the "first part" of our argument, because the evidence and explanation we have put forward thus far raise important new questions. First and foremost, if flexible production is so effective and U.S. auto had a functioning version of it, why was it abandoned? A secondary question is examined in chapter 5: why didn't the Japanese abandon flexible production when faced with the same issues that led the U.S. producers to do so?

Explaining the differing trajectories of the U.S. and Japanese auto industries with regard to flexible production is key: If the answer to these two related questions is cultural differences, greedy unions, or industry maturity, then it undermines our entire argument. If, however, the differing trajectories are not the consequence of these popular explanations, we can explore the industry dynamics that actually determined the Big Three's abandonment of flexibility and their subsequent decisions that locked the U.S. industry into a forty-year decline that has yet to end.

This chapter takes up the first question, regarding the Big Three's shuttering of flexible production. We demonstrate that the explanation for the abandonment of flexible production is not cultural, but structural and historical. This change was also not a natural process, like industry maturity, but an agentic decision made by the captains of industry in the context of the history and structure within which they were embedded. Finally, the explanation does involve unions; however, it was not union greed that led to the downfall of American flexible production but rather the unwillingness of the capitalists to accept and accommodate union power that undergirded the irreversible abandonment of flexibility. Our analysis of this history rests on two important relationships: first, the relationship between flexible production and worker power, which we term "structural leverage," and second, the relationship between flexible production, worker immiseration, and the activation of worker structural leverage.[2] Before we delve into the history behind the decision to abandon flexible production, we discuss these two relationships.

Flexible Production and Structural Leverage

Structural leverage (similar to and based on the concepts of "positional power" and "workplace bargaining power") is the power associated with a group's position in the social structure.[3] Schwartz explains structural leverage in this way:

> Social structures create power relationships. . . . A familiar example is the power of an employer over his employees. The employees work because they desire the pay. Whenever the employer gives an order, it carries the threat of job loss behind it—the job situation is one that enhances obedience for payment.
>
> We see here the exercise of *structural power,* which is recognizable by the fact that the structure in question could not function without the consistent and routinized exercise of such power. It

is not possible to imagine a company functioning in any recogniz-
able way without the employer ordering his employees to do certain things. . . .

If employees suddenly began refusing to obey orders, the company in question could not function. . . .

Thus we see a subtle but very important relationship between
structural power and those who are subject to it. On the one hand,
these power relations define the function of any ongoing system;
on the other hand, the ability to disrupt relationships is exactly
the sort of leverage which can be used to *alter* the functioning of
the system. Thus, *any system contains within itself the possibility of a
power strong enough to alter it.*[4]

Thus, structural leverage is the power that results from a group
refusing to play its role in the social structure. We can then concep-
tualize differing levels of structural leverage. That is, the higher the
structural leverage of a group, the fewer members it needs to mobilize in order to disrupt normal function and therefore command
changes in the system.[5] An example of high structural leverage would
be the leadership of major corporations, who, by threatening what
Kevin Young, Tarun Banerjee, and Michael Schwartz call a "capital
strike," can generate the leverage required to alter the system.[6] If only
a handful of large corporations stop playing their role of investing
money in the economy and employing people, this can devastate a
geographical region as well as erode the government's tax base. Thus,
capital strikes are especially powerful owing to the high structural
leverage that corporations gain from controlling capital.

Workers generally have a low level of structural leverage because
corporations can easily replace the productivity of small numbers of
workers, either by hiring unemployed workers or by increasing the
workload of the coworkers of those considering a strike; thus, large
numbers of workers are necessary for a strike to generate enough leverage to result in change.[7] In the pre–World War II U.S. auto industry, however, the system of flexible production enhanced the structural leverage of workers. That is, when a group of workers refused to
keep making a part needed to produce a car, flexible production reduced the effectiveness of—or removed completely—the three strategies that management could use to limit the damage: (1) hire new

workers, (2) counter the parts shortage with stockpiled inventory, or (3) ramp up production of the part at an unaffected plant.

Just-in-time delivery kept stockpiles of inventory minimal and ensured that temporary interruptions at key choke points would quickly reverberate throughout the production system, making the (usually slow) process of recruiting strikebreakers a partial solution at best.

Finally, geographic concentration and sole sourcing eliminated the option of ramping up production elsewhere. Recall from our previous discussions of the features of flexible production (in general in chapter 1, specifically in the United States in chapter 2) that just-in-time delivery necessitates the geographic concentration of suppliers and assemblers (and long-term relationships between assemblers and suppliers) in order to limit transportation complications, leading to the use of flexible machinery and parts in order to reduce the downtime of machines and enable the quick modifications that it also requires. In the early U.S. auto industry, such geographic concentration and use of flexible machinery and parts by suppliers resulted in single plants that could produce every type of a given component for all of an assembler's different models. At GM, these were referred to as "mother plants."[8] Mother plants were a necessary result of flexible production, and the system would not have functioned without them. Yet they also heightened the structural leverage of autoworkers because the concentration of production in the mother plant removed the option of increasing the production of parts at another plant to counter a strike. In other words, since parts for all models were made at only a few plants located very close to each other, it was possible for a handful of workers to shut them down and cripple production.

The relationship between flexible production and worker structural leverage is important for two reasons: first, as we discuss later in this chapter, GM autoworkers used their structural leverage during the Great Flint Strike of 1936–1937 and continued using it in wildcat strikes throughout World War II and up until around 1960; and second, it was the clear relationship between the structure of flexible production and worker power that led the Big Three auto management to alter their structure of production and thus undermine and ultimately abandon flexible production.

Before we discuss those events, however, it is important to explore the ways in which worker activation of structural leverage is not accidental in flexible production. The high rates of innovation and huge surplus value associated with flexible production that we have documented do not flow out of some neutral process, but rather, like all surplus value, from the exploitation of workers. The system is thus good for management precisely because it increases the exploitation of the workers—vastly increasing production without increasing workers' remuneration. Moreover, the method of increasing production involves an exquisitely oppressive intensification of production—the increased speed of the moving auto assembly line. This inevitably oppressive and dramatically more exploitative character of flexible production increases worker discontent and eventually results in workers taking direct action (sometimes organized, sometimes disorganized) to alleviate their discontent. In addition, because flexible production *also* increases worker structural leverage, many forms of resistance are successful in disrupting production and thus creating leverage capable of extracting concessions from management. In most instances, the offered concessions are calibrated to alleviate just enough worker discontent to remove the incentive for direct action and maintain the required (relatively high) level of worker commitment to the production process.

We document the exercise of leverage when flexible production was first introduced in both the early U.S. auto industry (later in this chapter) and in the Japanese auto industry (in chapter 5). First, however, we detail the exploitive nature of flexible production.

Flexible Production and the Exploitation of Labor

Japanese scholars were the first to develop criticisms of flexible production, though their work, written mostly in Japanese, did not reach Western scholars directly.[9] Later negative reviews by Western scholars were conveniently summarized by Christian Berggren in *Alternatives to Lean Production,* based on an analysis of the manufacturing system at Volvo designed to demonstrate the existence of alternative production strategies that combined the high productivity of the Japanese system with a more humane labor policy.[10] Essentially, these criticisms can be grouped into four categories:

1. Ultimately, the work on the Japanese assembly lines was un-skilled labor, reflecting the same Taylorist division of the work process into unskilled repetitive tasks that was the key fault of American assembly lines.

2. The Japanese system placed enormous stress on workers to per-form at great speeds, thus straining their physical and emotional capacities; this reflected both the immediate pressure of the work and the more or less unlimited commitment to excellence, which together led to longer hours and escalating obligations.

3. Despite the emphasis on work groups, the system fostered brutal competition among workers trying to position themselves for desirable promotions.

4. The system of worker-management cooperation left workers with little real power and instead conferred on management the ability to harness worker creativity and commitment without abandoning any of the traditional management privileges over workplace decision-making.

Former GM autoworker and union member turned author Mike Parker refers to these features of flexible production as "management by stress."[11] In the next section, we detail how each of these aspects increases the immiseration and exploitation of workers and how the high levels of oppression eventually lead to direct action by workers (action that ultimately activates their structural leverage).

UNSKILLED LABOR

A key element in the Toyota handbook for supervisors and foremen was the mandate that no task take longer than three days to learn or 2.4 minutes to perform. New workers entering the system were ex-pected to easily master the physical and mental demands of their job. This freed them to concentrate on the more challenging task of mas-tering "company culture"—fitting in with coworkers, foremen, and engineers and responding to the vast array of new demands that de-rived from the constantly changing system.[12] The central importance of company culture to Toyota jobs reflects the dependence of the Toyota system on a high degree of commitment by the workers to supporting the process that is typically absent in manufacturing systems that employ classically alienated workers.

As a consequence, the work itself was consummately repetitive, broken only by movement from one station to another or by the (equally mindless) retooling of a machine to perform another task. That is, flexible production required constant change in what workers were doing. To briefly recap why: because just-in-time delivery necessitates little to no stockpiled inventory, workstations face downtime when their specific part is not needed. Flexible machinery and parts allow the station to switch tasks during downtime and produce a different component. This flexibility keeps the factory operating at full capacity and the workers constantly busy. But the workers are still performing very simple tasks that are more similar to those of ossified mass production than the skills of craft production. Berggren summarizes the situation:

> For most workers, the demands for flexibility mean they are alternating between similar repetitive tasks. This is multitasking, rather than multiskilling. . . . The bulk of the work still consists of very standardized and factory-specific operations. In contrast, genuinely skilled work is characterized by the possession of competencies of a general value to the labor market; individuals are endowed with independence and opportunities for choice.[13]

THE STRESS OF UNLIMITED WORK COMMITMENT

Even if the deskilling in flexible production was a less odious cousin to Taylorist mass production, the degree of stress for the workers may have been no less severe. Even though workers were often relieved of the tyranny of the machine-driven assembly line, other mechanisms coerced remarkable speed of execution and therefore created a debilitating work environment.

The key element in this coercion was the operation of just-in-time on the shop floor. Because of the demand to meet downstream requests for particular parts, work teams were required to respond quickly to production requests and to perform these tasks without error. Benjamin Klein quotes a production manager in an American plant that had recently adopted Japanese methods: "It used to be that you had a monthly goal and you really shot for it. Now they have targets every day. It used to be that you could loaf a little bit, and other days you knew you were under the gun. Now you're under the gun all the time."[14]

This stress was enforced by the very structures that were celebrated by advocates of the system as the sources of worker esprit and productivity improvement. In a peculiar reversal of assembly line coercion, for example, it became the work groups themselves—the classic source of resistance to the speeding line—that formed the hub around which pressure was generated for unmediated labor intensification. Since groups were collectively held responsible for defects in their departments (and liable to work overtime to make up lost work), they became the principal agent for enforcing the intensification among their members.[15] And since promotion rested on individual performance and not on the rigid seniority rules of Fordist plants, the evaluations made by immediate supervisors—who were usually members of the work team itself—were the medium of exchange for upward mobility and gave even greater weight to the daily surveillance that was inherent in work groups.

Beyond the daily discomfort of this regime lay an extension of the workday, as workers stayed late to meet quotas, to meet the QC (quality circle) obligations, and to participate in the changes associated with ongoing innovation. This triggered physical and emotional problems that plagued workers, first in Japan and later in American and European transplants, including incidental injuries that sometimes reached three times the rates of comparable American plants and cumulative trauma injuries, like carpal tunnel syndrome, that reflected long-term overwork.

The unremitting pace and the stress of meeting deadlines, combined with the absence of organized resistance, created a pressurized situation that led to worker breakdown, withdrawal from the system, and the threat of long-term emotional and physical debilitation.[16] Even partisans of the system acknowledged these problems:

The NUMMI [New United Motor Manufacturing, Inc.] production system undoubtedly contains some disadvantages for the workers and the union. The increased pace of work and associated safety problems are mentioned most frequently by interviewed workers, union representatives and dissidents, and by management. The work intensity is exacerbated by no layoffs and reduced absenteeism, resulting in many more days of work.[17]

Robert Perrucci, in a reasoned review of the evidence from American transplants, suggests that the brutality of the system derived from the problems of translation from Japan to the United States and Europe, as well as from the focus of critics on these sites.[18] There is ample evidence, however, that the same sort of problems arose in Japan from the very beginning of the just-in-time system. In 1983, for example, Masaki Hayashi summarized the considerable body of Japanese evidence, anticipating most of the criticisms that would later develop among Western scholars who focused on transplants.[19] Michael Cusumano cited an ongoing series of exposés of the system that focused on the brutal pace of the work and included claims that Toyotism generated very high accident and suicide rates.[20] A book widely read in Japan, *Japan in the Passing Lane*, reported that Toyota workers felt emotionally isolated because of the company's tendency to think of its workers as "disposable parts."[21] Even Taiichi Ono conceded the strain on his workers, commenting to Cusumano that if he had faced an American union, "I might have been murdered."[22]

COMPETITION IN THE CONTEXT OF COOPERATION

The virtues of what Ouchi called "non-specialized career paths" had their dark side as well. Although system expansion guaranteed upward mobility based simply on longevity, the most successful individual workers earned their promotions in competition with other line workers, even those within their work team. This created a form of cutthroat competition that could not be fully expressed because of the ethics of cooperation that prevailed within the teams themselves.

Workers thus found themselves competing within a context that did not offer individual credit for what was considered a collective effort. Instead, their individual worth was judged by work team leaders, who operated for the most part as members of the groups, but who also had supervisorial responsibility and ongoing interactions with higher-line officers. Most significantly, the first-line supervisors were responsible for maintaining the *satei* scores that were secretly recorded in workers' files and became the principal basis for promotion.[23]

In this context, two virtues of Toyotism exacerbated both the competition and the coerciveness of the situation. The guarantee of lifetime employment and the specific removal of hiring and firing from the purview of first-line supervisors relieved workers of the fear of losing their job if their foreman disliked them, but it also kept the attention of these supervisors focused on judgments about their suitability for promotion. At the same time, the rigid work rules that dictated the exact best way to perform a task removed a degree of "over-the-shoulder" supervision from foremen, but it also left them without immediate technical criteria for judging the quality of work. In combination, these factors amplified the already prevalent impression that promotion would be based on the worker's attitude—his (or occasionally her) "unreserved commitment to the company." As a consequence, it became difficult "for employees to refuse overtime or take off paid holidays, since such actions are assessed as evidence of a poor attitude. In the same way, the evaluation practice renders it hard for workers to decline to participate in nominally voluntary activities outside of working hours."[24]

The pressure on workers was exacerbated further by the tendency for the first-line supervisors to also hold union office, thereby removing the possibility of a countervailing force within the work team.[25] In fact, most shops lacked the traditional "no-go" areas "where foremen fear to tread"—places where workers could congregate to develop group resistance to arbitrary decisions or oppressive conditions.

The denouement of this structure was the elimination of the sort of work-group resistance, made famous by the Western Electric studies, that are ubiquitous and effective in most industrial settings:

> Traditionally, the reaction of the working class to rationalizations has been characterized by spontaneous self-defense against what the Norwegian sociologist Sverre Lysgaard has called "the technical/economic system's insatiable, inexorable, unilateral demands." The extensive literature on output restrictions in American indus-

trial sociology and economics indicates the significance of this behavior pattern. . . . The maximal employment relationship of Toyotism entails turning this pattern upside down. By means of a far-reaching integration of employees in the technical and economic system, based on employees' dependence on the company as well as the promotion and personnel evaluation system, tendencies toward collective worker action—in Lysgaard's sense—are eliminated. . . . [Instead] "workmates put each other under massive moral pressure" to turn in a good performance. Peer pressure in the work group is thus a functional part of the production-control system.[26]

Like the previous two problems—unskilled work and work intensity—the problems of unfettered interworker competition and the vulnerability to exploitation were wedded to a virtue of flexible production: the widely celebrated cooperativeness of the system and the willingness of workers to constructively participate in both the demanding schedule and the process of innovation. It seems unlikely that one could construct a system that generated ongoing collegiality between management and workers without exposing workers to the risk that management would exploit their willingness to work longer hours, absorb difficult working conditions, and forgo complaint in exchange for the possibility of future promotion.

THE POWER DIFFERENTIAL IN WORKER-MANAGEMENT COOPERATION

Perhaps the most troubling of the criticisms of Toyotism were the claims of asymmetrical cooperation, with management retaining all of the decision-making power and workers playing the subordinate role of *offering ideas* to those in authority and *contributing* to whatever changes management chose to undertake.

The crux of this criticism is that worker participation ultimately did not involve any joint decision-making or veto power on the shop floor. The participation of the workers was strictly part of a consultative process that gave them input into the choices made but never guaranteed that they could impose their own program or veto one of management's programs. This point was underscored by Robert Cole, one of the earliest American analysts of the Japanese system: "A second characteristic of job redesign at Toyota Auto Body is that the emphasis is not on participation *per se,* but rather on achieving the consent of the workers for policies which management wants to pursue, as well as on guiding workers in the direction in which management would like to see them move."[27]

These exploitive aspects of flexible production present another puzzle. Berggren and other critics offered ample evidence that the workers were well aware of the difficulties that the work process presented for them, and that they disliked its exploitative aspects and wished for it to change. Moreover, it was clear to both workers and management that their positive commitment was essential to the success of the system, thus creating a kind of consciousness paradox that combined active discontent with positive involvement in the source of that discontent. This calls out the consistent finding by most analysts, pointing to ample evidence of workers' willingness to accept these same elements without protest. Perrucci, for example, cites two noncoercive union recognition elections in North American transplants in which workers with long union histories rejected unions in Japanese-owned plants.[28] Claire Brown and Michael Reich cite the drastic decline in grievances, absenteeism, and turnover at NUMMI in Fremont, California.[29] And more generally, the workers in transplanted facilities willingly worked overtime, participated in developing new techniques (some of which intensified their work), and involved themselves in various collective enterprises that they would have resisted in the earlier context of American management.[30]

Why did workers accept the system? The answer is that they didn't at first—in either the American context of the 1910s or the Japanese context of the 1950s. Rather, the exploitive nature of flexible production yielded discontent and disruption, and it was management compromise in the form of a generous effort bargain that won the acceptance of the system. We detail the Japanese effort bargain in chapter 5. Here, we discuss the effort bargain used to placate workers in the early U.S. auto industry. For now, it is worth noting that the two effort bargains were very similar. It is what happened after the effort bargains were first struck that explains why the United States abandoned flexible production while the Japanese have been able to maintain it.

The Effort Bargain in Old Detroit

Hilde Behrend first enunciated the concept of an "effort bargain" in 1957.[31] In an insightful article about labor contracts, she explained that:

> Every employment contract (whatever the method of wage payment) consists of two elements: (1) an agreement on the wage rate (either per unit of time or per unit of output), i.e., a wage-rate bargain; and (2) an agreement on the work to be done, i.e., an effort bargain. The employment contract thus fixes the terms of exchange of work for money.[32]

This is, in some sense, a restatement of Marx's original conceptualization of work under capitalism as the exchange of labor power for money. In Marx's rendering, this exchange was problematic in one important respect: the level of compensation delivered by the employer was negotiated through a complicated process that involved both the labor market and socially determined levels of subsistence. In effect, the class struggle germinated in the negotiation over compensation.[33]

Behrend focuses our attention on the other half of the arrangement and allows us to see that it too is subject to controversy and the same enduring struggle:

> Effort is not a substance that can be measured. Only the effect of the application of effort—output—can be measured. Effort itself is a subjective experience, like utility. An individual can say whether the effort he expends in performing a particular operation in a fixed time is equal to, greater than or smaller than the effort he expends on another operation in the same amount of time, but he cannot quantitatively define the amount of the difference. . . . [As a consequence] there is likely to be concealed bargaining about effort intensity, and the entrepreneur is likely to employ various devices of effort control such as supervision and machine pacing.[34]

These devices, even when effectively and subtly applied, can never fully measure or control the effort invested by the worker because they cannot determine what rates are within his or her physical capacity and which rates either exceed or underexploit that capacity. If management wishes to develop the work process effectively, it is dependent on workers to define the appropriate, viable, or most efficient level of effort for a particular job: "The belief [that there is] a correct rate for a job appears to work satisfactorily in practice although it has no scientific validity [that is, cannot be objectively measured]. The worker's reaction to the rate, not scientific judgment, determines whether the rate is considered correct, loose or tight."[35]

But this sort of cooperation depends on the commitment of the worker to accurately report on the appropriate effort levels, to react to changes in the system by measuring and recalibrating appropriate effort levels, and to work with technicians to alter work processes to be consistent with maximized effort. If management wishes to avoid this dependence on workers' goodwill and honesty, it must control work pace through a combination of time-study research and machine pacing, and it must anticipate and control the various forms of collective resistance and union bargaining that workers utilize in these circumstances.[36]

THE FIVE DOLLAR DAY

Ford's introduction of the moving assembly line in 1913 represented an attempt to control work pace. It also transformed automobile manufacturing from a boutique industry catering to a handful of wealthy sportsmen into the central sector in the American economy, supplying the primary transportation for the American working class.[37] The development process occurred on the floor of the constantly enlarging Highland Park plant, with continuous collaboration among engineers, product and tool suppliers, and line workers. The interactive process yielded new tools, novel uses of existing tools, frequent reorganization of the assembly process, creative resolution of production bottlenecks, and subdivision of the work into time-commensurate sequential tasks.

Although Ford was not operating a fully flexible production system yet, its process did contain some of the features that would later characterize flexible production, such as the physical proximity of assemblers and suppliers, a partial reliance on hand-to-mouth delivery, and cooperation among suppliers, engineers, and assembly line workers. These features of flexible production produced enough structural leverage that even disorganized action was massively disruptive. Thus, when workers' discontent over the combination of immiserating wages and the brutality of the constantly accelerating assembly line reached a crescendo in 1913, their resistance quickly led to compromise by Henry Ford in the form of the Five Dollar Day.[38] The compromise dramatically reduced turnover, as evidenced by Henry Ford's discussion of the program: "In 1913, in the Highland Park plant, we had an average monthly turnover of 31.9 per cent. In 1915, we introduced the five-dollar-a-day minimum and the turnover dropped to 1.4 per cent."[39]

Turnover, however, was part of a larger problem: the unwillingness of most employees to invest their own resourcefulness in improving both the process of production at Ford and the product that emerged from it. The other symptoms of this malaise were the large absentee rates and the vast amount of soldiering by line workers, who seized every opportunity to slow down, rest, and otherwise resist the efforts of management to increase the intensity of the work.[40]

Thus, the Five Dollar Day was not simply a method of reducing turnover: it was part of a more extensive and far-reaching effort to facilitate increasing productivity at Ford by raising the level of worker commitment to the company.[41] In other words, the Five Dollar Day was the result of concealed bargaining about effort intensity and ultimately reflected Ford's attempt to control and minimize collective resistance by workers. The irony is that it did not address the source of the discontent: the enormous stress created by the more intense and monotonous work enforced by machine-paced production. Instead, it represented a brilliant and effective substitute for alleviating the problems of the line: giving workers other benefits— notably higher wages and job security—that made the oppression of the line more palatable.

The result of Ford's program was dramatically increased productivity among autoworkers. Daniel Raff and Lawrence Summers have calculated the minimum increment in productivity during the next two years at between 40 and 70 percent.[42] Karel Williams and his colleagues have demonstrated that the increased commitment of workers, combined with the ongoing innovations at the plant, kept the cost of labor steady at $65 per Model T produced, despite a virtual doubling of wages.[43] That is, *the increased productivity from worker com-*

CLASS CONFLICT | 113

mitment and ongoing innovation absorbed the entire cost of the five-dollar-a-day program in the first year after it was implemented.

By 1918, Ford's at-first-experimental Five Dollar Day program had been adopted by both Chrysler and GM, and by 1919, the wage was raised to $6 and became the industry standard.[44] Thus, the Five Dollar Day became the key element in establishing the effort bargain for the industry as a whole. As Wayne Lewchuk comments in arguing this point:

> It is reasonable to conclude that Ford workers disliked the new pace of work, disliked authoritarian supervision, disliked being set to a mechanical pace setter, and disliked company intrusions into their private lives. However, they made a choice, albeit from a limited set of possibilities given the realities of the Detroit employment relationship, and they chose to accept managerially set effort norms and, at least in 1914, good wages.[45]

Once Ford established the bargain around superb wage levels, this became one of the central elements in the effort bargain in Old Detroit: it constrained management to keep raising wages to ensure that auto would remain at or near the top of the national wage hierarchy. The increases in wages—first to $6 a day and then to $7—were not acts of generosity, but rather management's effort to negotiate the minimum concessions needed to stop workers from resorting to disruption to control the intensity of the labor process.

In addition to the high wages that were part of the compromise, Ford also provided job security through a form of lifetime employment that quickly was adopted by the rest of the industry: the practice of rehiring laid-off workers. Since layoffs and furloughs were a necessary part of the constant changeovers featured in the innovative flexible productions system of the early U.S. auto industry, the promise of restoring furloughed workers' hours and rehiring laid-off workers when the new innovative models increased consumer demand became a key feature of the effort bargain.

The compromise worked, forestalling worker activation of structural leverage for more than twenty years. It worked not just by giving high wages, but by establishing a moral economy where the exploitation of the flexible system was seen as part of a larger pact of shared suffering and shared reward between company and worker.[46] Just as the workers came to accept the constant speedups of the line and the periodic furloughs that punctuated the economic cycle, they also came to expect a share of the prosperity when the industry expanded and became the most profitable in the country. It was this sense—of sharing in both the positive and negative fate of the owners—that defined the effort bargain for the workers and constituted the "traditional rights or customs" that informally governed labor-management relations at the Big Three for the two decades prior to the Great Depression.[47]

The role that the axiom of shared suffering and reward played in labor-management relations is illustrated by the changeover from the Model T to the Model A at Ford, which we discussed in chapter 2.[48] First, production was abruptly halted in May 1927, and sixty thousand workers were furloughed indefinitely. Beyond the abrupt closing of the line, which left tens of thousands of workers without income to support families and mortgages, lay the failure of the vaunted "welfare capitalism" that had always promised to support them in these sorts of crises. The privation that workers experienced became national news, reported regularly in the *New York Times, Barron's,* the *Wall Street Journal,* and other national media. When the workers were rehired, Ford was no longer the leader in wages or in benefits.

Despite this clear breach of the effort bargain, the workers returned to Ford with a commitment to making the new car work—and therefore to ensuring that their recently threatened jobs would be made secure again. This reflected the foundation of the workers' moral economy: that workers would share in the fate of the company. The decline of the Model T was visible to the naked eye, as were the huge losses absorbed by management during the eighteen-month redesigning and retooling process. So, despite the profound deprivations they suffered during the furlough, workers saw their suffering as part of the larger moral economy. Protest was at best muted, and no job actions were undertaken in or around the idled River Rouge plant. At the same time, workers expected that they would share in the anticipated success of the Model A, and they invested themselves in that project. In other words, the workers endured the wrenching immiseration created by wage cuts, layoffs, and speedups during the transition from Model T to Model A production at Ford because the concept of shared suffering made these acceptable under the moral economy derived from the effort bargain, and the concept of shared rewards held the promise that their suffering was not in vain. A return to productivity would mean compensation for their hard work and sacrifice.

This effort bargain was still exploitive in the sense that workers still produced far more value than they were compensated for, but it was generous when compared both to what autoworkers had previously received and to what other similarly skilled workers were receiving at the time.[49] For instance, Gartman reports, in 1914, after the first round of wage increases at Ford, the auto industry stood seventh in average wage. Just after World War I, as Ford's Five Dollar Day spread to the rest of Detroit, the industry rose to fifth, despite a substantial decline in average skill level, and then rose to first in 1925 as skill levels continued to decrease precipitously. It remained first or second in average wages until the beginning of World War II, despite the fact that it had one of the lowest proportions of craft or skilled workers.

In addition, the auto industry evolved an attractive benefit package that was similarly superior to the offerings available in other work settings. Perhaps the most dramatic innovation was once again at Ford, where a fully equipped hospital was attached to Highland Park to treat workers for on- and off-the-job injuries and ailments. In the context of the times—when no medical plans were available and injuries on the job were a daily danger—this was an extraordinary fringe benefit that (at least temporarily) set Ford apart from the competition. Ultimately, as Detroit employers emulated Ford, its medical benefits set the auto industry apart from other core manufacturing sectors.

The benefit package did not stop at the factory gates. One element that helped auto earn the label of "enlightened capitalism" was the concern of the major firms in helping their workers effectively manage the munificent wages and, in particular, to aid them in purchasing houses. Each of the major producers and many of the parts suppliers offered a range of services in this realm, including mortgage programs, subsidized housing, and free legal help in executing house purchase agreements. Although this concern had originated in Henry

Ford's desire to ensure that his workers were fiscally responsible and had stability in their lives, the housing programs eventually became unadorned services that reduced the cost and stress of house purchase.[50]

These medical and housing benefits were part of the shared benefits aspect of the moral economy of the early auto industry. When it came to shared sacrifice, the automakers put policies in place that helped workers deal with the furloughs and temporary layoffs that were part of the ups and downs of auto production in Old Detroit. By the mid-1920s, automakers had subsidized welfare plans—with both worker and management contributions—that created forced savings to cushion the impact of such furloughs. At GM, for example, management contributed 50 cents for each dollar the worker deposited; fully 89 percent of employees participated, though many did so involuntarily. Moreover, since the money was invested in GM stock, it often accrued very high interest. During the early 1920s, when GM was experiencing geometrical expansion and overtaking Ford as the leader of the industry, interest rates averaged nearly 30 percent per year.[51] And a host of other benefits were made available to workers, including death benefit plans that paid funeral and burial costs (nearly all employees took advantage of this program), high-interest savings plans, English-language classes (compulsory at first at Ford), and a host of less universal services. The profile of these varied from employer to employer, but by the mid-1920s few auto industry firms were without an impressive array of ancillary services that sought to ameliorate various problems on and off the job.

Finally, Ford established job security as a critical adjunct of high wages. The lifetime employment systems of Japanese manufacturers were among the most visible of the virtues that the transplants brought with them to North America, but in the context of 1920s Detroit, they were virtually invisible. The removal of foremen's right to hire and fire during the implementation of the Five Dollar Day made job security the sine qua non of automotive employment; the policy was emulated by the other assemblers and finally adopted by the rest of the industry. Unlike the Japanese industry, temporary layoffs were the norm in Detroit (except for the most senior workers), but there was a commitment—usually honored, but unspoken—to keep these furloughs short and to restore jobs in an orderly manner. And the constant increase in employment in Detroit as a whole ensured that these promises were kept up until the Great Depression began in 1929. Functionally, workers in the flexible production era of Detroit had a system of lifetime employment.

The relative generosity of the effort bargain and moral economy was necessary for the functioning of the flexible production system, and it was made necessary by the dialectical relationship between the structure of flexible production, worker disruption, and worker power. Specifically, the exploitive nature of flexible production incentivized disruptions, and its tightly coupled and concentrated structure maximized worker structural leverage. Thus, the system gave workers both the motivation and the tools to successfully disrupt the functioning of the system. The effort bargain and moral economy were needed to remove the motivation to disrupt. If the effort bargain ever ceased to deincentivize disruption, however, the dialectics of class conflict under flexible production also made it logical to shutter the entire system.

THE END OF THE MORAL ECONOMY IN DETROIT

At first, everyone thought that the Great Depression would end quickly, so business as usual was the order of the day.[52] Thus, in auto, Henry Ford went ahead with his pending increase of wages to $7 per day. This was, after all, the tried-and-true solution to declining sales: increase wages for workers, thus increasing their willingness to participate in new rounds of innovation and intensification, while giving them the wherewithal to buy the new cars they are manufacturing. As usual, the industry followed Ford's lead: the new rounds of innovation began, including the introduction of brand-new models of Ford and Chevrolet, prices declined drastically, and Plymouth made its incredible descent into the low-priced field.[53]

Once it became apparent that hard times were not temporary, however, Ford and the other assemblers began to behave more like traditional capitalists. They continued to introduce production innovations that reduced costs through enhanced efficiency, but they also sought to decrease labor costs. Most immediately, there were massive layoffs.[54] At Ford, for example, there were rounds of layoffs totaling 45,000 in the winter of 1930–1931, followed by (after some rehiring) an additional 50,000 in 1932–1933. At GM, employment declined 50 percent, to 116,000, by 1932. Among Detroit autoworkers, in general, the unemployment rate reached about 50 percent, soaring to 80 percent among the substantial black workforce, which was, as always, differentially targeted. Given the central position of the auto industry in Detroit, these trends were reflected in the city's employment rates during the period. Specifically, employment at the end of 1931 was about half of the 475,000 it had reached before the crash in 1929, and it did not substantially increase again until 1937.

Among those who escaped unemployment, a large majority experienced substantial declines in earnings, since the industry augmented the massive layoffs with equally massive temporary furloughs. In 1931, about two-thirds of all employees worked less than a full year, with many working less than half the year. In August of that year, only 37,000 were actually working at Ford, less than one-third of the 128,000 count in March 1929.[55] Though the wage rate had not yet drastically declined, the income for the average *employed* individual decreased by one-third in 1931, placing enormous strains on all families, especially those with mortgages to pay and children to feed. (Statistics on the annual income of the vast number of officially unemployed are not available.)

One analyst estimated that 20 percent of the children in Detroit were undernourished in 1931.[56] Even *Fortune* magazine—then as now the voice of business—obliquely acknowledged the brutality of these events: "The sharp fluctuations in employment, both seasonal and cyclical, are of course the blackest mark—perhaps the only black mark—on the record of the automobile industry."[57]

This widespread privation led to the first successful protests in Detroit since its transformation into the center of American automotive production. Animated by the realization that the massive initial layoffs would not soon be reversed, inspired by the culture of collective action that immigrant workers brought with them from Europe, and nurtured by the already formidable organizational capabilities of the Communist Party, the Detroit Unemployed Councils grew rapidly. By 1932, the Ford Hunger March, along with other major protests, forced substantial improvements in the local relief program and provided the organizational foundation for effective resistance to the evictions that plagued unemployed workers.[58]

Despite these successes, union organizing was at first unsuccessful, at least in the plants of the Big Three. Rather, collective action was generally directed against the more immediate symptoms of suffering, such as hunger and evictions, rather than the policies of the Big Three automakers.[59] As the historian Joyce Peterson has reported, "the presence of union power in the industry was so small as to be almost unnoticed."[60] So, while there was collective action, it did not leverage the power inherent in the flexible production structure.

One significant factor explaining this was the difficulty for labor organizers of building a union in a company town like Detroit—as well as in its satellite cities, notably Flint (GM) and Dearborn (Ford). These cities had physically present upper classes, comprising mostly executives and stockholders of the Big Three and its multitude of suppliers; they sought to dominate public life in the region and to control government and public spaces so as to foreclose collective action deemed antagonistic to management's interest. Equally important, however, especially at the beginning of the Depression, was that the massive cuts in wages, benefits, and employment levels did not violate the industry's moral economy of shared sacrifice and shared reward. The companies were also suffering visible losses. Specifically, Ford and Chrysler logged major losses starting in 1930, while GM's profits sunk each year, from a record $296 million in 1928 to $8.5 million at the trough of the Depression in 1932.[61] Thus, though top management retained their more-than-ample salaries, the companies themselves absorbed tremendous declines in sales, revenues, and profits, the benchmarks used to evaluate sacrifice.

During the early years of the Depression, then, workers viewed the calamitous conditions as shared suffering, with workers, management, and owners all experiencing (hopefully temporary) austerity. They therefore directed their collective action against the more immediate symptoms of immiseration, such as hunger and evictions.

As the Depression lengthened, however, the underlying reality became more and more apparent. While the workers experienced increasing immiseration, the major assemblers were suffering much less, and eventually they were not suffering at all. Instead, they were becoming immensely profitable again. General Motors registered a profit every year, and Ford and Chrysler, after losing money at the beginning of the Depression, more than compensated for these losses with record profits after 1934. In direct parallel to previous hard times for individual firms or for the industry as a whole (such as the 1919 recession and the period of development of the model A at Ford), worker commitment and willing sacrifice proved instrumental to early recovery. The recovery was most spectacular at GM, whose after-tax profits reached $240 million by 1936.[62]

In previous iterations, workers had shared in the rewards of recovery—the companies often rehired the laid-off, gave wage increases, and put an end to furloughs—but the Depression-era recovery did not bring the same level of reward to workers. Before the onset of the Great Depression, General Motors employed 208,981 hourly workers making around $1,195 annually.[63] In 1936, employment at GM had been increasing and stood at 171,711—still over 30,000 fewer jobs than before the crash. Hourly wages saw a similar trajectory, almost returning to their previously high levels (reaching $6 a day). However, while hourly wages were recovering in 1936, incomes for GM workers were not. Sidney Fine describes the situation: "The irregularity of employment in the automobile industry meant that the well-publicized high hourly wages of the auto workers did not necessarily become translated into equally high annual earnings."[64]

Workers claimed that furloughs forced them into seasonal work that saw them receive around two-thirds of their pre-crash annual incomes, or $800 a year on average.[65] Official GM records indicate that 85 percent of the workforce (145,860 workers, or 63,000 fewer than before the crash) worked full-time and made $1,541 annually; Fine estimates that the actual annual average was between $1,200 and $1,300. Even if we accept the higher official numbers, the annual wages were still below estimates of a maintenance-level budget in Flint at the time. The Works Progress Administration estimated that $1,434.79 was needed annually for a family of four (the average GM worker earned around $200 below that figure), and Hartley Barclay, the editor of *Mill and Factory*, estimated that $150 per month was needed (full-time workers at GM made only $128 a month). The situation at Ford and Chrysler was no better: many of their workers received between 40 and 75 percent of their pre-crash annual wages.[66]

In addition to depressed incomes, which violated the effort bargain's promise of high wages, autoworkers in 1936 faced production speedups that coerced "prodigious new quotas" from "lines that had been fast and taxing" before the Depression, such that workers "were convinced that standing up to such a pace was aging and debilitating."[67]

Thus, notwithstanding the small but visible improvements in hourly wages for all workers and annual wages for some workers, autoworkers in 1936 were essentially working harder, producing more, and receiving less annual income than they were before the Great Depression. In the eyes of the workers, the traditional right and custom of ownership and labor sharing in the sacrifices needed to grow the industry and, in turn, sharing the rewards of that growth had been violated. Management had breached the moral economy of the auto industry, and the autoworkers felt justified in challenging management's actions.[68] This sense of injustice regarding the worker share in GM's return to profitability might have been best expressed during a debate about the ongoing Flint sit-down strike detailed by Henry Kraus, a UAW organizer and the union historian of the strike.[69] The debate matched United Auto Workers union president Homer Martin against prominent Michigan minister R. L. Lee. In opposing the strike, Lee invoked a familiar metaphor for the pre-Depression effort bargain, calling General Motors "a big family of 250,000 people," within which strikes were alien ways of resolving disputes. To this point, Martin responded that GM was "the kind of family where father eats the bacon, mother eats the gravy and the kids can lick the skillet."

The Activation of Structural Leverage

The violation of the moral economy of the auto industry during the Great Depression spurred direct action by industry workers, who had been working in the flexible system long enough to know the key leverage points in the structure. For example, workers at GM had adopted management's term "mother plant" to refer to facilities that represented the single source of parts for various other GM plants located within Detroit and across the country.[70] Although the activation of worker structural leverage culminated in the defeat of America's largest and most powerful corporation (GM) during the Great Flint Strike, that historical event was dependent on (1) mobilizing enough workers to engage in a successful shutdown of GM's production; (2) rediscovering the sit-down strike as the strategic weapon that would best leverage the structure of flexible production; and (3) developing an organizational structure responsive enough to local rank-and-file workers that the sit-down strike would be aimed at the key leverage points in the system. It turns out that the structure of flexible production facilitated all three.

MOBILIZING WORKERS IN FLEXIBLE PRODUCTION

The organizing process in the auto industry involved building unions capable of imposing on the Big Three at least some of the elements of the effort bargain at the heart of the autoworkers' moral economy. The success of this campaign relied to a considerable degree on exploiting the specific characteristics of the production system in southern Michigan. Among these, the central point of vulnerability was the high concentration of suppliers and assemblers, a foundation for industrial cultures of innovation.[71] This concentration was also a foundation, however, for systematic communication among workers, unmediated by management. Workers from the many GM establishments—as well as workers from other Big Three plants and myriad suppliers—lived in the same neighborhoods, socialized in the same bars, and played in the same parks. The tightly coupled southern Michigan production culture therefore created enduring personal and community relationships among workers who, in a dispersed production system, would have had few useful relationships unless they deliberately sought them out.

Beyond the organic connections created by the geographical concentration of production lay the myriad employee benefit programs that had developed as part of the effort bargain and were bulwarks of the production culture. Consider, for example, Fine's description of the Industrial Mutual Association (IMA) of Flint:

> The IMA offered its members gymnasia, bowling alleys, billiard tables, card rooms, chess and checkers, facilities for dancing, an auditorium seating sixty-five hundred, and a summer resort at Potters Lake. It carried on an elaborate intra- and inter-company sports program in cooperation with the personnel departments of various plants, and sponsored gardening, stamp, hiking, bridge,

cribbage, youth, and similar clubs, a male glee club, a women's chorus, several bands, and classes in such things as handicrafts, sewing, and modern dance.[72]

Fine points to the functionality of this program (and others): fostering loyalty among workers (and hence providing a layer of protection against union organizers) as well as providing a locus for systematic surveillance over workers' personal lives and any effort at collective action.[73]

Henry Kraus also recorded the management functionality of these welfare services, observing that they "multiplied the number of hidden ties between man and company" and provided an important locus for the companies' extensive espionage network.[74] When describing the impact of the IMA and the many other programs operating at GM, however, he also noted a perhaps unintended side effect: fostering a sense of community by multiplying the number of unmediated ties among the rank-and-file workers. That is, by providing a platform for socializing outside of work, the IMA increased the possibility that workers from different factories knew each other, creating a city- and even regionwide interpersonal network that facilitated the type of grassroots organizing used by UAW organizers in Flint and elsewhere in the auto production culture. It also guaranteed the kinds of rank-and-file connections that are essential to and generative of union democracy and allowed for optimization of direct action strategy to local structural conditions.

The necessity of word-of-mouth organizing to the labor movement in the auto industry was increased by the fact that the towns at the center of auto production—not just Detroit but also its satellite cities, notably Flint (GM) and Dearborn (Ford)—were essentially (or actually) company towns with physically present upper classes. Stanley Nowak, a union activist at the massive River Rouge plant, described the sort of political control that Ford exercised over the localities where its plants were located and its workers resided:

The Ford Motor Company . . . actually controlled the municipalities: Dearborn, all of Lincoln Park . . . Ecorse, River Rouge . . . all of the municipalities down the river. Because that's where the Ford workers lived. They controlled it—well, they had all kinds of municipal acts against distributing leaflets, against organizing meetings, and in Dearborn particularly. So to get in front of the Rouge plant, nearby where workers were going to work, it was impossible. You'd be arrested for violation of a city ordinance.[75]

At the time of the first sit-down strike, Flint's city manager, mayor, and police chief all had close ties to General Motors executives, and they continued a long history of enacting and enforcing public policies that GM favored.[76] This sort of domination, combined with the ferocious antagonism of the Big Three to any independent unions, meant that organizing efforts faced explicit repression from local police and other public officials. Difficult daily barriers to organizing were posed by tactics such as injunctions against mass picketing enforced with targeted or mass arrests; the denial of public permits for handing out literature, also enforced with arrests; the refusal by local papers to print anything that would offend GM; and a virtual blackout of radio news or announcements about collective protest.[77] Unable to mount large demonstrations, activists who did engage in public actions were subject to immediate firing from their jobs, especially at GM, where the spy network allowed quick identification of protest participants.[78] The social control tools available to management made public agitation more difficult and less fruitful, and it worked well to suppress and defeat the traditional organizing strategies, which focused on building support through formal rallies and official leaflet and literature distribution (such as the failed 1934 organizing action undertaken by the AFL).[79]

Labor organizers were able to work around these social control tools by exploiting the vast interpersonal networks that both the production system and the benefit system had created, conducting word-of-mouth, grassroots campaigns to build support for direct action while eschewing any initial effort to create large formal membership in union locals infiltrated by GM spies. The historian James Prickett describes the strategy of Wyndham Mortimer, one of the leaders of the Communist group within the UAW, when he arrived in Flint in May 1936 with the daunting task of organizing in the heart of the GM corporate empire:

Mortimer slipped secretly, he thought, into the company town of Flint, and checked into a hotel room. As he was taking off his coat, the phone rang, and a man told him, "You better get back to hell

where you came from, you S.O.B., or we'll take you out in a box."
Mortimer attributed the threat to the Black Legion, a semi-fascist
organization widely credited with the murder of several union organizers.

There were other difficulties in organizing in Flint. City ordi-
nances forbade the distribution of leaflets and the use of sound
equipment. The five locals in Flint had a total membership of 122,
out of a potential of 45,000, and most of those were considered
company spies by the workers. Open meetings were out of the
question, since only company spies and ardent unionists would
show up. The spies would report the unionists, and the company
would fire them.

So Mortimer simply went door-to-door in Flint, talking to
workers and their wives, discussing their grievances, and signing
them up in the union. Their membership cards were sent directly
to [national UAW secretary-treasurer George] Addes in Detroit,
thus bypassing the spy-infested local leadership. Some of the
workers visited by Mortimer would invite him back for a second
meeting with their friends present.

Before the summer was over, Mortimer was mailing a weekly
mimeographed newsletter to seven thousand working class families in Flint.[80]

Friendship ties thus became the main vehicle for recruiting new
members. As Mortimer described the process, the door-to-door campaign was simply "leavening the dough," through which "a few men
joined the union and then they got their friends in."[81] This process
also resulted in a flat organizational structure, featuring rank-and-
file democracy and informal local leaders created through interpersonal ties.

The effectiveness of using the existing social structure can be confirmed by underscoring the simple (but quite amazing) statistic reported by Prickett: Mortimer, the only full-time organizer in Flint
during the summer of 1936, went from a standing start to a mailing
list of seven thousand families who supported unionization and were
willing to take the (moderate but measurable) risk of receiving (and
almost certainly reading) his union newsletter.[82] He recruited, therefore, about six families per day; perhaps even more extraordinarily,
this foundation would yield, only three months later, a forty-four-day

strike ultimately involving tens of thousands of workers and community members that would shut down virtually all of GM's automotive production and establish industrial unionism in the United States.

This rapid and thorough mobilization reflected a process that social movement scholars have identified as the (often) invisible foundation for most (or perhaps all) explosions of social protest. Such explosions are marked by a process by which, once the constituency has (implicitly or explicitly) arrived at a unity of purpose, new movements borrow preexisting structures to mobilize coherent collective action.[83]

While the dense interpersonal networks created by flexible production and the number of ancillary benefits that had been part of the now-broken effort bargain facilitated organizing in a company town, the growing commitment to unionism among rank-and-file workers was restrained by a widespread understanding that union activism risked jobs, physical well-being, and even lives. These dangers were measured against a growing history of union organizing that had an at-best checkered history of success.[84] As Fine notes, by the end of 1936, the UAW had only around 10 percent of the GM workforce as members.[85] And the even weaker presence of the union in Ford and Chrysler was one reason why Wyndham Mortimer and the other union activists selected GM as the target.[86]

This lack of a critical mass for a general strike in GM necessitated that the union stage successful actions despite having a relatively small proportion of autoworkers enrolled, in order to demonstrate that workers could win and thus change the political calculations of the art of the possible among workers who were not enrolled.[87]

Flexible production aided in the task of staging successful direct action with small numbers, since only a few plants had to be shut down in order to stop all of GM's production. What the workers needed was a strategy capable of prolonged shutdown of mother plants in the face of the inevitable violent repression that GM would mobilize through its ties to the town's elites.

REDISCOVERING THE SIT-DOWN

The key to leveraging the workers' structural leverage was the use of the sit-down strike, which allowed workers to stop production while frustrating the huge arsenal of countermeasures that management could usually apply to workers' demands.[88] For example, with workers occupying the factory, employers could not hire scabs; the factory served as a defense against the type of police brutality often faced by strikers on picket lines. Most importantly, occupying the factory protected the union's structural leverage by stopping the employer from moving equipment to non-unionized plants and resuming production.[89]

Flexible production made using the sit-down strike more effective, because shutting down a key supplier to many downstream factories (recall that these suppliers were referred to as "mother plants" by both workers and management) cripples a flexible production system, whereas shutting down plants in a dispersed system causes only temporary losses while production at other plants is increased. The structure of the system also makes it easier to engage in successful action, because fewer workers are needed when a single plant being shut down will do major damage. As Beverly Silver describes it, this structure of production meant that "a relatively small number of activists could bring an entire plant's production to a halt" and that "when the line stopped, every worker necessarily joined the strike."[90]

The selection of the sit-down strike as the weapon of choice was the result of a more than yearlong trial-and-error process by the world's working class and the diffusion of these lessons to the UAW through organizational learning. The collective learning by the UAW was made possible by the democratic nature of the union structure being built and its responsiveness to rank-and-file input through informal local leadership. The diffusion of successful collective action repertoires through social movement networks has been documented in many different circumstances.[91] The manner in which the sit-down strike as a tactic gained currency in 1936 exemplifies this phenomenon and adds substance to the idea that collective learning is always a part of the process.

Starting as early as 1906, the tactic was used sporadically in various locations inside the United States, most notably by the International Workers of the World (IWW, or Wobblies), but it was not until late 1935 that workers and union organizers began to appreciate the exceptional leverage that it conferred in assembly line manufacturing, especially in company towns like those where the auto industry was located.[92]

The process of learning worked its way through a series of smaller and larger strikes, not all of them in the auto industry. Fine offers this summary of the prehistory:

There was a three-day sit-down at the Hormel Packing Company in Austin, Minnesota, in 1933, some brief sit-downs in the rubber factories of Akron in 1933, and quite a few sit-downs of the quickie variety in the automobile industry, especially in body plants, in 1933, 1934, and 1935; but it was not until the next year, 1936, that the sit-down strike began to receive widespread attention and to become a matter of some public concern. There were forty-eight strikes in 1936 in which the strikers remained at their jobs for at least one day; in twenty-two of these work stoppages, involving 34,565 workers, the strikers stayed inside the plants for more than twenty-four hours.[93]

Among these many precursor strikes inside and outside the Detroit production culture, some became key nodes in the learning process that defined the strategy and execution of the Flint strike at the end of 1936.

Perhaps the earliest of these learning moments occurred at the Toledo Chevrolet plant, the site of the only militant AFL strike in the auto industry, beginning on April 23, 1935.[94] Without the endorsement of the national union, a relative handful of critically placed workers sat down at their stations, quickly idling almost the entire plant. After a few hours, when the bulk of the 2,300 workers had registered support for the strike, the sit-downers left their stations and joined the outside picket line. Confronted with this fait accompli, the national AFL leadership reluctantly offered its endorsement without acknowledging the sit-down tactic.[95] Because the Toledo plant was the sole source of Chevrolet and Pontiac transmissions, within ten days seventeen plants employing 32,000 workers were idled, and Chevrolet and Pontiac dealers around the country faced the imminent prospect of vacant showrooms and business lost to Ford and Chrysler.

On May 11, with the Toledo plant idle for eighteen days, GM executive vice president William Knudsen offered unprecedented concessions, including the first instance of (de facto but not publicly acknowledged) sole bargaining rights to the local union, together with substantially increasing wages, improving seniority, and slow-ing the speed of the assembly line.[96] Though this offer did not answer most of the workers' demands, Knudsen told the union negotiators that continuing the strike would result in Chevrolet moving the en-tire operation to a non-union location, depriving all 2,300 workers of their jobs.[97] Under this pressure, and against the resistance of the more militant unionists—who felt that they could defeat the threat by widening the strike to other plants (particularly the Flint Buick facility, which would interrupt Buick, Oldsmobile, and Cadillac pro-duction)—the leadership endorsed the settlement and won a rank-and-file vote.

Even this less-than-complete victory created an indelible mark on workers' understanding of how to leverage GM into restoring key el-ements of the pre-Depression moral economy. The initial sit-down demonstrated that a relatively small band of well-placed militants could initiate an effective plantwide strike, embraced by the bulk of previously uncommitted workers. This lesson would be applied re-peatedly for the next four years. The more important lesson, however, was that a militant strike at a mother plant could force even GM to offer unprecedented concessions. The AFL national newspaper pointed out why the victory was so important: "For the first time in history, one of the major automobile manufacturing concerns has agreed to recognize and meet with a spokesman for its employees."[98]

Despite the agreement to negotiate with the union exclusively, GM did not negotiate around—or unilaterally address—either the lost jobs or the multitude of other issues that remained after the strike. Long-term success would therefore depend on effective in-plant mechanisms to coerce adherence to negotiated settlements as well as the tattered effort bargain. Ultimately, the threat or reality of sustained sit-downs would become the answer to this problem.

Rubber workers in Akron, Ohio, provided the first overwhelming victory for militant strikes in the early months of 1936, mounting a series of short sit-downs against the four largest rubber manufactur-ers and a sustained militant strike against the Goodyear Rubber Company.[99] The first big explosion occurred on January 29, when the tire builders in one corner of the main Firestone Rubber Company plant initiated a sit-down strike, provoked by a speedup and the fir-ing of a protesting union official. The journalist Ruth McKenney, who spoke to the workers soon afterward, described the start of the strike as a cathartic moment for the assertion of workers' power in the tightly coupled system of manufacturing.[100]

After two days, with one plant completely idle and workers at a second poised to initiate a sit-down of their own, Firestone capitulated, granting all the strikers' demands. This success was repeated at Goodrich, which answered the sit-downers' demands in less than a day.

These preliminary victories set the stage for the workers to challenge industry leader Goodyear. On Friday, February 14, a tiny cohort of 137 tire builders in Department 251-A of Plant No. 2 "shut off the power and sat down."[101] As in earlier sit-downs, this small action rendered the entire plant inoperative and inspired the vast majority of the now-idled other workers to join the strike in an "endless human chain" around the factory. On Tuesday, five hundred Plant No. 1 workers sat down and remained inside for twenty hours, then marched out and joined ten thousand strikers who surrounded the plant in what they claimed was the longest picket line in history.

It took a month involving a full array of tactics—ranging from publicity campaigns through recruitment of vigilantes to police violence—for Goodyear to satisfy itself that only concessions would end the strike. Although the company postponed signing a formal contract, the final resolution granted virtually all of the workers' immediate demands, most notably a companywide agreement, the cancellation of the layoffs and speedup, and routinized meetings with union officials around these and other issues.

In the next few weeks, Akron workers pioneered the use of spontaneous sit-downs to enforce the recently won agreements. As one United Rubber worker told *Nation* reporter Louis Adamic, sit-downs "put teeth in the agreement."[102] Since management sought to follow its prestrike pattern of failing to implement most elements in new (formal and informal) contracts, the sit-down as enforcement mechanism became a daily fact of life in Akron.[103]

The events in Akron definitively validated the Communist/CIO organizing strategy of mounting strikes in plants without a strong union presence, using the strike to validate union effectiveness, and thereby building the union based on successful militant action. At their annual convention in the fall of 1935, prior to the sit-downs, the

United Rubber Workers had three thousand dues-paying members in an industry employing one hundred thousand. In the spring of 1936, just after the conclusion of the Goodyear strike, membership had reached thirty thousand, on its way to almost fifty thousand by the end of the year.[104]

Many UAW leaders, including Homer Martin (the sitting UAW president) and Walter Reuther (a future UAW president), traveled to Akron for the victory celebration. Without yet embracing the sit-down as a necessary weapon, they concluded that Akron had validated all the elements in the overarching strategy of strikes initiated by small numbers of workers and sustained by a flood of workers into the nascent union organization.[105] They returned to Detroit with this confidence and were soon joined by a new cadre of organizers among whom were sit-down veterans from Akron and Toledo, newly moved to Detroit to help fulfill Martin's prediction that "we'll be next."[106]

Two months later, the first sustained sit-downs—with workers remaining in the plants until a settlement was reached—occurred in Europe.[107] Similar to the Akron strikes, the strikes in France were not centered in industries with existing union organization (fewer than 7 percent of workers were union members). Rather, they "occurred precisely in the under unionized manufacturing sectors of dynamic France, among semi-skilled factory workers."[108]

By early June, almost 2 million French workers were on strike, with 8,941 of the nearly 11,000 shuttered plants occupied by their workers. Instead of leaving the plants once production stopped, the French workers announced that they would remain next to their machines while negotiating an acceptable settlement. Despite many threats from various management and government officials, no violent effort was made to dislodge them. On June 7, the French premier, Léon Blum, brokered the Matignon Agreements, which gave the trade union movement official recognition and workers the right to freely organize.

Even before the French strikes ended, sit-downs spread throughout Europe, with noteworthy movements in Yugoslavia, Hungary, Spain, Poland, and Scotland. Although the tactic of the sustained sit-down strike was eventually adopted by U.S. autoworkers, its diffusion was not aided by major newspapers, which published almost nothing about the French sit-downs. The lack of coverage made the path of diffusion easier to trace, however, as the few news sources that did carry articles with substantive content about the conduct of the national strike and its resolution were labor-oriented publications: *The Daily Worker* (the Communist Party national newspaper) and *The United Automobile Worker* (the UAW organ in the Detroit area).[109]

Activists took note of three aspects of the strike that would figure in the Flint strike, which was at that time only six months away. First, reaffirming the lessons learned earlier in the year in Detroit, the French strikes demonstrated that sit-downs could be successful without an already established union presence. Second, a sustained sit-down—never before attempted in Detroit—could guarantee that the plants remained shut down, that the machines could not be moved and activated with non-union labor, and that the workers would have a far less arduous task in sustaining solidarity and commitment. Third, the absence of violent police action in France convinced them that sit-downs were far less susceptible to physical repression than other strike strategies, since the risk of destruction of valuable machinery (by either the workers or the police effort to dislodge them) in any attempt to violently remove strikers made corporations and government less willing to adopt such strategies.

The French strike may have convinced key activists and some rank-and-file workers in Detroit of the efficacy of the sit-down strike, but it did not convince William Knudsen, the top GM operating executive, of the strategy's applicability in the United States. When warned against the tactic by French auto executives, Knudsen told them, "That could not happen in the United States. The American people would not stand for them."[110]

On November 17, 1936, the first sustained sit-down strike in the American auto industry took place in South Bend, Indiana, at the Bendix Products Corporation. The strike sought to enforce union recognition and wage increases negotiated in June but never implemented. GM, which owned 24 percent of the company's stock, participated in a settlement with the union after six days of the factory occupation, agreeing to honor the previously promised wage increase, while partially recognizing the UAW local. Henry Kraus, the editor of the *United Automobile Worker* during this period, concluded that it was the Bendix strike that convinced the mass of autoworkers of the "basic advantages of the technique for the auto industry, and especially employer-ridden cities like those of Michigan."[111]

Two days after the Bendix settlement, the UAW used the sit-down strike for the first time in Detroit. At the Midland Steel Products Company, which made bodies for Chrysler and Ford, twelve hundred workers halted production and caused the layoffs of fifty-three thousand workers at the Plymouth, Dodge, Chrysler, Lincoln-Zephyr, and Briggs plants, which used frames manufactured at Midland. Given its position as "an important feeder plant . . . in the highly synchronized automobile industry, the strike's effect was immediate."[112] In a little over two weeks, on December 4, Midland management agreed to a wage increase, abolition of piece rates, and time-and-a-half pay for overtime (more than forty-five hours a week) and for work on Sundays and holidays. This strike further demonstrated that a work stoppage at a key plant could paralyze production in a large part of the industry.[113]

In the month of December, Detroit saw a rash of sit-down strikes at parts companies. Each strike had a negative effect on the production of the auto companies, and it was often pressure from the Big Three that led to relatively quick settlements.[114] These victories also confirmed an argument that the Communists had been making for several years: that a show of union power in even small shops could lead to support for unionization across the Detroit region. Immediately following each strike, union membership for the striking local boomed and spread to other companies. In December 1936 alone, the UAW added more than ten thousand members in Michigan.[115]

WORKERS' LEVERAGE ACTIVATED:
THE GREAT FLINT STRIKE

Buoyed by the success of previous sit-down strikes, the Detroit-based UAW organizing committee (though not necessarily the national officers) was committed to the strategy of initiating a full-scale conflict with General Motors by stopping production in two "mother plants" that could choke off 75 percent of all GM production—the Cleveland Fisher plant and Flint Fisher Body Plant No. 1.[116] Henry Kraus, labor historian, editor of the *Flint Auto Worker*, and a key Communist UAW organizer, described the meticulous logic that informed this choice:

The union's strategy held that the chief burden of the strike must be borne by Flint's Fisher One and by Cleveland-Fisher, with the former taking the lead. These two plants were the major body manufacturing units of the corporation—"mother plants," according to GM terminology—being responsible for the fabrication of the great portion of Chevrolet and other body parts, which were then shipped in so-called "knocked-down" form to the assembly plants throughout the country. All the stampings for the national Chevy production were turned out in Cleveland. Fisher One, on the other hand, manufactured irreplaceable parts for Buick, Oldsmobile, Pontiac and Cadillac. In particular the great dies and enormous presses needed to stamp out the mammoth simplified units of the new "turret top" bodies were concentrated in the Cleveland and Flint body plants. Possibly three-fourths or more of the corporations' production were consequently dependent on these two plants; an interlocking arrangement that was not unusual, moreover, in the highly specialized auto industry and especially among the leading corporations. There were perhaps a dozen other plants equally crucial to General Motors, but in only the two designated was the union strong enough to halt production.

The entire blueprint of the union's organizing schedule depended upon this type of careful selection, for its forces were terribly limited and the power it opposed so commanding.[117]

Though the activist workers in the targeted plants were anxious to get started, the leadership wanted to wait until January, after the promised five-dollar Christmas bonuses would be paid, and when Frank Murphy, the newly elected governor of Michigan who sympathized with organized labor, would take office.[118]

The workers at Cleveland Fisher, though aware of the January target, initiated the soon-to-be national strike several days early. On December 28, 1936, after a month of brief work stoppages, the workers in the "strongly organized quarter panel department" sat down in protest against a newly announced wage cut. Unlike previous job actions in Cleveland and elsewhere, this dispute did not remain restricted to one section while the involved workers sought immediate response to their grievance by local management. Instead, the origi-

CLASS CONFLICT | 135

nal instigators successfully recruited the support of the other departments and expanded their demands, culminating in the first articu-
lation of the global slogan that would become the mantra for the
GM-wide shutdown: "No Settlement without a National Agreement."[119]

Once it became clear that the Cleveland sit-down would be part of
a larger struggle, events began to overwhelm the plans of the UAW
organizing committee. At 7:00 AM on December 30, while the organizing committee continued to prepare for the Fisher Body Plant No.
1 strike in early January, fifty workers at Fisher Body No. 2 in Flint "sat
down and tied up production" in the entire plant. The provocation
in this instance was the transfer of three inspectors for refusing to
quit the union.[120] Though Fisher No. 2 was not a mother plant (it produced only 450 Chevy bodies per day and no critical components),
the workers there sought to join the national strike signaled by Cleveland Fisher, and the successful shutdown shattered the image of
Flint—GM's company town—as invulnerable to anything more than
hit-and-run work stoppages.

In the meantime, the Fisher Cleveland strike had alerted GM management to the "mother plant" strategy, and they moved to preempt
the expected takeover of Fisher No. 1. Twelve hours after the Fisher
No. 2 sit-down, the company began loading key machinery from
Fisher Body No. 1 onto freight cars, apparently headed for the less
militant plants in Grand Rapids and Pontiac. The process by which
the union responded to the threat posed to their structural leverage
by GM's transfer of equipment to less unionized plants illustrates the
importance of the responsiveness of the democratic structure of the
new union to local rank-and-file workers. As a superintendent and
other workers who were unaware of the strike began loading machinery onto freight cars, they were spotted by John Ananich, a swing-
shift worker at Fisher Body No. 1 and a union member. Ananich
slipped out of the plant to call CIO organizer Bob Travis with the
news. Travis immediately called an 8:00 PM lunch-break meeting of
the UAW stewards at the union office across the street from Fisher
Body No. 1. As described by UAW organizer Henry Kraus, the entirety
of the meeting consisted of the following discussion, called to order
by chief UAW organizer Bob Travis:

"Boys, we'll make this snappy," he said. "I understand there's something happening over there on the press room dock."

"That's right," one of the men called out, "they're taking dies out of the press room. They got four or five [railroad] cars lined up there."

The men from the die room substantiated this.

"Well, what are we going to do about it?" Travis asked, looking slowly about the room.

There was a cold sort of pause. A chap raised his hand and stood up.

"Well, them's our jobs," he said quietly. "We want them left right here in Flint."

"That's right!" several others exclaimed.

"Boys," Travis said, still holding himself back, "I'm not going to tell you what you ought to do. That ought to be plain enough to you if you want to protect your jobs. In my plant in Toledo, General Motors walked off with 1,500 jobs a year ago and in Cleveland the Fisher Body boys struck just Monday to save theirs. What do you want do?"

"Shut her down! Shut the goddam plant!"

The cry was taken up by the whole room till it was nothing but one big shout.

"Okay, fellows, that's what I wanted to hear you say. . . . Roy [Reuther] and I will come in after you've got the plant down and help you get everything organized. . . ."

"Everybody stays in till the warning whistle!" I yelled from the door.

"That's right," Travis said. "We don't want any stooges tipping the company off ahead of time."[121]

Within days the magnitude of the strike had become apparent. GM production ground to a halt as national attention focused on Flint, Detroit, General Motors, and the auto industry, accompanied by ferocious debates within local and national media about the strike's origins, legality, viability, and ultimate fate.[122]

The beginning of the strike became the denouement of the process that led auto industry workers to rely on class struggle—specifically the militant strike—as the central tool for reestablishing key elements of the pre-Depression effort bargain. Several noteworthy elements in this process underscore the embeddedness of the workers' action in the production structure of the Detroit "keiretsu":

- The fact that the leaders—even the on-the-ground organizers—did not ultimately decide on the timing of the strikes illustrates the rank-and-file absorption of the logic of the strike as a strategy, and their own sense of control over its use. The yearlong organizing process convinced semiskilled workers—previously ignored or excluded as agents of unionization—that they could effectively harness their structural leverage in the production process. The workers who stopped the assembly line asserted a form of agency that had been a latent (but rarely manifest) part of the tightly coupled mass production system in the auto industry at least since the institution of Henry Ford's assembly line.[123]

- The willingness of Cleveland Fisher workers (and subsequent sit-downers in mother plants) to forgo their immediate demands in favor of a national settlement that served (with a few exceptions) all GM employees (including those with insufficient structural leverage to impose concession) ensured the broader support of GM workers and the surrounding working-class communities. This class consciousness constituted a commitment to the strategic orientation required for the successful application of structural leverage. Without this strategic orientation, even the most successful plant shutdown would have yielded gains for only the workers involved, and then necessitated myriad local struggles, with many doomed to failure in plants without strategic leverage.

- The "rallying to the cause" by concentric circles of supporters—workers in the same factory, those in connected plants, the surrounding (working-class) communities, and ultimately a considerable proportion of national public opinion—provided the workers with validation of their own belief that "taking the law into their hands" was justified. To a large degree, it was this belief in the justice of their cause—in the moral economy that their actions enunciated—that animated the drastic actions they took and gave them the energy to risk their own safety, their jobs, and even the welfare of their families.

- The fact that the surrounding workers quickly rallied to the cause—and therefore ensured that there would be little inside-the-factory pressure to return to work—validated the "strike first, union second" strategy that CIO militants and the Communist Party had been advocating for the better part of two years. This success thus served notice to other workers, to plant managers, and to the captains of the U.S. automobile industry that even the most quiescent workforce might be galvanized into proactive class struggle with little visible (to management) forewarning. Each production bottleneck in every mother plant thus became a powerful tool in the hands of the workers to build a union capable of extracting concessions or resisting policies initiated by management.

On January 4, the UAW sent a letter to GM's Chief Executive Officer Alfred P. Sloan and Chief Operating Officer William Knudsen, detailing the union's specific demands.[124] Two key demands—union recognition and collective bargaining on a national level—immediately emerged as the axes of conflict.[125]

The conflict did not last long. GM had delivered 50,000 cars in December; in the first week of February production had dwindled to 1,500.[126] No longer able to resist the financial pressure, GM agreed to a settlement on February 11. As part of the settlement, GM consented to rehire workers who had participated in the strike, to allow union members to wear buttons and other insignia on company property, and to give the UAW-CIO six months as the sole negotiator in the plants that had gone on strike.[127] This last term of the settlement amounted to the exclusive bargaining rights that the UAW and CIO had desired, even if just for a limited time.

As it turned out, six months was all the union needed. Riding a wave of momentum created by the victory over GM, the UAW-CIO increased its membership from about eighty thousand in February to around four hundred thousand in October 1937.[128] Given that UAW membership had stood at twenty thousand in December 1936, and zero just a few months before that, this turn of events confirmed not only the Communists' theory of taking action to build support—rather than building support in order to take action—but also the power that flexible production gave to the small groups of radical workers who were taking direct action.

At this juncture, we want to briefly address the role of the political opportunity structure in the success of the Flint sit-down strike. We have emphasized the interaction between movement strategies and the structure of flexible production in our retelling of the Flint strike. This is necessary to illustrate the central role of the Flint strike in creating the conditions that led to the abandonment of the U.S. version of flexible production. An astute reader, however, would be correct to wonder how much of the success of the Flint strike and the labor movement was due to the structure of flexible production, and how much was due to a friendly political opportunity structure created by a labor-friendly U.S. president and governor of Michigan. President Franklin D. Roosevelt had set up the National Labor Relations Board (NLRB) in 1935 and refused to denounce the strikers during the sit-down, and Governor Frank Murphy sent in the National Guard to keep the peace after the "Battle of the Running Bulls," protecting the strikers from local police and GM goons rather than joining the effort to dislodge the workers.[129]

Although this political opportunity structure most definitely contributed to the labor movement's success, it was not the primary factor that it may seem to have been on the surface. First, the NLRB played no role in the Flint strike, and the strike was resolved two months before the Supreme Court upheld the National Labor Relations Act (NLRA).[130] Additionally, the local rank-and-file workers employed key strategies that took advantage of the political opportunity structure. For instance, it was the strikers' sense of ownership over their jobs, their stewardship of the occupied factories and the equipment inside, and the general peacefulness with which they conducted themselves (aside from self-defense during the Battle of the Running Bulls) that allowed the labor-friendly president and governor to give any measure of support to the workers. In fact, Governor Murphy cited worker conduct as integral to his decision to use the National Guard, not to remove the strikers, but to keep the peace.[131] In addition, GM's President William Knudsen released a statement supportive of Governor Murphy, saying that GM did "not believe labor disputes [could] be helped by violence."[132] It should be noted that GM used violence as a tactic in labor disputes many times. In fact, the company used it at the Guide Lamp plant in Anderson, Indiana, three days after the Flint sit-down at Fisher Body No. 1, when an army of city police and deputized foremen attacked workers picketing outside the plant. General Motors defended this action, saying that the police and its employees had a "right" to use violence to disperse the picket line.[133] What was different about Flint and Anderson (and every other case of GM supporting the use of violence against striking workers) was that in Flint the workers were occupying the plant. In Anderson, the sit-down strikers had been tricked into leaving the plant before they were attacked. Attacking workers in the plant risked damaging valuable equipment, and this was the real reason why GM supported Governor Murphy's use of the National Guard to protect the workers from police violence—Murphy was also protecting GM equipment.

The workers' stewardship of the plant equipment, which acted as a shield against violent removal, was made possible by the fact that they used the sit-down strike rather than a traditional picket line. The decision to take care of the plants diffused through the workers quickly and was adopted by all participants because of the democratic nature of the union organization. Recall our demonstration earlier in this chapter that the sit-down strike was the optimal strategy because of the tightly coupled nature of flexible production. We also discussed the union's ability to develop a democratic structure because of the strong social networks among workers, which were the result of the personal relationships created by the constant interaction of different departments during the trial and error that was a part of the flexible system. Thus, the interaction of worker agency with the structure of flexible production was the most significant factor in the success of the Flint strike, not friendly politicians and brand-new untested legislation.

THE PURPOSE OF ABANDONING FLEXIBLE PRODUCTION

The UAW's victory over GM in Flint demonstrated the potential power available to workers when they activated their structural leverage. This lesson quickly spread, first throughout the auto industry and eventually to most of the labor force in the United States. For instance, in 1937, there were 4,740 strikes in the United States, including 477 sit-down strikes in the auto industry.[134] Between 1938 and U.S. entrance into World War II, there were more than 12,000 additional strikes, with the auto industry at the center of labor insurgency.[135] The success of sit-down strikes led directly to the organization of virtually all workers employed by the Big Three and their direct suppliers and eventually the widespread adoption of industrial unionism in the United States.[136]

Although victory for the labor movement, in terms of adoption of unionism, came relatively quickly after the Flint strike (five years), Ford was not easy to defeat. The struggle to unionize Ford taught important lessons to both workers and management.[137] Ford had been the most visibly ferocious anti-union company in North America for two decades, with its leadership resorting to "sheer physical force" on many occasions during the 1930s.[138] In fact, violence was the first and last line of defense at Ford. The Flint strike demonstrated that if a strike took place in the flexible system, Ford would lose, just as GM had. Ford hoped to block any strikes at River Rouge through sheer intimidation by having its private security force beat any union organizers coming near the plant. This strategy backfired in the 1937 "Battle of the Overpass," when a *Detroit News* photographer captured pictures of a brutal attack on UAW organizers and released them to the public. Rather than dampening support by sowing fear, the attack resulted in the skyrocketing of worker and community support for the union.

By 1941, the long winning streak for labor made the leverage of workers so visible that even Henry Ford Sr. could see that further resistance was fruitless—as was expressed perfectly by Ford when he told his chief negotiator, Harry Bennett, to grant both the union shop (compulsory membership for all employees) and dues checkoff (management collection of union dues) in the first formal contract. Bennett protested against this "generosity," since the union was not (yet) demanding these concessions and the workers had not (yet) won them at GM and Chrysler. According to Bennett, Ford replied with perfect capitulationist logic: "If we gave the union just a little, then they'd be right back at us for more."[139] In the end, Ford negotiated full union recognition without any climactic strike or significant interference from the NLRB. The surrender of Ford thus demonstrated to workers—and to corporate leadership in the country as a whole— that even the most determined management could be defeated just from the threat posed by activated worker structural leverage.

Radical Democracy and Workers' Leverage in World War II

World War II interrupted all civilian automobile production and transformed the Detroit regional economy into the primary supplier of military equipment to the U.S. government and many of its allies. The urgency of war production foreclosed any systematic alteration of production methods. For instance, GM had shown interest in shifting production to non-union locations. First, as we mentioned in the last chapter, they tried to avoid the Flint strike by loading key equipment onto freight trains to be shipped to non-union plants (but were blocked by Flint's astute workers). Second, as we demonstrate later in this chapter, GM began opening plants far away from southern Michigan immediately after the Flint strike. This strategy was stopped by the war. Yet there was no stop to the determination of management to "regain autonomy over setting workplace rules"— that is, to prevent workers from using their now fully activated strike leverage to force or veto changes in work process.[140] To accomplish this, the leadership of the Big Three turned to the federal government.

It may seem strange to claim that the auto companies thought government would be on their side, given the Roosevelt administration's reputation as pro-labor. In fact, the pro-labor nature of FDR and the NLRB are so taken for granted that many liberal analysts now assume that it was the primary cause for the success of the labor movement. Yet the actual actions of the administration and the NLRB during the key time period between the Flint strike and the beginning of World War II suggest that corporate leaders were right to expect the government to come down on their side in the class war.

First, both the NLRB and the Supreme Court ruled sit-down strikes illegal in 1939. Workers at Fansteel Metallurgical Corporation had made a failed attempt at a sit-down strike in 1937, resulting in the dismissal of workers involved in the sit-down. The NLRB took the company to court to get them to rehire the workers. In litigation, however, the NLRB characterized the sit-down as an illegal strike in violation of the National Labor Relations Act. Their argument for rehiring workers rested on the company violating the NLRA first. The Supreme Court agreed that the sit-down was illegal, but decided that workers who violate the NLRA are no longer protected by it. Thus, the NLRB and the courts made a major strike against labor's most powerful weapon.

Second, President Franklin Roosevelt had energetically invoked the federal commitment to increasing military production in an attempt to dampen the crescendo of strikes in 1941. Despite his rhetorical efforts, 1941 was a record strike year, involving 8.4 percent of all workers in the country (significantly higher than the 7.2 percent of workers who went on strike during 1937, the previous peak year).[141] This failure of federal rhetoric led to Roosevelt's cosponsorship with industrial leaders of a no-strike pledge in all basic industry, which the AFL, CIO, and United Auto Workers leadership eventually supported. Following a contentious conference among government, labor, and industrial leaders on December 17, 1941, Roosevelt publicly announced a no-strike agreement with three elements: (1) the full cessation of all work stoppages (mainly strikes but also lockouts); (2) the settlement of all disputes by the peaceful means mandated by union contracts, including a compulsory grievance procedure; and (3) in the event of the failure of these methods, the settlement of disputes by the National War Labor Board (NWLB) established and appointed by the president.[142] The CIO tried to leverage cooperation with the government on the no-strike pledge to advance broad working-class interests by pushing the Murray Industrial Plan, which would have granted them participation in the administration of basic industry, but the Roosevelt administration rejected it.[143]

Thus, the corporate strategy of using government and the law as a weapon against worker structural leverage seems successful given the historical record. First, the NLRB and courts ruled the most powerful type of strike illegal and deincentivized its use by making loss of protection under the law a consequence of its use. Then FDR took away strikes entirely.

The actions taken by government on behalf of corporate interests were important given automakers' limited options at the time. To recap, there were essentially two strategies that could diminish the threat of worker structural leverage. One involved revising the production system itself to undermine the structural basis of power. This strategy would require major changes in the overarching structure, including the abandonment of sole sourcing (which created production bottlenecks and mother plants), the reestablishment of large stockpiles (which could buffer against local area work stoppages), and decentralization (which made strike coordination more difficult). Given the urgency of ramping up war production, these sorts of changes were impractical.

The alternative strategy for retilting the balance of power involved developing mechanisms to prevent or deter workers from using their structural leverage. In the past, such as with Ford's Five Dollar Day, a generous effort bargain had been enough to placate workers. Since the Flint strike, however, management of the Big Three had capitulated on much of what the union asked for—union recognition, collective bargaining, raised wages, increased benefits, rehired laid-off workers—and yet the strikes kept coming.

Two key differences marked the post-Flint auto industry compared to the Five Dollar Day industry, and these differences explain the differing effectiveness of the effort bargain. First, in 1913–1914, the autoworkers were unorganized. The absenteeism that motivated the original effort bargain was an individual reaction, taken simultaneously by many workers, to the oppressiveness of the production system. The Great Flint Strike, on the other hand, was organized and strategic about leveraging flexible production against management. It is easier to secure the consent of unorganized workers acting purely because they are unhappy with the system than it is to respond to workers organized around taking collective power over the conditions of their labor. This hints at the second difference: after the initial effort bargain, the auto industry developed a moral economy that bred trust between workers and management. For example, when Ford rehired laid-off workers at new and higher wage levels after the successful introduction of the Model T, this signaled to workers that management could be trusted to abide by the maxim of shared sacrifice and shared rewards, and that any violation of the effort bargain was temporary and necessary for the greater good. When GM exceeded pre-Depression profitability in 1936 but failed to rehire laid-off workers and instead hired new workers at low entry-level wages, this signaled to workers that management could not be trusted. It signaled that the automakers were now operating according to a new maxim: workers make all the sacrifice, management gets all the benefits.

Thus, the Flint strike is a key moment when the ideological hegemony of the automakers collapsed. The moral economy of shared
sacrifice and shared reward had not truly been a reflection of reality—neither sacrifice nor reward was shared equally. Rather, it functioned as ideology—turning the world upside down, in the words of
Marx—that made the oppressiveness and exploitive nature of flexible
production seem natural and moral.[144] Once the automakers violated
the moral economy, it ceased to serve its ideological function, and
workers became woke to the fact that the only thing guaranteeing
that they would benefit from their labor was the exercise of their own
power. Thus, the same concessions previously made by management
could not stop the tide of direct labor actions in the post-Flint U.S.
auto industry.

These events led management to realize that they would continue
to endure endemic disruption of production whenever even a few
workers felt that changes in production methodology created undue
or unremunerated intensification of the work. They could either find
a way to convince their semiskilled workforce to stop utilizing the
power conferred on them by the structure of flexible production and
their now-activated organizational capability, or they could find a
way to neutralize workers' disruptive power, which was challenging
management's previously unchallenged control over the structure
and speed of production. GM chief executive Alfred P. Sloan summarized the industry's attitude to the sudden onset of what was soon
going to be called "collective bargaining": "Our rights to determine
production schedules, to set work standards, and to discipline workers were all suddenly called into question."[145]

From the perspective of those corporate leaders who supported
the no-strike pledge, its virtue thus rested largely on the hope that
the pledge would convince workers to forgo activating their structural leverage in order to constrain and channel the vast changes in
production process that the war economy mandated. That is, auto
executives hoped that either the workers would voluntarily give up
work stoppages or their leaders could and would compel workers to
channel their discontent into the grievance process.

This logic of worker constraint rested on the implicit theory that
post-Flint strikes did not spring from the structural conditions of
auto production and the desires of the rank and file, but were driven

by union organizations and leadership. MIT professor Leonard R. Sayles, writing in the *Harvard Business Review*, characterized this commonly held position among top management as the "generally assumed" view that strikes resulted from "demagoguery and deceit" by union leadership.[146] The testimony before the U.S. Senate of George Romney, chief spokesperson for the automobile industry during the war, reflected this opinion: "The desire of a majority of workers who want to do more work and get this war over with is being thwarted by an unrestrained militant minority group of workers, stewards and union representatives."[147] Under this logic, if the "stewards and union representatives" did not support or agitate for strikes, work stoppages would decline precipitously. According to Sayles, many managers operationalized this view as "find the leader and you eliminate the problem."[148]

The problem with this anti-democratic view of unions—that union leadership imposed radical action on the rank and file—is that flexible production made it impossible. As we demonstrated in the last chapter, the structure of flexible production contributed to the development of a democratic union organization that was responsive to rank-and-file workers through informal local leadership.

Though they may not have realized this at first, management learned that the union was, in fact, radically democratic as they observed an increasing tide of strikes, almost all unauthorized and many actively and even ruthlessly opposed by formal union leadership. The U.S. *Monthly Labor Review* counted nearly three thousand strikes in 1942, the vast majority in the second half of the year. Then, in 1943—the first fully mobilized war year—the official statistics recorded a 33 percent increase in the number of strikes, a 200 percent increase in the average size of strikes, and a 300 percent increase in the amount of working time lost. After another 33 percent increase the next year, the sociologists Jerome Scott and George Homans concluded, the 1944 count of 4,956 strikes was "greater in number if not in duration than any other year of the country's history."[149] Though 1945 showed a slight decline in the number of strikes (to 4,750), the strikes were dramatically larger and longer: the loss of 38 million labor days was 40 percent above the previous high of 28 million, recorded in the summit year of 1937.[150] According to the labor historian Art Preis, U.S. workers "chalked up more strikes and strikers during the period from December 7, 1941, to the day of Japanese surrender three years and eight months later, than in any similar period of time in American labor history."[151] Virtually all of these strikes were wildcats, unauthorized by formal union leadership, since both the CIO and the AFL had fully endorsed the no-strike pledge.

The auto industry led the national trends.[152] In 1943, despite strenuous opposition from the national and Detroit-area leadership of the UAW, 27 percent of all autoworkers participated in work stoppages, including five major wildcat strikes at Chrysler plants in Detroit. In 1944, the growing wave involved 50 percent of the workforce, including 6,500 strikers at Chevrolet Gear and Axle, 5,600 strikers at the Ford Highland Park plant, a wave of very large wildcat strikes that shuttered the Ford Rouge plant, and a shutdown of the Chrysler Highland Park plant. The wartime peak arrived at the end of that year, when, from December 1944 to February 1945, 126 work stoppages involved the majority of U.S. autoworkers. In 1945, fully 75 percent of autoworkers were involved in strikes.[153]

As the historians Martin Glaberman and Nelson Lichtenstein clearly document, the strikes percolated upward from the shop floor, where they originated in the daily confrontation between supervisors and workers over control of the work process.[154] What the crescendo of strikes demonstrated was that the vulnerable structure of production, combined with the organic democracy of the UAW (which had been engraved in the CIO structure by the Flint strike and then diffused through basic industry), gave shop-floor workers the tools and willingness to organize strikes without the impetus of formal leadership and to sustain them long enough to outlast management. As *Harvard Business Review* author Sayles put it: "It is necessary to acknowledge that [a wildcat's] source is likely to be rank-and-file dissatisfaction."[155] Or as the business scholar Garth L. Mangum observed (also in the *HBR*), "Often a high wildcat strike rate is accompanied by a high degree of local democracy."[156]

Management Confronts Workers' Power

In some sense, World War II production and the no-strike pledge constituted an immense social experiment designed to test whether the class struggle within auto (and other mass production industries) could be adjudicated by convincing workers to cease the chronic work stoppages that had emerged from the reconfigured effort bargain of the late 1930s. The answer was a resounding negative, underscored by the record strike years in 1945 (the last war year) and 1946 (the first full year of postwar production). This crescendo—with over 80 percent of the strikes unauthorized by union leadership—was destined to continue with only modest declines until 1960.[157]

What the experiment had shown was that the unionization process—taking place as it had in Detroit—had created a class-conscious working population that grasped the usefulness of applying pressure on the shop floor by attacking the point-of-production vulnerability of flexible manufacturing.[158] One potential challenge to the class consciousness that auto labor had developed throughout the 1930s was an influx of new workers (including many black and women workers) to Detroit, Flint, and other auto production centers. Even though the millions of new workers flooding into the industry as part of the mobilization of the economy to wartime production transformed the labor force, most of the new workers joined the existing unions.[159] For example, from 1942 to 1947 (during the no-strike pledge), total employment increased 3.3 million, while union membership increased 4.4 million.[160] The unionization of new workers provided an avenue for the diffusion of class consciousness. That is, as new workers joined the union and became integrated into labor movement networks, they gained access to the collective knowledge that workers already in the union had of structural leverage and class solidarity. The diffusion of collective action repertoires through social movement networks has been documented in many different contexts.[161]

One of the strongest pieces of evidence for the class solidarity of the wartime workforce is the UAW's response to inequality in wages within the union created by the influx of new workers.[162] Among the wartime auto workforce, there was inequality both within and across plants on the basis of race, sex, and region. Facing immense pressure from the rank and file, the UAW took complaints about unequal wages to the National War Labor Board. This cross-race and cross-sex solidarity did not come without struggle. The initial onset of racial diversity in Detroit was met with a rash of "hate strikes" by white workers who felt that black workers were a threat to their jobs.[163] By 1943, however, wildcat strikes over other issues continued to increase, but hate strikes had almost vanished.[164]

The many wildcat strikes during the war are themselves evidence of the diffusion of class consciousness. Although some have argued that the wildcat strikes represent a *lack* of union solidarity by new workers, Lichtenstein argues—and we agree—that this view ignores "much of the empirical evidence to the contrary and reject[s] most of what we know about the consciousness of workers who engage in strike actions."[165]

For the Big Three automakers, the lesson in rank-and-file solidarity was clear, and it authoritatively disproved management's thesis regarding the role of leadership in fomenting discontent among their workers. That is, the frequent strikes were not the result of a contented workforce being called out to strike by union leaders or demagogic shop-floor activists. Instead, the massive strike wave reflected exactly the desires of the rank-and-file workers in their shops, and the demands they raised were a reflection of a radical democracy within the union. This democracy delivered to the workers the right to decide—with or without the support of their union leaders—which issues to raise as points of contention, and then the right decide—again, with or without the support of their union leaders—when to disrupt, stop, or slow production in order to force response to these demands. The strike waves after Flint, during the war, and immediately after the war had demonstrated to auto management, which stood at the core of the U.S. capitalist class, that workers would not honor any commitment—whether made by the president of the United States, by their union leadership, or even by themselves in the form of a union contract—to abandon the disruptive tools that flexibility conferred upon them if they felt that they were subjected to unfair labor practices. As a consequence of this unequivocal proof of the willingness of workers to exercise their newly activated power, auto industry management had two choices, which we mentioned earlier: negotiate production changes with the shop-floor workers or deprive shop-floor workers of their direct power to disrupt production.

The first possibility, which might be called a "workers' peace," could be glimpsed in the behavior of Chrysler during the immediate postwar years. Among the Big Three, Chrysler was most susceptible to the leverage that shop-floor workers could exercise, largely because its production structure was by far the most tightly coupled. As a result, its plants and suppliers were riddled with choke points, creating many points of leverage that could severely disrupt production. Moreover, the crucible of class struggle before and during World War II had created fully realized union solidarity at Chrysler, where strategically located workers were now willing to sit down in support of demands made by those with less production-conferred leverage.[166]

Because workers could so effectively threaten disruption of production, Chrysler management fell into the routine of "constant bargaining about rates [of production and pay]."[167] Although "constant bargaining" could be quite contentious, in many areas of the Chrysler system such negotiations became routine and were conducted with minimal disruption. In effect, a form of "worker-imposed peace" prevailed, based on granting a veto to the affected workers (often represented by shop stewards) over many work process changes initiated by management.[168]

The degree to which this was a "workers' peace" and not acceptable to management can be found in the description by one final assembly worker of his job in Dodge Main: "The standards were pretty much decided by the workers on the job. We would decide how much we could do. Without jeopardizing my job I could make 15 minutes [of relief time] for myself every hour. The foremen knew what was going on. But there was time to do good quality work."[169] This degree of control was unsatisfactory to management because it constituted a severe constraint on what they considered managerial autonomy— the right to alter the work process and, if they deemed it proper or necessary, intensify it (as they had repeatedly done at the beginning of the Depression). Fifteen minutes of idle time per hour may have been reasonable (or even necessary) from the perspective of workers trying to endure the long haul on assembly lines that were "really tough" on their bodies and their health. But for management, 25 percent downtime constituted an assault on their bottom line. Chrysler management believed—and they may well have been right—that this sort of shared governance over the work process (as practiced in Dodge Main) was the principal reason for their profit levels trailing those of Ford and GM.[170]

This managerial logic—that unfettered control over the work process would increase profit margins—was impeccable as far as it went, but it was faulty in a larger sense. If Chrysler had sought to impose its will, the workers' "readiness to sit down and refuse to work" would have translated into a rash of work stoppages that would most likely have resulted in even lower profit levels.[171] In effect, final assembly workers could bank fifteen minutes of downtime an hour, because it was more profitable for Chrysler than enduring the constant disruption of wildcats.

It is important to note in this context that this sort of workers' peace did not deprive Chrysler of the ability to increase productivity and remain profitable. At the plants and companies where "appeasement" became the accepted practice, the workers did not continually escalate demands to the point of unprofitability. Instead, they accepted increased quotas produced by improved production methodology when "they thought it was fair," while resisting those deriving from unremunerated intensification of labor; in making that distinction, "the standards were pretty much decided by the workers."[172] Some scholars of wartime production have argued that the willingness of management to concede to the demands of the workers during World War II was largely a consequence of either cost-plus contracting or tight labor markets. However, the continued profitability of Chrysler and other companies that continued the appeasement policy after World War II, when unemployment increased and the companies could no longer rely on "cost-plus" contracting, suggests that "labor-imposed peace" was not solely the result of market forces. Appeasement was a viable option, and the choice involved human agency.

One route to resolving the chronic production disruption, then, would have been to allow for the sort of cogovernance of the production process that many union activists and shop stewards on the left wing of the union movement explicitly sought. However, such cogovernance—often mischaracterized as "worker control of production"—would probably have resulted in profit levels considerably below those achieved during the pre-Depression and late-Depression years. In effect, management would have had to become reconciled to three sorts of constraints on their autonomy:

1. Workers would be able to veto changes in production methodology that intensified their effort.

2. Workers would extract substantially increased compensation for the increased effort.

3. Workers would share in the increased profits resulting from
   changes in work process that increased worker productivity
   without intensifying the work process, including technology
   innovation and improvement in production methodology.

In other words, institutionalizing shop-floor negotiation around
work processes would have resulted in a profit-sharing system enforced and imposed by workers' structural leverage. Equally important to management, however, is that it would have resulted in management's loss of power. Given that profit is the result of surplus
value generated by labor, profit-sharing between labor and management is still a win for management. Power makes all profit possible,
because power is what allows management to appropriate the value
produced by the labor of others. Thus, at the core of management's
choice between accepting appeasement and dismantling flexible production was class struggle. Auto management represented the interests of company ownership, but when it came to labor conflict, they
also represented the interests of the capitalist class. As managers of
the largest industry in the nation, they faced off with the most powerful labor union. When auto unionized in the late 1930s and early
'40s, the rest of American industry followed suit in a matter of years.
Similarly, if auto management had made appeasement their policy,
that would have had ramifications for the larger class struggle.
    While Chrysler management drifted toward a de facto acceptance
of the workers' peace, Ford and GM remained determined to (re)es-
tablish unfettered autonomy over the work process. In the context of
this ongoing determination, the World War II experience offered an
important lesson: that union leadership—even when highly motivated to support management prerogative (as it was during the no-
strike pledge)—could not prevent workers from using their shop-
floor leverage to assert their demands. The wildcat strikes had
accomplished more than vitiating the no-strike pledge: they had created an ultra-democratic union structure that was capable of coordinating even large strikes. By the end of World War II, not only could
rank-and-file workers stop production in specific areas with grievances and use the structure of production to spread the stoppage to
wider areas, but they could also—through the lateral structure developed among shop stewards within the Detroit production system—

organize companywide and potentially industrywide strikes, with or without the support of the top leadership.

GM first, Ford second, and Chrysler much later concluded that avoiding a "workers' peace" and preserving the full autonomy of management would require applying the lesson that Leonard Woodcock—the regional director of UAW-Chrysler during the latter part of World War II, and destined to become UAW president in the 1960s—had sought to teach Continental Motors, and that various scholars had pointed to—that only the defeat of the strike weapon would ultimately convince workers not to use it.[173] But, as Mangum and other scholars pointed out, defeating the strike weapon would require altering the equation of forces, so that management could endure—without suffering grievous losses—a sustained strike.[174] And the ability to endure such a strike required altering the production system to eliminate the choke points from which workers' power derived.

THE DIRE CONSEQUENCES OF ABANDONING FLEXIBLE PRODUCTION

4

Having laid out our case for the role of class conflict in motivating the shuttering of American flexible production, we want to focus in this chapter on detailing when the system was abandoned and documenting the consequences for innovation. That there is an objectively measurable moment when the Big Three shifted from flexible production to parallel production, and that this moment marks the start of a major decline in innovation, demonstrates that the Japanese advantage we documented in chapter 1 is not simply a case of the Japanese being naturally more innovative than the United States. Rather, it is the result of U.S. automakers under an ossified parallel production system being less innovative than *any* automaker under flexible production—be it the Japanese since the 1970s or the earlier version of themselves before World War II.

The Rise of Dispersed Parallel Production

In the face of the massive worker leverage conferred by flexible production, the Big Three automakers had to find a way to defeat strikes (especially the type of bottom-up, wildcat strikes they faced starting during World War II). The system that emerged from efforts to counteract worker power made three significant departures from the existing flexible production system: parallel production, large stockpiles, and dispersion from the Detroit and southern Michigan region. Thus, we term the new U.S. system "dispersed parallel production."

The ways in which dispersed parallel production deviated from flexible production had two types of consequences: first, these deviations insulated the production system from work stoppages, resulting in a reduction of worker structural leverage; and second, they necessitated a number of other changes to the production system, ultimately making it impossible to uphold flexibility, along with its associated high rates of innovation.

The new production system was insulated from strikes in several significant ways:

1. Dispersion made coordinating direct action more difficult by creating large physical distances between workers. No longer could a strike at one plant quickly spread to other plants the way it had during the Flint strike.[1] More than just making coordination difficult, however, dispersion also contributed to a change in how decisions were made.[2] When workers were concentrated in production centers, the UAW was able to have a more democratic decision-making structure, with informal local leaders emerging and serving as a bridge between the rank and file and the national leadership. In chapter 3, we demonstrated that this radical democratic structure was a key to the success of the Flint strike. Dispersion made responsiveness to the rank and file more complicated with the growth in the number of different groups of workers who now faced vastly differing local conditions.

2. Stockpiles allowed stations downstream to continue working if a strike disrupted production upstream. Thus, worker structural leverage was directly reduced, as more workers needed to join a strike in order to shut down an entire plant.

3. Parallel production further reduced structural leverage by eliminating mother plants. That is, rather than a single plant producing parts for most vehicles produced by a company, now every part was built in at least two plants. Hence, even if the union mobilized enough workers to shut an entire plant down, the companies now had the option of ramping up production at one of the parallel plants producing the same parts. This capacity deprived wildcat strikes of their power, as something approaching a national work stoppage became necessary to have any significant impact on auto production.

As each of these changes reduced worker leverage and protected automakers from work stoppages, they also had the unintended consequence of necessitating complete abandonment of the rest of the features of flexible production. In this chapter, we summarize the relationship between these changes and the abandonment of flexible production. For full details about each of these relationships, see chapter 1.

In short, dispersion, by geographically separating suppliers and assemblers, made just-in-time production difficult to coordinate, and the large stockpiles made it expensive. Thus, just-in-time delivery was abandoned. Stockpiles made flexible machinery redundant. Flexible machinery's main role in flexible production was to allow upstream workstations to stay active by making different parts once the downstream stations had all they needed of one type of part. Stockpiles allowed those workstations to keep making the same part and the downstream stations simply stocked backup inventory.

Finally, the incentive to maintain long-term supplier relationships under flexible production had been the need to coordinate just-in-time delivery and the buy-in needed on the supplier end to keep pace with rapid innovation (see chapter 2). With just-in-time delivery abandoned and innovation slowing because of the other structural changes cited here, trust between suppliers and assemblers was not as immediately necessary. Predictably, automakers began exploiting competition between suppliers in order to reduce costs. Thus, the rise of dispersed parallel production was the death knell of flexible production in the U.S. auto industry.

In this section, we detail the implementation of dispersed parallel production for each of the Big Three.

GENERAL MOTORS DISCOVERS THE
POWER OF DISPERSED PRODUCTION

Ford and Chrysler would not begin to implement a spatially decentralized production system until after World War II, but GM began to disperse production immediately following the 1935 Chevrolet strike in Toledo and consciously reduced its dependence on Detroit and the southern Michigan region following the Flint strike.[3] There may have been many market-based advantages to building facilities outside of

Detroit, but the new policy was designed to neutralize the newly activated shop-floor power of the sit-down strikes. This was the conclusion of Arthur Kuhn, who accessed the documents that describe GM's
decision-making during the post-Flint period. Referring, for example, to the 1937 decision to build a new Chevrolet engine and axle
plant in Buffalo, New York, rather than in the Detroit region, Kuhn
found that it was motivated by a desire "to get away from labor-torn
Flint" and to provide GM with "more sources of supply; that, of
course, lessened the impact of a strike at a particular plant."[4]

Despite Kuhn's conclusion that the dispersion process at GM was
animated primarily by a desire to weaken labor's structural leverage,
this relationship has not become integrated into the standard history
of the period. This failure to understand that decentralized production was an explicit policy—not the natural expression of market-
driven product life cycles—was masked by the conjunction of ob-
scuring events during that critical moment. First, GM's origins as a
holding company for a number of autonomous producers had kept
production from being as fully concentrated as it was at Ford, where
nearly all production before World War II took place at River Rouge
in Dearborn, Michigan. Thus, GM's early dispersion efforts were not
of the immediately noticeable (to use the parlance of autos) "zero to
sixty" type. Second, while GM began to decentralize production after
the Flint strike, this reorganization of production was interrupted by
World War II. Thus, there was a ten-year gap between GM's initial
reaction to the Flint strike and its full implementation of dispersed
parallel production. Furthermore, it took another twenty years before
the concomitant decline in innovation hurt the bottom line of the
Big Three and alerted analysts to the existence of a problem.

Nevertheless, GM did engage in dispersal of production (beyond
moving production of some Chevy parts to Buffalo) before World War
II. Table 4.1 lists the new component plants operated by GM in 1939.

Out of the eighteen new GM component plants, thirteen were located outside of southern Michigan. The point of management's new
production strategy was to create redundancy and reduce dependency. For that to work, not only were new plants outside of Michigan
needed, but plants producing the same parts had to be far enough
away to make coordinating work stoppages more difficult. This locational element of the parallel production strategy is illustrated in

Table 4.1 *New GM Component Plants, 1924–1939*

City	State	Components Produced
Bristol	Connecticut	Drivetrain and chassis
Meriden	Connecticut	Drivetrain and chassis
Anderson	Indiana	Drivetrain and chassis
Kokomo	Indiana	Electrical
Muncie	Indiana	Electrical
Bay City	Michigan	Engines
Flint	Michigan	Electrical
Pontiac	Michigan	Drivetrain and chassis
Pontiac	Michigan	Electrical
Saginaw	Michigan	Electrical
Harrison	New Jersey	Drivetrain and chassis
Buffalo	New York	Drivetrain and chassis
Rochester	New York	Drivetrain and chassis
Tonawanda	New York	Engine
Dayton	Ohio	Drivetrain and chassis
Dayton	Ohio	Engine
Moraine	Ohio	Drivetrain and chassis
Warren	Ohio	Electrical

Source: Authors' compilation. Adapted from Rubenstein 1992, 109–20.

table 4.1. For instance, drivetrains and chassis were now built in Indiana, Ohio, Connecticut, New Jersey, and New York in addition to southern Michigan. A similar dispersal of production of electrical components and engines can be seen. It should be noted that GM had an assembly plant in Norwood, Ohio, that was about two and a half hours from the new Indiana component plants and about an hour from the different Ohio-based component makers. It also built an assembly plant in Linden, New Jersey, which was just down the road from its new Harrison plant and only a couple of hours from its Connecticut plants. That said, its New York plants were more than six hours away from any assembler, and all of the new plants represented moves away from the "home" plant cities of Pontiac, Lansing, Detroit, and Flint, where labor militancy was greatest.[5] Flint especially stood out as a center for GM facilities.[6] Thus, it is notable that of the new plants in 1939, only one was in Flint. And most of the seventeen new plants outside of Flint were far away from the center of labor militancy: the average distance between these new plants and their Flint counterparts was 322 miles.

GM paused its dispersal actions during World War II. As detailed in the last chapter, the Big Three thought that the use of government and courts to rein in union leadership would solve their problem just as well as dispersal. Yet the rash of wildcat strikes during the war signaled to the industry leadership that a continuation of the policy of dispersed parallel production would be a necessary condition for defeating shop-floor disruption of production. After the war, GM restarted and intensified its move to dispersed parallel production. For instance, engine production shifted from each car division producing all of its engines in its home "mother" plant in Flint, Lansing, or Pontiac to each engine plant producing a specific size of engine. Thus, a strike in Flint could shut down only the production of the Buick and Chevrolet models that used a specific size engine, not all production of all Buicks and Chevrolets. Other models of Buick and Chevrolet that used different-size engines could go on being produced.

Creating redundancy in engine production, however, also constituted an abandonment of flexibility. With each engine plant producing only a single-size engine, flexible machinery and parts were not needed. This lack of flexibility created a self-reinforcing loop that necessitated full abandonment of the flexible system: without flexible machines and parts, stockpiles were needed to keep upstream stations busy, providing justification for a policy that GM was following anyway as an anti-labor strategy. Eventually, plants with inflexible machinery that produced one size of engine found it cost-effective to have very long production runs for each engine. Finally, this situation lent itself to automation.[7]

In addition to producing engines for all models at different plants in southern Michigan, GM also expanded engine plant production to Tonawanda, New York, and St. Catharines, Ontario. The expansion of parallel production represented a general postwar trend in GM component production.[8] For instance, in 1946, when Central Foundry was created, it included plants that were a minimum of 300 miles apart—in Saginaw, Michigan; Danville, Illinois; and Lockport, New York. Between 1948 and 1958, Central Foundry added new facilities in Defiance, Ohio, and Bedford, Indiana—245 miles apart.

Finally, GM further intensified its production dispersion when it moved most electrical component production from southern Michigan to the U.S. South, starting in the late 1960s. Unlike its post-Flint locational choices, GM's motivation to avoid labor conflict was explicit here. For example, Rubenstein states that through labor's use of strikes at key supplier plants, GM learned "that the local labor climate could be more critical than transport costs in selecting new plant sites," and that this was what motivated the "southern strategy" with regard to electrical component parts.[9]

FORD AND CHRYSLER ADOPT DISPERSED PARALLEL PRODUCTION

Although Ford and Chrysler were slower to disperse production, they too learned the lessons taught by the wildcat strikes during World War II. Prior to the war, both automakers' production was almost entirely located in Detroit. Chrysler's only major component plant outside of Detroit was a transmissions producer in Kokomo, Indiana, and Ford maintained only two conventional component plants as feeders to River Rouge that were not in Dearborn: glass production in St. Paul, Minnesota, and steering wheels in Hamilton, Ohio. After World War II, however, both companies joined GM in decentralizing production, although at different rates. Table 4.2 lists the fifteen new component plants built by Ford in the 1950s and '60s.

Like GM in the late 1930s, Ford built a number of redundant plants (duplicating production already taking place at River Rouge) that were far enough from Dearborn to make coordination between workers producing the same component much more difficult. This constituted a major departure from Henry Ford Sr.'s policy of centralized sole sourcing, but it allowed Ford to endure local strikes within the Rouge complex—by the most militant of all UAW locals and the most willing to undertake unauthorized strikes—by ramping up production at another plant.[10] The average distance from the fifteen new plants to River Rouge was 136 miles, and these new plants were not concentrated in one locale: the average distance between any two of the new plants that produced the same components was 106 miles.

Although these new Ford plants were clearly not as widely dispersed as GM's, it is important to remember that flexible production

Table 4.2 *New Ford Component Plants, 1950–1969*

City	State	Components Produced
Livonia	Michigan	Transmission
Monroe	Michigan	Stamping
Mount Clemens	Michigan	Paint
Rawsonville	Michigan	Electrical
Sterling Heights	Michigan	Suspensions
Utica	Michigan	Trim
Woodhaven	Michigan	Stamping
Brook Park	Ohio	Casting
Brook Park	Ohio	Engines
Canton	Ohio	Forge
Fairfax	Ohio	Transmission
Lima	Ohio	Engines
Sandusky	Ohio	Electrical
Sharonville	Ohio	Transmission
Walton Hills	Ohio	Stamping

Source: Authors' compilation. Adapted from Rubenstein 1992, 102–04.

at Ford had included the construction of self-sufficient automobile factories capable of producing a completed vehicle with few to no outside suppliers. Thus, the use of many new component suppliers that were not part of any single assembly plant represented a departure from flexibility. This change is also reflected in an increase in the average number of independent feeder plants used to supply final assembly plants. Figure 4.1 illustrates this trend at Ford. The dramatic increase in its feeder plants in the 1950s and 1960s brought Ford a long way toward "catching up" with GM in creating dispersed parallel production.

Chrysler lagged even further behind, partly because it had been the most dependent on independent suppliers within the Detroit production culture and therefore had few resources for creating parallel production facilities. This technical handicap was probably amplified by Chrysler's policy of accepting the "workers' peace" that conferred on its workers veto power over production methods and thus created another barrier to removing production from Detroit. It was not until the 1960s that Chrysler opened more plants outside of Detroit: an engine plant 23 miles from Detroit in Trenton, Michigan; an

Figure 4.1 *Average Number of Outside Feeder Plants Used by Ford, 1910–1972*

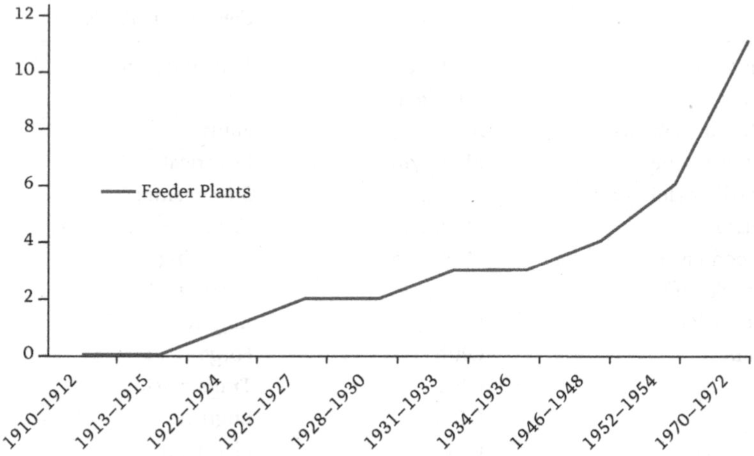

Source: Adapted from Abernathy 1978, 108.

aluminum casting plant 244 miles from Detroit in Kokomo, Indiana; and a foundry 287 miles away in Indianapolis, Indiana.[11] From that point forward, Chrysler became a full partner in the migration away from Detroit.

It is important to note that this process of dispersal—which has escaped the attention of virtually all the theorists of deindustrialization in Detroit and elsewhere—was fully actuated by the late 1960s. The dispersal process initiated by GM and followed by Chrysler, Ford, and then other major parts of the Detroit production culture was in full swing long before it became a public issue in the 1970s. Not only did the dispersal process deprive Detroit of virtually any new facilities that would have expanded the workforce in the region, but by 1962 it had led to the loss of 134,000 manufacturing jobs and 10 percent of the population of Detroit.[12]

As the policy of decentralization matured, an elaborate stockpiling system evolved in which downstream plants maintained large inventories of components produced in bottleneck plants. Abernathy, Clark, and Kantrow refer to this inventory system—in contrast to Japan's "just-in-time" system (or, although they do not mention it, Old Detroit's hand-to-mouth system)—as a "just-in-case" system that treats inventory as a hedge against the interruption of long production runs.[13]

The Consequences of Abandoning Flexibility

The wartime strategy of securing no-strike pledges from union leadership and relying on the union leadership to rein in the radical democracy that flexible production conferred on the rank and file had definitively failed, producing record strike years during and after the war—despite the best efforts of management, union leadership, and the various levels of government. The postwar reorganization of U.S. auto production—which created a more decentralized and redundant system that drastically reduced the leverage of line workers—had the intended effect on work stoppages. As previously noted, there were 477 sit-down strikes in the ten months following the 1937 Great Flint Strike and 126 wildcat strikes in a three-month period during late 1944 and early 1945, a time when the UAW had a no-strike pledge in place.[14] Just after V-J Day, autoworkers led a national strike wave that included uncounted numbers of wildcats as well as a 113-day formal strike against General Motors.[15]

In contrast, there were only 504 wildcat strikes in the twenty-seven-year period from 1946 to 1973.[16] During that period, the auto industry signed landmark labor contracts, specifically in 1948 and 1950. It seems intuitive that the labor contracts brought about the decrease in wildcat strikes. That is, one could see the Treaty of Detroit as the new effort bargain in the U.S. auto industry and view this new effort bargain as having the effect, like the Five Dollar Day before it, of placating workers' discontent and putting a stop to their militant actions. This view of the effect of the Treaty of Detroit on worker militancy is incorrect. It might have been accurate had management honored the agreement on the shop floor, but as they had since the Depression, management violated the effort bargain and proved themselves untrustworthy. This is why the rank and file kept engaging in unauthorized strikes, just as they had done during World War II. The difference this time was that the Big Three were constructing a dispersed parallel production system. Flexible production was not abandoned all at once by all of the Big Three, but rather over the course of the period from 1946 to 1960, with Chrysler being the last to fully abandon it. So the wildcat strikes that followed the Treaty of Detroit contract gradually grew less and less effective, because, as the dispersed system replaced flexible production, strikes required the involvement of more and more workers in order to exert enough structural leverage. Specifically, under parallel production with stockpiles, if a factory making one component was shut down, production could be increased in other factories making that part. Workers had to be able to shut down all the factories making the part. Under flexible production, shutting down one or two mother plants had the consequence of shutting down the rest of the factories. In the postwar period, the need to have most or all union members involved in strike actions required having leadership on board with the action in order to mobilize the rest of the union. In other words, management's abandonment of flexible production made wildcat strikes a losing weapon for labor. Once workers learned that the wildcat was not as effective, they abandoned it as a tactic.

A close look at key details of this time period reveals that this story is consistent with the facts, and that the view of the Treaty of Detroit as bringing labor peace is not. For instance, if the contract brought labor peace by placating the workers with benefits such as indexed pay wages and company-paid health care, then we would expect that rank-and-file workers were happy for a time after the contract was signed and that wildcat strikes immediately and significantly declined. Instead, as Ruth Milkman notes, "settlement at the national level obscured ongoing turmoil at the local level," where "the factory . . . remained a site of intense conflict and deeply rooted discontent."[17]

This turmoil shows up in the wildcat strike data compiled by James Zetka. While the peak years for wildcat strikes were during the war, his analysis shows that the bulk of the 504 wildcat strikes from 1946 to 1973 took place between 1950 (when the Treaty of Detroit was signed) and 1960 (by which time all of the Big Three had fully abandoned flexible production).[18] The fact that wildcats were used significantly less often (1) just after World War II when GM abandoned flexibility and Ford began to move to dispersed flexible production and (2) after 1960, when both Ford and Chrysler had fully joined GM in abandoning flexible production, also supports our reading of the period. Finally, Zetka also provides statistical analysis of the determinant of wildcat strikes.[19] He finds that, controlling for other factors, a wildcat strike was most likely to take place at Chrysler and least likely to take place at GM, with Ford in the middle. Furthermore, his analysis finds that the odds of a wildcat strike dropped over the course of the period from 1946 to 1963. That is, the highest likelihood of a wildcat strike was during the 1946–1950 time period, when only GM had begun to institute a system of dispersed parallel production, and the lowest chance of a wildcat strike was during the 1960–1963 time period, by which time all of the Big Three had moved to dispersed parallel production.

THE END OF PRODUCT INNOVATION

Viewed from the point of view of management's ongoing struggle against the shop-floor workers taking advantage of flexible production methods to disrupt production and extract concessions, the policy of dispersed parallel production with large stockpiles appeared to be a win-win situation for management. Not only did it seriously reduce labor conflict by reducing the structural leverage of workers, but there was no apparent impact on the appeal of the automobiles they produced. In the period after the Flint strike, but before World War II, the average annual auto sales per one thousand people was thirty-one, while from 1951 to 1955 the industry sold an annual average of forty-five automobiles per one thousand people.[20] In addition, in 1955 GM became the first corporation to make $1 billion in profits.

The huge negative and unintended consequence of this drastic shift in production methodology was the dramatic decline in product innovation. The consequences of declining innovation remained invisible to auto executives, scholars, and the press alike, however, because the entire U.S. industry abandoned flexible production.

Although the impact of the decline in innovation was not noticed or analyzed until after the Japanese imports began arriving in the 1970s, there are good historical data on U.S. auto innovation documenting the decline, the fruit of a ten-year study by William Abernathy and his colleagues at MIT. Table 4.3 shows the mean weighted innovation index in U.S. auto before the Flint strike and after World War II.[21]

From 1910 to 1936, when GM, Ford, and Chrysler all used a form of flexible production, the mean weighted innovation index score was 219.71. In the twenty-six years after World War II, significant innovation in the industry was more than cut in half, with the mean score

Table 4.3 *Average Weighted Innovation Index in the U.S. Auto Industry before the Great Flint Strike and after World War II*

	Mean Weighted Innovation Index Score	Standard Error
Pre–Flint strike	219.71	30.93
Post–World War II	103.67	19.37
Difference	116.04	50.25

Source: Authors' calculations. Adapted from Abernathy, Clark, and Kantrow 1983, 180.

falling to 103.67. In addition, the level of innovation that the industry produced without flexible production was lower than at any other time in the industry's history, with the exception of the troughs of the Great Depression and the immediate aftermath of World War II.

Earlier we discussed figure 4.1, which demonstrates a trend of an increasing number of outside feeder plants during this time period. If we compare the number of feeder plants before and after the war, this becomes even more evident: before the Flint strike, the mean number of outside feeder plants used by Ford was 1.57; post–World War II, that mean number was 7.00, representing a 446 percent increase. Finally, the correlation between the number of outside feeder plants and the weighted innovation index score is –0.47, which indicates a strong negative relationship between decentralization and innovation. That is, as production becomes more dispersed, innovation declines.

Although observers have generally recognized a decline in innovation within the U.S. auto industry, the significant role played by dispersed parallel production (and the associated stockpiles of inventory) in that decline has largely been missed. Without an appreciation of the role of the structure of production in innovation, and of the changes made by the Big Three to that structure in response to labor power, analysts tend to focus on the culture of the Big Three organizations. For instance, Rubenstein characterizes 1960s U.S. auto executives as "making decisions designed to minimize risk and avoid innovation."[22] This view has been explicitly applied to analyses of both GM and Ford. Robert Monks and Nell Minow point to GM's long tenure at the top as the reason for a mind-set that "failed to see the need for change."[23] The *Fortune* reporter Carol Loomis cites a Wall

Street source that suggested replacing the top five executives at GM with individuals from outside the company.[24] Alex Taylor attributes Ford's inability to successfully implement innovations to constant conflict between Ford family members and nonfamily executives, while he characterizes GM's culture as preferring "stability over change, continuity over disorder, and GM's way over anybody else's."[25]

The evidence we have presented thus far in this book demonstrates that there is more to the decline in U.S. auto innovation than the personality characteristics of leadership. To briefly summarize our four major points: (1) Japanese auto currently uses flexible production and is highly innovative; (2) U.S. automakers do not use flexible production and are not highly innovative; (3) U.S. auto used flexible production before World War II and was highly innovative at that time; (4) when U.S. auto abandoned flexible production after World War II, significant innovation in the industry dropped by more than half. This is not to say that insider accounts of the culture of management at the Big Three are false; there is most likely some truth to these descriptions of the different organizational cultures of the Big Three. But these cultures developed, we contend, in interaction with certain structural constraints created by decentralized production.

The relationship between structure and management culture is best understood through the psychological phenomenon of cognitive dissonance.[26] Essentially, humans seek consistency between actions and beliefs, and when that is not possible, dissonance forms, leading individuals to take measures to resolve it. In the case of U.S. auto executives, the recognition that certain innovations were needed in order to compete conflicted with a reality in which they were unable to implement those innovations profitably owing to the structure of decentralized parallel production. Faced with a cognitive dissonance between what they believed was the best course of action and what they were actually able to do profitably, management at the Big Three changed their beliefs to justify their inaction. That is, if GM executives preferred stability to change, it was because change was too costly under a decentralized production system.[27]

The tendency of company culture to be shaped by the actions that are most profitable in a given structural context is best illustrated by the evolution of management culture at General Motors. In 1934, the company's officially designated historian, Arthur Pound, described GM's approach as not so much "Shall we change?" as "How and when shall we change?"[28] As we have documented, from the 1920s to the 1940s, the one constant at GM was change, which was made possible by its use of flexible production. By the 1960s, however, General Motors executives were being characterized as seeking to minimize risk and avoid change, and that characterization has persisted to the present day.

General Motors had ten presidents, two CEOs, and four chairmen of the board before World War II, and all of them saw the value of innovation and change. Since 1960, GM has had ten presidents, eleven CEOs, and twelve chairmen of the board, and all of them have valued stability rather than change. The difference in company culture during the two time periods clearly cannot be assigned to any individual leader. The question, then, is: what changed between early GM and mature postwar GM? The argument we have made extensively in this book is that the major change at General Motors, and in the U.S. auto industry in general, was a switch from flexible production to dispersed parallel production. Early executives, who operated in a system that facilitated innovation, valued change and creativity, while later executives, who operated in a dispersed system that made innovation difficult and costly, tended to value stability. The differences between U.S. and Japanese management when it comes to innovation are rooted in structure, not culture. (Although culture, once shaped by structure, can certainly reinforce the relationship between structure and innovation.)

In his archival research on the decline of GM, Robert Freeland focuses heavily on the culture of upper management.[29] Two of his findings support our argument. First, GM culture after 1920, Freeland found, was characterized by conflict, egotism, and hubris. That is, GM's upper management culture during the time when they were most successful was marked by the same problems that analysts would later blame for their decline (minus the risk-aversion). And second, the conflict at the top of GM was between upper management and an ownership coalition of Dupont and J. P. Morgan representatives, and it was over the ownership group's desire to decentralize the management of the production system. According to Freeland's archival research, management resisted dispersal until

1940, after which they went along with the edict, fully decentralizing control of the production system by 1958. Thus, control over the production system was decentralized at nearly the exact time that, as we show, the production system itself was being dispersed.

PARALLEL PRODUCTION AS A BARRIER TO THE IMPLEMENTATION OF INNOVATION

In chapter 1, we detailed the ways in which flexible production facilitates innovation. The geographic concentration of production created by mother plants and long-term supplier relationships—which is necessary for the functioning of just-in-time delivery—results in a concentration of engineers, designers, planners, managers, and rank-and-file workers. This concentration of principal actors makes ongoing, long-term, face-to-face interaction of people with diverse perspectives a regular feature of the production culture, and this in turn increases the odds of innovation. Flexible production also facilitates the implementation of innovations by making coordination easier between suppliers and assemblers—both because there are fewer assemblers and suppliers to coordinate and because they are right next to each other spatially. In addition, flexible machinery and parts allows for trial-and-error implementation without stopping lines.

If the presence of these factors facilitates innovation, then their absence inhibits innovation. First of all, discovery becomes less likely because dispersal decreases face-to-face interaction. Even when the parallel production system is overcome and a new product or process is invented, a decentralized system throws up barriers to its implementation through the mechanisms of cost and coordination. That is, implementing innovations becomes prohibitively costly, and the cost is derived largely from the difficult logistics of coordinating innovation among as many as two dozen spatially dispersed plants.

One example of how dispersed parallel production hurts implementation is the initial response of the American producers to the demand for smaller cars in the 1960s. The demand for fuel-efficient cars created by the entrance into the domestic market of European cars (led by the VW Beetle) eventually spurred U.S. producers to import compacts from their European subsidiaries. They chose to import small cars rather than make them in the United States because dispersed parallel production made it too expensive. That is, in order to compete with Volkswagen's small cars, the Big Three would have had to implement some new production methodologies and equipment. In a dispersed parallel system, that would have caused the traditional shutting down of production that takes place during model changeovers to take even longer, cutting into profitability. With no flexible machinery, moving from making large autos and trucks to making small cars would have required changing out all the machinery. Buying all new machines and getting rid of the old ones would have been not just time-consuming but also expensive. In addition, mistakes probably would have been made at first in implementing new methodologies, since dispersal made face-to-face contact between rank-and-file and engineers and designers more difficult. We want to emphasize here, however, that the Big Three *were already producing small cars in Europe*. Thus, this example illustrates an inability to *implement* innovation rather than a lack of technical knowledge.

Importing cars from one's own foreign subsidiary is not cost-effective either. Thus, the Big Three abandoned small cars for a time, with the claim, "small car, small profits."[30] When the Japanese proved definitively in the 1970s that big profits could be made by selling high-quality small cars in the U.S. market, the Big Three tried again to make small cars in the United States. The U.S. automakers' small cars were generally of lower quality than the Japanese versions—and still are, we contend, because of differences between the production systems. Two cases in particular, unit body construction and aluminum engines, exemplify the structural inability to implement the changes in production that were necessary to produce low-cost, high-quality small cars. We have already discussed (in chapter 1) the details of these cases within the context of flexible production and innovation, but it is worth coming back to them briefly here to buttress our point that U.S. automakers' failure to compete in small cars was due to the structure of U.S. auto production.

With both unit body construction and aluminum engines, the reasons for slow innovation had little to do with the discovery process and everything to do with structural impediments to implementation. For instance, in both instances the Big Three had discovered the innovation long before foreign competition brought it to our shores.

GM had successfully used unit body construction in the production of the Vauxhall Ten in Britain and the Opel Olympia in Germany as far back as 1937, and aluminum engines were standard on cars produced in Europe by Big Three subsidiaries by the 1950s.[31] Rather, each of these innovations was delayed in the United States owing to costs associated with implementing the innovation in a parallel production system.[32] To recap the evidence from chapter 1, unit body was held up primarily by the cost associated with implementation in the numerous distant plants in the decentralized production system, and converting to aluminum engines would have required eating the costs already invested in cast-iron technology (a symptom of single-purpose, as opposed to flexible, machinery).

DEINDUSTRIALIZATION

The final consequence of abandoning flexible production was the deindustrialization of the U.S. economy, which accelerated in the 1970s and '80s and has decimated former production centers like Detroit and Flint.[33] As the largest and most central industry in America at the time, auto led the way for other manufacturers. For instance, GM employed around 350,000 production workers throughout the United States in the 1960s. By 2016, this number had fallen to 135,000 total production workers, only 55,000 of whom were employed domestically.[34] Once auto assemblers started leaving, the effect was felt on suppliers and then spread to industries such as steel and glass. For example, about 22.7 percent of the U.S. civilian labor force was employed in manufacturing jobs in 1960. That number had declined to only 7.8 percent in January 2018.[35]

Because manufacturing jobs had been transformed by organized labor into engines of middle-class creation, their loss has contributed to soaring economic inequality.[36] It is true that the percentage of workers employed in manufacturing jobs has declined in most developed countries, including Japan. But the Japanese comparison is instructive. In 1970, 27.4 percent of the labor force in Japan worked in manufacturing. This figure declined to 16.7 percent in 2015.[37] So the decline of manufacturing employment in Japan from 1970 to 2015 was 39 percent. In comparison, from 1960 to 2018, U.S. manufacturing employment declined 66 percent, and if we look only from 1970 to

2015 (to make the time span equal to the period examined for Japan), the U.S. decline is still 65 percent. Thus, even though manufacturing has declined in Japan owing to factors such as automation and rising productivity, the decline of U.S. manufacturing has been much larger. This difference probably stems from multiple causes, but one of those causes is the U.S. auto industry's reliance on cheap labor to take the place of innovation.

When foreign imports began arriving in the United States in large numbers in the 1970s, the migration of the auto industry out of Detroit had already been under way for decades as part of the change-over to dispersed parallel production. The movement of auto manufacturing away from Detroit, and even out of the United States, accelerated starting in the 1970s because the foreign imports' use of flexible production placed the U.S. industry at a significant disadvantage in terms of the cost of auto production, and the Big Three began to lose market share. A seemingly simple solution would have been to readopt flexible production in order to compete. Readoption, however, was undermined by a number of structural constraints (which we discuss in more depth in chapter 5). Thus, the easy option was what Beverly Silver has identified as a "spatial fix": inefficient (labor-intensive) manufacturers migrated to low-wage areas in order to offset the cost-of-production advantage through more efficient competition, leaving behind devastated local economies.[38]

This analysis flies in the face of standard market-based explanations for deindustrialization. The market narrative is closely related to the product life cycle perspective on industrial decline. That is, the market narrative takes as an assumption the claim of product life cycle theory that all industries eventually mature to the point that the capacity for innovation reaches its limit, leaving labor costs as the only form of competition. Other than innovations in the production process, the two ways to reduce labor costs are to automate (replacing expensive workers with cheaper machines) or to move production to cheaper areas (replacing expensive workers with cheaper workers). U.S. automakers have used both tactics, although outsourcing was more prevalent early on when new communication technologies made globalizing production an option. As a consequence of U.S. auto's efforts to reduce labor costs, the former production centers have suffered deindustrialization.

Market forces supposedly make deindustrialization a natural and unavoidable outcome, but the example of Detroit's sister city in Japan, Toyota City in Aichi prefecture, demonstrates that there was nothing "natural" about the decline of Detroit.[39] Toyota City is the location of Toyota's first plant, built in 1938. Like Detroit, it was the center of Japanese auto production. Unlike Detroit, however, Toyota City did not face deindustrialization in the 1970s and '80s, even as Toyota globalized its production, including to the United States. In fact, according to the Japanese census, Toyota City's population grew from 105,165 in 1960 to 421,141 in 2010. Since 2010, there has been a slight decline (of 0.3 percent), to 420,000 in 2015. What distinguishes Detroit from Toyota City is that Toyota explicitly built its production system around flexible production and recognized the necessity of worker cooperation to the functioning of that system. Thus, Toyota did not use globalization to replace more expensive domestic workers with cheaper foreign workers. It did not close down factories in Toyota City and replace them with new factories in cheaper areas. Instead, Toyota built new production complexes overseas that included assemblers and suppliers, leaving its existing flexible production centers in Japan untouched. Toyota chose locations for the new overseas complexes partially on the basis of labor cost (that is, it wanted to exploit cheap labor in the new locations). But key to the firm's ability to keep flexible production and not create the misery of massive deindustrialization in Japan was that it did not use globalization to replace costly workers in the old home city, as was done in the United States. In fact, in Toyota City, the local government invested in infrastructure and services to keep Toyota's production running smoothly, while the corporation itself took responsibility for meeting the social consumption needs (welfare, health care, and so on) of residents.

In chapter 5, we discuss how this effort to maintain the trust of their workforces has been key to Japanese automakers' ability to maintain flexible production. For now, we note the stark contrast between the way Toyota treated its eponymous city and the way the Big Three treated their production centers like Detroit and Flint. The differences undermine any market-based explanation and make sense only when analyzed through the lens of production structures. For the Japanese automakers, flexible production depended on geographic concentration and worker trust and cooperation. In their structural context, it would have been suicide to start closing factories and dispersing production around the globe, wherever it was cheapest. The savings in labor costs would have been more than offset by the losses in productivity as a result of losing the ability to innovate. For U.S. automakers, which had already abandoned flexible production, there was no impetus to avoid dispersing production around the globe. As a result, they had also already dispersed production around the United States when they set up their system of parallel production in order to reduce worker structural leverage. By the 1970s, the United States found itself in a context where it would have been suicide *not* to close factories and outsource production to developing countries—precisely because abandoning flexible production had made cheap labor the only way for U.S. automakers to compete against the Japanese.

Viewing U.S. deindustrialization through the lens of production structure and history reveals that its consequences—including the deepening of both class and racial inequality, as Thomas Sugrue details in his seminal study—are ultimately collateral damage in a class war waged by U.S. auto management against its workers.[40] In fact, a close look at all of the consequences associated with abandoning flexible production cements our case for the decline of U.S. auto. The "second industrial divide," as Michael Piore and Charles Sabel term it, is the result of choices motivated by class conflict—in other words, the relentless desire of auto top management to prevent rank-and-file workers from exploiting their strategic position in production to delimit management control of the process of production.[41]

In the next chapter, we move on to answering two remaining questions: Why were the Japanese able to maintain flexible production and not succumb to class conflict? And why didn't the U.S. auto industry reinstitute flexible production in the past several decades?

THE JAPANESE COUNTERFACTUAL: MAINTAINING FLEXIBLE PRODUCTION

5

In chapter 3, we documented the role that flexible production played in the labor movement of the 1930s and '40s and how the decision to abandon it was motivated by class conflict. In addition, we argued that this set of events is endemic to flexible production. That is, flexible production is especially oppressive to workers, and as such, it is a system that motivates workers to take action to alleviate their suffering. Flexible production also confers high structural leverage to workers, making their direct action remarkably successful. The only way flexible production can function for management is to ensure that workers do not exercise their structural leverage—that is, that they do not regularly engage in strikes and other direct actions to extract concessions. In the United States, this requirement led automakers to abandon flexible production, a strategy that, as detailed in chapter 4, brought an end to the wave of wildcat strikes that started during the war. (The chapter also demonstrates that the decline in wildcats was not due to contracts like the Treaty of Detroit.) An unintended consequence of abandoning flexibility, however, was a decline in innovation, which set the United States on the path to deindustrialization.

The Japanese case seems to contradict this narrative that the decline of flexibility was an inevitable consequence of the system itself energizing the relentless resort of workers to disruptive work stoppages. Toyota and other Japanese auto manufacturers have not abandoned their version of flexible production over the seventy years since it was instituted, even as they have globalized their production. This chapter seeks to explain how the Japanese have maintained flexible production rather than succumb to the forces that, we argue, motivated the U.S. industry to shift to dispersed parallel production. Our analysis underscores the importance of the interaction of contingent historical moments, existing structure, and the agency of the top managers and owners of the Big Three U.S. companies in charting and implementing the dismantling of flexible production, which then guaranteed the dramatic decline in the U.S. automobile industry.

The Resilient Effort Bargain at Toyota

Toyota's initial implementation of aspects of flexible production led to worker discontent and collective action, just as it had at Ford in 1913–1914. The early worker actions at Ford, however, were not organized, whereas at Toyota they were associated with a strong, organized, and militant union movement.[1] These unions were the descendants of the prewar Communist-led movement that had been suppressed by the fascists but had nevertheless survived as an underground component of the resistance to the Tojo regime. Because their resistance won them enormous respect among Japanese workers and citizens, these unions were immediately revived once the fascist regime was ousted by the U.S. victory (to the consternation of the commanders of the American occupation). As the intensity of the just-in-time system became more general and more permanent, the automobile unions began resisting the most intense elements of the system—along with the low wages and inadequate job security that characterized the initial experiments—by demanding short-term changes as well as the sort of long-term power-sharing that Berggren poses as a central issue in Toyotism. This led to massive strikes in 1950 and 1953.[2]

In 1950, in response to a recession, Toyota planned to cut 25 percent of its labor force. The union went on strike, but after a long standoff, during which the company almost went bankrupt, the union was defeated and agreed to the "voluntary retirement" of 1,600 workers.[3] In 1953, the union again struck, this time demanding a minimum seniority wage. As in 1950, the conflict was lengthy and very costly to Toyota, but the company responded by cutting the wages of the workers on strike. These losses took their toll on worker solidarity. In 1954, skilled-worker opposition to the leftist union won, and this ushered in the enterprise union system that has since become associated with the Japanese automobile industry.

The compensation and promotional system that would become identified with Toyota arose from the ashes of these confrontations. It was only after the defeat of the union that the lifetime employment, munificent wages, and other features of the system were initiated, and Toyota's management made no effort to conceal the fact that these features of the system were a result of the strike. There was an explicit understanding that, without this compensation system, they could not extract the work intensity they needed; they could not generate the levels of commitment necessary for the system to work; and there would continue to be major disruptions of production whenever the workers experienced a new breaking point.

The high level of structural leverage conferred on workers by the flexible production system allows us to understand why, even though Toyota management defeated each of the major strikes in the 1950s, they nevertheless granted major concessions on key issues that had animated the strike, including wage increases, employment guarantees, and substantial changes in working conditions.[4] These concessions were made because Ono and the management team above him, like Henry Ford in 1914, knew that a flexible production system cannot function if a relative handful of workers can stop production. At Ford, it was the fact that totally unorganized worker action did such damage that made management realize the necessity of placating workers. In Toyota's case, Ono and Eiji Toyoda eventually understood that they had to take positive actions to deincentivize workers from using their structural leverage. Toyota's management made no effort to conceal the fact that the concessions to worker welfare and power contained in the new effort bargain were a result of the strike.[5] Toyoda simply acknowledged, as Howard Kimeldorf has aptly put it, that the workers had "increased the costs of disruption to the point that . . . [there was] little economic advantage in continued resistance."[6]

Also in parallel to the early U.S. auto industry, the concepts of the effort bargain and the moral economy are useful in understanding why the workers "agreed" to the bargain that was struck after the 1950s strikes rather than continue to use their structural leverage. On the one hand, the Japanese workers lost the strikes, and in 1954 their union was destroyed and replaced by company unions, which may have affected their willingness to immediately strike again. On the other hand, one loss cannot explain the lack of direct labor action in the Japanese flexible system for more than half a century. In most industrial settings, broken strikes have not yielded high levels of commitment and willing acquiescence to a demanding system. Instead, workers tend to undertake various forms of on-the-line resistance that slow production while protecting the workers from the ravages of the pace desired by management. The willingness of Toyota workers to forgo such resistance, which would have been particularly devastating in the context of a flexible production system, is only explainable by attributing to them the same calculus that early U.S. workers engaged in when they accepted Ford's Five Dollar Day as enough to stop rampant absenteeism. That is, in the context of a broken strike, postwar Japanese industry, and a history of low wages and grueling work, Toyota workers found the offer of high wages and the willing repair of problematic working conditions— combined with the promise of future considerations—an impressive offer that justified a form of cooperation that would otherwise have been withheld.

Workers in Japan in the early 1950s were unhappy with the work intensity, with their lack of control, and with the various health hazards that they had to endure. They demonstrated this by making these key issues in a ferocious strike. But the strike failed, taking with it the possibility of achieving the radical changes they would have liked to enact. In this context, the immediate wage increases and the long-term promise of personal and financial security were more than adequate. These concessions were sufficient to strike the effort bargain: workers were willing to invest the energy and commitment that management needed to make its nascent system work. In another time, or another place, they might have felt differently.

Once the workers had agreed to this effort bargain, it diffused from Toyota to the rest of the Japanese auto industry (as it had earlier from Ford to the rest of the U.S. automakers) and expanded into a moral economy in which the sacrifice of doing deskilled work at high speeds with unlimited equipment was accepted as a fair trade-off for sharing in the profits of the system. In the next section, we detail the key components of the Japanese effort bargain and its similarity to the early U.S. effort bargain.

HIGH WAGES

As we discussed in chapter 3, Henry Ford doubled the wages of his workers in 1914 in order to deincentivize the turnover and absenteeism that workers engaged in to protest the low wages and dire working conditions associated with the production system he was building. At Toyota, the wage increase given after the 1950s strikes was not quite as large as Ford's increase to $5 a day. However, the manner in which the wage increase was implemented at Toyota—the wage policy tied pay to collective worker output—directly contributed to the formation of a similar moral economy of shared sacrifice and reward.[7] Thus, when all the workers collectively increased productivity and the company benefited, the workers saw an increase in their wages. In the context of flexible production designed to continuously implement increased productivity at each station, this wage system resulted in constantly increasing wages for Japanese autoworkers. It also created a commitment to the success of the company and to the demands of the flexible production system, because the success of the system directly translated into benefit for the workers.

The American effort bargain was also predicated on tying the workers' benefits to the success of the company, but in Japan it was a visible and formal aspect of their daily routine. In Detroit, workers relied on the periodic increases in wages delivered at the discretion of management and therefore had only an informal guarantee that raises would derive from growing productivity. During the 1920s, when regular wage increases were delivered, this informal guarantee was sufficient, but after the crash, the continued increase in productivity was associated with lower remuneration, thus breaking the moral economy and creating deep distrust among the workers. At Toyota, no such betrayal occurred during recessions, and this became a key factor in the continued commitment of workers.

LIFETIME EMPLOYMENT

In Japan, lifetime employment was not so much a policy as a nexus of patterns, including slow evaluation and promotion and nonspecialized career paths, with the most visible consequence being the expectation of workers that they would spend their entire working life with a single company. In fact, there was no actual guarantee of lifetime employment, and many workers were in fact fired, but these terminations generally occurred for cause and usually near the beginning of their tenure. Most workers who fit into the system (and chose over the years not to move for personal reasons) could expect continuous employment until retirement.

The most significant aspect of this policy was what was called in the United States "job security," and it reflected the willingness of Japanese firms to find work for their employees even during slack times when the production of automobiles was slowed or halted. This policy became one of the most visible features of the Japanese transplants in the United States, surrounded as they were by Big Three plant closings, mass layoffs, and repeated furloughs.[8]

This job security was the centerpiece of Japanese workers' willingness to embrace automation, robotization, and other drastic changes in the job structure of the factory. Whereas American workers in the post–World War II industry were constrained by the threat of permanent displacement to protect their *specific* jobs in order to guarantee their future employment, workers in Japanese firms could and did embrace drastic changes that eliminated their section of the plant (or even the plant itself), since they could look forward to the challenge of mastering new skills in a new work site without any decrease in wages. Moreover, it was the very changes that U.S. workers feared and opposed that provided Japanese workers with the opportunity to pursue the nonspecialized career paths and long-term promotional possibilities to be found in a pantheon of differences between Ouchi's flexible production system and the ossified U.S. mass production system.[9] Similar to the U.S. industry in the 1920s, the combination of rapid innovation and expanding markets in Japanese auto required constant reorganization on the shop floor, and the assurance of lifetime employment therefore became an implicit but very reliable guarantee of upward mobility within the firm. For many workers, this was largely a matter of constantly rising wages and continuously improved benefits, but the changing technology and ongoing reformulation of the assembly line nevertheless contributed to a sense of personal progress, particularly since manual labor tended to be replaced by machine operation—and ultimately by computers manned by former line workers.[10] For many others, however, it also involved promotions into positions of supervisorial responsibility, as some workers were chosen to become team leaders and then trained as technical personnel. As previously discussed, Toyota even established its own Technical Institute, where ambitious line workers could get formal training that would smooth their upward path.

FRINGE BENEFITS

In addition to high wages and lifetime employment, a broader system of fringe benefits and perquisites has occasionally been portrayed as the essence of Toyotism. These include low-interest mortgages, health clubs, golf clubs, and a variety of other off-the-job benefits, as well as the informal but usually reliable guarantee that the sons (not daughters) of Toyota workers will have first preference for jobs.[11] These benefits also worked to create commitment, as much of employees' lives outside of work came to depend on the continued success of the company. They also reinforced the moral economy by serving as another way in which workers shared in the benefits of flexible production and making the stress and tedium that they endured an acceptable trade-off.

This aspect of the Japanese effort bargain is also found in the early U.S. system. In chapter 3, we detailed the ways in which the auto leaders in the pre-Depression era became known as "enlightened capitalists" by offering their workers benefits such as on-site hospitals, mortgage programs, subsidized housing, social clubs, and recreation facilities.

The striking similarity of the pre-Depression U.S. and postwar Japanese effort bargains and moral economies provides significant support for our contention that both were compromises rooted in the same logic: a desire to deactivate worker structural leverage and allow the flexible system to function smoothly. Despite these similar origins, however, the U.S. and Japanese systems met different fates. The Japanese effort bargain managed to inhibit any activation of worker structural leverage, allowing for the maintenance of the flexible system of production up to the present day. By contrast, U.S. workers reactivated their leverage and used it to effectively challenge what they considered unfair changes in the production methodology during the next decade. Ultimately what accounts for this difference is the role of trust in the flexible system and the effect on trust of the decisions made by U.S. management during a key contingent moment: the Great Depression.

Differences between the U.S. and Japanese Auto Industries

As we discussed earlier in the chapter, when flexible production was first implemented, the Japanese auto industry had been plagued by labor conflict, suggesting a lack of trust between labor and management. Once Toyota established its effort bargain with the workers, however, trust was established and the moral economy of shared sacrifice and shared reward became accepted throughout the industry. Such a bargain is not unique to Japan, and indeed, as we have documented, it has striking similarities to the early U.S. effort bargain. The difference between the two cases is that U.S. auto broke the trust it had established with workers, while the Japanese did not. To understand this dynamic, it will be useful to take a look at how trust is established.

The effort bargain rests on the idea that in exchange for an agreed-upon level of effort, management will provide benefits. For such a moral economy to take hold, workers must trust that management will hold up their end of the bargain. Workers can rely in part on immediate proof of management commitment: their wages are sufficiently high to make the job an attractive one despite its physical demands; major changes in productivity are accompanied by raises in pay; or corporate expansion produces immediate opportunity for line workers to move upward in the company or receive regular wage increases. Such solid symbols of an effective effort bargain could be consistently found in both Old Detroit after the institution of the Five Dollar Day and Japan after the defeat of the early 1950s strikes and the institution of Toyota's version of the effort bargain, especially during times of industry and corporate expansion.

As we documented in chapter 3, these kinds of immediate evidence of a functioning effort bargain are held in abeyance during times of austerity for the industry or for particular corporations. For example, in the 1919 recession, workers in the auto industry experienced layoffs, declining wages and benefits, and degraded working conditions, and throughout the 1920s workers in specific firms (notably Ford workers during the changeover to the Model A) experienced these kinds of setbacks. For the most part, they endured these hard times, maintained a cooperative attitude toward the demands of a constantly changing work process, and did not activate their latent power to disrupt production if they were not granted immediate relief. This forbearance was a result of workers' trust that the future restoration of corporate profits and prosperity would restore and perhaps enhance their own pre-austerity status.

This trust was also key to the Japanese effort bargain—in 1953 and ever since. The degree to which trust continued to be at the center of the process at Toyota is revealed in observations at Japanese transplants in the 1980s, where the construction process was most visible. Brown and Reich, for example, observed:

> The crucial difference between Van Nuys [a GM-managed plant] and NUMMI [the Toyota-managed plant] is in the union and management strategies used to build trust. . . . Both sides must take risks in trying new forms of labor-management relations and of work organization. In order for workers to be convinced that working both harder and smarter will not cost them their jobs, they must be given job security. In order for the companies to be convinced that providing secure jobs will not result in long-term commitments to an inadequate workforce, they must be assured of improvements in productivity and quality.[12]

This trust is not only difficult to construct but organically fragile, and it can be rapidly undermined if either side shows signs of flagging commitment. This is exactly what happened during the Great Depression. At the start of the Depression, the Big Three automakers kept themselves afloat by repealing much of the effort bargain. Wages were drastically cut, job security was violated by massive layoffs and furloughs, and the extensive fringe benefit programs were discontinued. In 1936, when profits soared and benefits did not return to—let alone surpass—previous levels, it became clear to workers that what had taken place was actually a wholesale violation of the effort bargain and a betrayal of the industry's moral economy.

The central casualty during the 1930s was any faith among rank-and-file workers that auto industry management could be trusted to voluntarily meet any agreements, formal or informal. Moreover, since shop-floor disruption had been the only mechanism that had—so far—yielded effective results in enforcing their demands against management, workers utilized it whenever they had a complaint that needed attention. It is possible to establish trust where none has existed—such was the case with Ford's Five Dollar Day and Toyota's concessions after defeating the 1953 strike—but there is a difference between an initial lack of preexisting trust and the distrust produced when established trust is broken. A relationship in which trust has been violated can be repaired, but it takes more effort than was necessary to initially establish trust.

In the relationship between autoworkers and management, the process of establishing trust is represented by the effort bargain to which both eventually agreed. After U.S. automakers violated the trust of their workers, it took more than a return to the old effort bargain to repair that trust—as Chrysler management discovered when they temporarily ended the wildcat strikes that threatened the firm's viability by accepting a labor peace. Unlike the original effort bargain, which offered benefits in exchange for oppressive conditions, the labor peace gave union stewards control over conditions by accepting virtual veto power over changes in production methodology. Collectively, however, U.S. automakers rejected the labor peace and instead changed the structure of auto production to remove worker leverage. Chrysler followed suit, abandoning it shortly thereafter.

Like their U.S. counterparts, Toyota and other Japanese automakers also had to establish trust with their workers through an initial effort bargain, but Japanese management never violated the established trust significantly enough to break faith with the workers. To be clear, Japanese auto management were far from ideal partners to their workers. Just like any capitalist, they sought to exploit their workers as much as they could. Yet there was never a moment in Japan when trust was completely broken, as it was during the Great Depression in the United States. This helps to explain the different trajectories of flexible production in the two industries.

JAPANESE COMMITMENT TO FLEXIBLE PRODUCTION

Would the Japanese have made the decision to dismantle flexible production had they faced the same situation as the U.S. automakers after the war—namely, a relationship with their workers in which

trust had been shattered? It is impossible to know for sure. The answer depends on fully understanding the interaction of management
agency with existing structures, and human agency is often unpre-
dictable. Human agency, however, is also informed by actors' bounded
rationality—the idea that the rationale they bring to a decision is
limited by the information available to them.[13] We leverage that in
the next section to develop a set of educated guesses about the plausible rationale informing the U.S. decision to abandon flexible production, and we compare it to the information on which we know the
Japanese are operating.

Why the Big Three Abandoned Flexible Production

It is clear that during the era of flexible production, the Big Three
knew that the way they produced cars was very profitable.[14] It is not
clear that they knew why. It is clear from the historical record that
U.S. automakers were aware of the usefulness or profitability of the
various components of flexibility, including mother plants, geographic clustering, long-term relationships with suppliers, multipurpose machinery, just-in-time delivery, and the superior productivity
of committed workers. But an appreciation of the elements of flexibility might not have translated into an understanding of the larger
system of which they were a part. The U.S. flexible production system
evolved organically, through trial and error, without self-conscious
planning by leadership with authority to enforce an overarching vision. Hence, it is more than plausible that the leadership of the Big
Three after World War II may not have appreciated that the system
as a whole was more productive than the sum of its parts, and that it
was foundational for the breathtaking pace of innovation that continued at least through the early 1930s.

WERE U.S. AUTO EXECUTIVES UNAWARE
THAT THEY WERE SACRIFICING INNOVATION FOR
CONTROL OF THE WORKERS?

Many of the early developments in the industry suggest that the
management and ownership of the major companies were unaware
of the overarching virtues of flexible production. The creation of Ford's

ill-fated branch assembly plant system, which symbolized the glorious rise of the Model T and then fell into disarray with its decline, is powerful evidence that Henry Ford, the pioneer builder of what became the Detroit flexible production system, did not appreciate the extent to which future innovation depended on—among other elements of flexibility—continued concentration of production. To Ford, there was a once-and-for-all aspect to the changes that took place at the central factory. Once the assembly line system was applied to the production of a certain commodity, the major work was finished. The later tweaks to the now-established production system could take place in the hinterlands without the surrounding support system of the central facilities. This false belief was fully articulated by Ford when he wrote in 1927, at the pinnacle of flexible production in Detroit:

> A big factory sometimes pays. Our Fordson [River Rouge] plant pays because it brings raw materials together economically. Our finished product . . . goes out with a minimum transportation charge. But if Fordson did not deal in heavy, bulky raw materials it would not pay. It pays because it combines quick transportation both inward and outward.[15]

In valorizing the "minimum transportation charge" as the primary virtue of the fully integrated River Rouge plant, Ford betrays little understanding that the innovative dynamics at Ford depended on other factors within the immense complex: the concentration, sole sourcing, "hand-to-mouth" inventories, and high level of nondisruptive worker commitment.

An added irony of Ford's comment is that it was written just before River Rouge became the venue for one of the most remarkable demonstrations of the innovative power of the flexible system in Detroit: the miraculously rapid eighteen-month development of the Model A, which saved the Ford company from bankruptcy and reconsolidated its continued role as a central source of product and process innovation in the Detroit production system.[16]

The opaque view of production explicitly articulated by Henry Ford—but also less directly expressed by a surprising range of Detroit executives—contrasts sharply with the highly conscious approach of Eiji Toyoda, who intentionally modeled the Toyota system after

Ford's flexible production and was fully cognizant of its virtues.[17] Other Japanese automakers copied Toyota, making the structure of flexible production an explicit part of the strategy of Japanese auto management. Consequently, they created mono-regional production complexes, exemplified by Toyota City outside Osaka, Mazda's huge presence in Hiroshima, and Nissan's devotion to Tokyo. When they built factories in the United States, they expressed a similar commitment by insisting that their suppliers locate close to their new plants.[18]

If it is the case that the Big Three management did not really know what they were losing when they dismantled flexible production in order to strip labor of its power, then maybe the Japanese (fully aware of the virtues of the system) would have been willing to compromise, even in the face of a fully organized labor movement that would demand a degree of worker control over the production process. We may yet see an empirical test of this hypothesis.

DID U.S. AUTO EXECUTIVES ABANDON FLEXIBILITY BECAUSE THEY BELIEVED THAT IT HAD OUTLIVED ITS USEFULNESS?

It is also conceivable that the Big Three management—who rapidly applied their labor-debilitating solution as soon as World War II ended—understood that they were sacrificing their innovative capacity in hopes of establishing a system that could generate equal or greater profits by slowing (and eventually reversing) the increase in wages (mainly through industrial migration) and collectively abandoning competition through product improvement. They may have thought—along with many economic "experts"—that their (at least domestic) monopoly was permanent and that no "better product at lower price" could invade their market.[19] One might argue that the miscalculation made by U.S. management was in assuming that no foreign competition using flexible production would invade their domestic market—even though they were correct in this assumption for two decades of record profits.

If this were true, Toyota and other Japanese automakers would not be expected to copy the Americans' decision, because their own history would have precluded them from making the same mistake.

That is, since the Japanese *were* the foreign competition that bested a rival using flexible production, they were intimately acquainted with the long-term consequences of choosing ossified mass production. Given their positive experience with global expansion and their subsequent reliance on the U.S. and European markets, the idea that they could afford to stop innovating and rely on a monopoly of domestic markets would not have been plausible.

WHAT THE JAPANESE EXPERIENCE TEACHES US
ABOUT ABANDONING FLEXIBILITY

Both of the scenarios presented here—that U.S. auto executives believed that flexible production was no longer useful and that they did not realize they were sacrificing innovation for control of workers—are plausible, and both are supported by some anecdotal historical evidence. It is even possible that both scenarios were partially true. That is, the U.S. automakers could have realized that restructuring the industry would require a trade-off with the ability to rapidly innovate, but without fully grasping the extent to which this would be true. Lacking a full appreciation for what they were giving up, the trade-off might have seemed reasonable given the lack of competition on the horizon. Whatever the case may be, it is not possible to know for sure what the Japanese would do given a similar situation. Our hunch is that they would react differently, because the information informing their rationality is different. Yet the fact that the Japanese are fully aware of the virtues of the system and the pitfalls of abandoning it may also be the reason they have not faced a similar situation. That is, their commitment to the effort bargain and their ability to keep their workers' trust is probably due to the fact that they realize the importance of worker commitment to the system and their ability to innovate.

The key takeaway, then, is that Japanese and American automakers faced very different conditions: the Japanese were more explicitly aware of the value of flexible production, they were more familiar with the threat of competing against flexible production using a different system, and they never violated their industry's moral economy and lost the trust of their workers. Given these differences from

U.S. auto, the different trajectory of the Japanese in maintaining flexible production is not the huge mystery it seems at first glance.

Path Dependency and the Inability to Reinstitute Flexible Production

Having established that some combination of a lack of foresight and a determination to reduce and deactivate the workers' structural leverage led U.S. auto manufacturers to abandon flexible production, we are left with one more puzzle to solve: why couldn't hindsight animate a reverse transformation?[20] It makes some sense that U.S. auto would lose domestic share to Japanese automakers in the 1970s and early '80s. Given that the Big Three had just enjoyed more than twenty years of record profits when the Japanese first arrived, U.S. management probably thought their production system worked fine. Once they started losing market share to small Japanese cars, the U.S. automakers first tried to make small cars to compete. When that failed, they convinced themselves that the demand for small cars was due to the oil crisis of the mid-1970s. Their assumption that once the energy crisis was averted consumers would be back to demanding large gas guzzlers slowed their diagnosis of the underlying structural problem.

Once decision-makers figured out that the Japanese advantage did indeed lie in a more efficient system of production, it is reasonable to think that it would have taken some time to readopt the principles of flexible production. But we are now almost two decades into the twenty-first century, nearly fifty years past the arrival of the first Japanese imports. Why have U.S. automakers *still* not reorganized their production and readopted flexible principles?[21]

U.S. automakers did attempt to reintegrate flexible principles into their production system as early as the 1980s, but consistently failed. The analytic concept of path dependence is useful for understanding these failures: the cumulative weight of auto management decisions at contingent moments in their history yielded a tangle of institutional practices, fixed costs, and human capital that created monetary and engineering barriers to reconversion. The rest of this chapter is dedicated to detailing the role of structural constraints in undermining all efforts by U.S. automakers to reimplement flexibility.

SUNK COSTS

As we discussed in chapter 4, the Big Three reduced the structural leverage of autoworkers by creating redundancy in their production system. They accomplished this in four ways. First, they eliminated the geographic concentration of production by building new plants and contracting with new suppliers strategically dispersed away from Detroit and each other so as to make organizing strikes more difficult. Second, they eliminated the use of mother plants, using the new dispersed facilities to create a parallel production system in which each part was produced in multiple plants that focused narrowly on a few models, rather than in single multipurpose plants servicing all models. This ensured that a shutdown at any single plant would damage only a few models, rather than all or most of production. In addition, automakers usually had at least two plants producing the same parts, so that if one was shut down, the other could increase production to make up for it. Third, they began to carry huge stockpiles of inventory. This tactic also reduced the damage associated with an interruption of production at any single point in the production system. These three changes together made just-in-time delivery of parts untenable, which removed all necessity of using flexible machinery. Thus, the fourth way in which automakers created redundancy in a parallel production system was in having the new plants use specialized machinery.

These four aspects of postwar U.S. auto production—dispersed plants, parallel production, large stockpiles, and single-purpose machinery—represented tremendous sunk capital for the Big Three. It took major investments to build new plants, stock them with new single-purpose machinery, and purchase extra inventory from suppliers. In the context of the booming postwar economy, when the Big Three were turning record profits, this investment was tenable. But the prospect of leaving already paid-for productive plants, machinery, and parts vacant and unused was a barrier to implementing flexible production. The necessity of then investing more capital in buying flexible machinery and new parts and reconcentrating assemblers

and suppliers constituted an even bigger barrier, especially while losing domestic market share in the post-1970s environment.

The costs of shifting from dispersed parallel production to flexible
production were made prohibitive by the availability of the much
cheaper option of cutting labor costs. This option is always a short-
term fix, and it results in the long-term consequence of continually
damaging trust. The broken trust between management and workers
constitutes another barrier to flexible production.

HALF-MEASURES AND BROKEN TRUST

The other major impediment to readoption of flexible production
has been the broken trust between U.S. autoworkers and management. We have detailed how management violated the moral economy of the industry during the Great Depression (and kept violating
it at every turn, from trying to take advantage of the no-strike pledge
during war production to failing to honor aspects of the Treaty of
Detroit on the shop floor). In the process, management shattered the
trust upon which effort bargains depend to function. As a consequence, we have argued, workers were forced to use the tools at their
disposal—activation of structural leverage—to enforce effort bargains. That is, rather than trust in management to uphold their end
of any bargain over the workers' share of the surplus, the workers
continually used the leverage stemming from disruptive work stoppages to assure themselves of a share in the benefits of the system.
This state of affairs continued—management breaking their end of
the bargain and workers resorting to wildcat strikes to enforce it—
until all of the Big Three had fully abandoned flexible production in
the early 1960s.

What is important here is that wildcat strikes did not stop because
management demonstrated their trustworthiness and won workers
back over. The strikes stopped because the shift to dispersed parallel
production reduced their effectiveness as a weapon; the union still
occasionally engaged in strikes, but they usually had to be unionwide
in order to be effective. Thus, another reason flexible production
could not be reimplemented was that trust had not been reestab-
lished between workers and management.

Had U.S. automakers shifted fully back to flexible production and committed to repairing the broken trust with their workers by offering the sort of shared governance that brought the brief labor peace at Chrysler in 1949, or even simply abided fully by the generous effort bargains they made with union leadership, there is no reason to doubt that the workers would have recommitted to the system, as they had done in the early U.S. industry and in Japan. Unfortunately, the Big Three could never seem to resist the option of increasing profits by squeezing labor through industrial migration and unremunerated speedups. As a consequence, U.S. automakers' attempts to reinstitute flexibility were always half-measures. In always seeking to maximally exploit labor, management undercut their own efforts at flexibility in two ways: (1) by undermining geographic concentration, since industrial migration leads to dispersal of production, and (2) by undermining the trust needed to make flexibility work by constantly demonstrating to the workers that management was not to be trusted and that the use of structural leverage was necessary to enforce any effort bargain.

Thus, trust and half-measures have a dialectical relationship: half-measures make rebuilding trust impossible, and lack of trust makes it impossible to go from a half-measure to a full measure. The next section details examples of this relationship.

CONFLICTING DESIRES AND HALF-MEASURES

The half-measure of partially reconcentrating and then further dispersing production through the quest for cheap labor that we document and discuss in this section is the result of the conflicting desires to reap the innovative benefits of flexible production while also keeping (both labor and supplier) costs low. These conflicting desires of U.S. automakers led to contradictory impulses, because the broken trust and sunk costs associated with the prior dismantling of the U.S. version of flexible production created a situation where geographic concentration increased both innovation and costs (especially labor costs as a result of the activation of structural leverage). Thus, when one desire is to be high (innovation) and the other is to be low (costs and the structural leverage of labor), neither concentration nor dispersion will be totally satisfactory.

The inherent contradiction in such a production system created what we have observed to be an almost schizophrenic style of management among the Big Three. On the one hand, the success of Toyotism—and their own constantly declining market share—provided U.S. automakers with a painful reminder of the virtues of flexible production. This spurred numerous attempts to reintroduce key aspects of the system of flexible production, most often flexible machinery, the clustering of parts suppliers around final assembly, and just-in-time delivery. On the other hand, each of these measures increased the shop-floor leverage of the workers, since even a weakened union—as well as rank-and-file workers without the support of their union—could shut down large chunks of production when these elements of flexibility were reintroduced.[22] In fact, the twenty-first-century UAW, although weaker than in its heyday, is much larger and more strategically located than it was in 1936, when it began the Flint sit-down strike that changed the industry. The structural leverage that concentrated production provides to workers is exactly what the Big Three had been seeking to minimize since the end of World War II, and the fear of it, along with the costs already sunk into factories and parts, inevitably led to actions that undermined every attempt at reintroducing elements of flexible production.

The first major attempt to reinstitute just-in-time production came in the early 1980s, when GM began to cluster parts manufacturers and final assembly plants (followed by a clustering of component suppliers) in Auto Alley—the corridor formed by I-65 and I-75 that runs from the southern Michigan region to Mobile, Alabama.[23] In fact, General Motors invested close to $60 billion in new products and manufacturing systems in the 1980s.[24] These efforts in Auto Alley were followed by the establishment of the New United Motor Manufacturing Inc. (NUMMI), an assembly plant jointly run with Toyota in Fremont, California. This experiment afforded GM "the opportunity to observe firsthand Japanese production methods and management practices."[25] It was followed by a series of ambitious new product development projects, none of which matched the Japanese in quality until the Saturn reached the market in 1991. At the same time, GM undertook wholesale closings of outmoded mass production plants and remodeled other facilities to accommodate just-in-time inventories and other features of lean production. These new and remodeled factories often initiated labor practices copied from the Japanese, including work teams and other innovations designed to increase morale and commitment on the plant floor.[26] Here again, only the new Saturn plant in Spring Hill, Tennessee, successfully mimicked the Japanese system.

In many cases, these positive changes coincided with the movement of production to developing countries like Mexico, where labor is much cheaper because of a lack of both labor regulations and strong unions.[27] In fact, building new factories in the *maquiladoras* in Mexico (zones where regulations and tariffs do not apply) was a major strategy designed to cut labor costs in the 1980s and early '90s.[28] These industrial migrations undermined efforts to reconcentrate production. They also led to massive layoffs (rather than lifetime employment), and they therefore undermined the reestablishment of trust and generated hostility and suspicion rather than cooperative commitment among rank-and-file workers.

In 1992 there was an attempt, explicitly modeled after the Japanese system, to establish cooperative relationships with outside suppliers. This time, it was not lack of trust between workers and management that sabotaged a new initiative, but lack of trust between suppliers and assemblers. Senior Vice President Jose Ignacio Lopez moved to the United States to implement the program that he had successfully put into practice in GM's European division.[29] GM offered to supply engineering assistance "free of charge to help suppliers find ways to reduce costs," and to reward those who did with long-term contracts, while forgoing price reductions until 1994. But the history of exploitation by GM, along with the fact that Lopez put potential suppliers through endless rounds of bidding in an effort to lower their prices, led to a lack of trust among suppliers. Ultimately, in 1993, Lopez gave up and left GM to administer Volkswagen's ambitious European expansion program. The key half-measure that had undermined the project was GM management's requirement that their suppliers trust them, without giving any indication that they themselves could be trusted or that they were willing to place the same trust in the supplier. That is, GM management could have offered sole sourcing contracts, which would have demonstrated trust on their end and invited reciprocation. Yet they chose not to, and the lack of trust undermined their attempt at reimplementing a key aspect of flexibility.

GM's creation of Saturn represents still another attempt at flexibility undermined by half-measures and a lack of trust. Saturn was CEO Roger Smith's attempt to address the issues of dispersed production at GM by starting a new, separate company that would combine all production processes in its own assembly plant in Spring Hill, Tennessee.[30] In addition, Saturn marked an attempt to forge a new effort bargain with the UAW and to restore the moral economy of shared sacrifices and shared rewards. Rather than use the standard UAW-GM contract at Saturn, management and workers collaborated to loosen workplace rules, give labor more autonomy over the work process, and link compensation to company profits.[31] This worked for a time at Saturn, but the attempt to restore the moral economy was undermined by the fact that the rest of GM did not follow suit in either production structure or labor relations. Not only was GM's half-measure a barrier to the flexibility in the rest of the company, but it hurt Saturn too, as a strike at a different plant—a supplier in Lordstown, Ohio—created a significant parts shortage and threatened to shut down Saturn production.[32] Rather than have the rest of the company follow suit and reconstruct their labor contracts and operations to be like Saturn's, GM slowly abandoned the experiment at Saturn. In fact, by 2004, GM had integrated Saturn's operations into its dispersed system of production and moved back to its standard labor contract at Saturn plants.[33] Yet the Saturn example demonstrates the potential had full measures been taken. Flexibility was working at Saturn until GM's choice to try to simultaneously squeeze labor undermined it.

By the late 1990s, GM had successfully reduced stockpiles and begun to implement a just-in-time delivery system. The move to flexible production was halted, however, after a 1998 strike at two key stamping plants in Flint shut down nearly all of its North American assembly plants and cost the company $2.8 billion.[34] Once again, the lack of trust between workers and management led to the immediate use of structural leverage to enforce the sharing of benefits. The company had been hammering the workers in Flint for two decades, demanding givebacks and cutting jobs. Now management added just-in-time without giving back even a fraction of what they had extracted. Had trust existed between workers and management, perhaps the workers would have waited for just-in-time to increase company profits, trusting that they would get a share of the reward. But trust was long gone, so as soon as workers grasped that they had disruptive power, they utilized it. This action pushed management to hedge against workers' structural leverage by maintaining the parallel production system they had built, rather than tearing it down and rebuilding a geographically concentrated flexible production system.

Aside from a lack of trust undermining a return to flexible production, sunk costs also served as a major impediment. For example, in launching the new-generation J-body Chevrolet Cavalier and Pontiac Sunfire in the mid-1990s, GM tried to model production after the GM-Toyota joint project NUMMI in Fremont, California.[35] The cornerstone of the project was GM's massive stamping and assembly plant in Lordstown, Ohio. The company invested nearly $1 billion to upgrade the Lordstown facility—along with plants in Lansing, Michigan, and Ramos Arizpe, Mexico—into a flexible production center that could produce everything needed for the Cavalier and Sunfire.[36] Immediately upon launch, the project faced problems with coordination and ended up months behind schedule, costing the company $2 billion in lost sales and a point in market share.[37] The root of the failure was an incomplete commitment to the geographic concentration of assemblers and suppliers. Unlike Ford's River Rouge plant up until the 1950s, or even the GM-Toyota NUMMI plant on which it was modeled, the Lordstown plant was not part of a single region of concentrated production. Instead, GM invested in three already-existing plants dispersed across North America in Ohio, Michigan, and Mexico. Rather than use suppliers clustered around the plants, GM had all three use the same suppliers, and instead of each plant being designed to build the entire automobile, the Lordstown plant provided stampings to the Ramos site. This dispersion made it impossible to truly take advantage of the benefits of flexible production, a reality recognized by future CEO Richard Wagoner, then the president of GM's North American operations: "The big issue is we bit off a big chunk. There were three orders of magnitude—three buckets. If it had been the same plant, same processes and same productivity it would have been easy. But if you vary all of those things it becomes more complex."[38]

Given Wagoner's insight, we are left wondering why GM did not shut down Lordstown and Lansing and build new plants next to the Ramos plant, thus creating the geographic concentration needed for flexible production to work. If management knew how important concentration was to their attempts at instituting flexibility, then the sunk cost fallacy should not be enough to explain this.

This is where the broken trust with workers reinforces the role of sunk costs. Under the old moral economy, during the height of U.S. flexible production, lifetime employment was informally guaranteed. It consisted of the company rehiring laid-off workers when production expanded and helping workers from closed factories find new jobs at other factories. This process was informal because workers trusted management to hold up their end of the bargain. After trust was broken in the Great Depression, workers had to use their power to enforce benefits such as lifetime employment. In 1984, the UAW used its power (which was weakening, but still strong) to formalize something approaching lifetime employment by negotiating the Jobs Bank Program, which gave laid-off workers a choice: take a one-time lump sum buyout, or keep getting paid for up to six years, during which time "they may receive training, fill in temporarily for more senior plant workers who are undergoing training, perform nontraditional jobs in the plant or in the local community, or be placed in a job opening at their home plant or another GM location."[39]

The idea behind the Jobs Bank was to provide job stability to the union's members, not just by securing income for them for at least six years after a layoff but also by deincentivizing the plant closings associated with outsourcing. It is impossible to say whether, without the Jobs Bank, outsourcing among the Big Three would have been even more common. It is clear, however, that the Jobs Bank did not stop the Big Three from closing many U.S. plants and replacing expensive workers with cheap workers in new locations. What the Jobs Bank did succeed in stopping was plant closings and layoffs associated with efforts at reconcentrating production. To understand why the prospect of paying laid-off workers stopped one type of plant closing and not the other, it is important to examine the costs and benefits of each type of closing and how those interacted with the Jobs Bank.

When closing a plant as part of a strategy to move production to areas with cheaper labor, the benefits are immediate. That is, the new factory using cheap labor immediately replaces the old factory's revenue as it produces the same volume as the old factory. The difference is that because labor costs are much less, profits are higher. Paying laid-off workers from the old factory for a few years (especially considering many took the onetime buyout) cuts into those new profits but does not erase them.[40] Thus, the Jobs Bank was not ideal for the outsourcing strategy, but it did not really discourage it.

When, on the other hand, the plant closing is part of a strategy to reinstitute flexible production, the Jobs Bank is an impediment because the benefits of flexibility are not immediate. Flexible production's primary benefit from the perspective of ownership is its facilitation of high rates of innovation, which improves production efficiency and product quality. Recall our discussion of innovation in chapter 1: it is a trial-and-error process that takes time to implement and perfect. During the time that innovations are being implemented, the process often costs the company profits. Once the innovation is in place, the lost profits are more than made back, but the prospect of taking short-term losses is part of the process. In addition, the new plants concentrated around production centers do not have the advantage of using cheaper labor. In fact, much of the effort is likely to center first on old production centers, where labor is more expensive. Thus, closing plants in order to reinstall flexible production combines a best-case scenario of the old profit level being cut into by payments to laid-off workers (meaning less profits overall in the short term) and a worst-case scenario of making less profits at the new factory and then further reducing them with the Jobs Bank. Hence, the Jobs Bank played a role in discouraging a move back to flexible production.

In short, under the old moral economy, when workers trusted management to uphold their end of the effort bargain, informal job security actually facilitated innovation, while job security enforced by a UAW that no longer trusted management to uphold any bargain impeded innovation.

CONCLUSION 6

In conclusion, we return to the question we posed at the beginning: how did the largest, most prosperous industry in the richest, most powerful country in human history crash and burn? In this book, we have made the case for an interpretation of the decline of U.S. auto that is rooted in class analysis, views history as path-dependent, and understands human behavior to be embedded in—and influenced by—social and economic structures. That is, U.S. auto was set on the path to decline when the captains of the industry reacted to the Great Depression by behaving as capitalists typically behave: trying to minimize the impact of economic downturns on their bottom line by shifting as much of the immiseration to the workers as they could manage. And when the industry began to revive, they sought—as capitalists typically do—to maximize their share of the rewards of the revival, while maintaining or even intensifying the immiseration of their workers. For the six years of the Depression, this strategy worked well for top management and their stockholders and lenders. Workers remained unorganized and powerless as management continued profiting off of their suffering and sacrifice, until profits exceeded pre-Depression levels in 1936.

But this successful application of capitalist strategy in the Detroit-centered auto industry took place in an industrial structure that gave workers the tools and opportunity for resistance. These policies broke with the effort bargain that was placating workers and violated the previous moral economy that had been established to justify the oppressiveness of flexible production. This set in motion a series of events after World War II, including the dismantling of the U.S. version of flexible production, that have driven U.S. auto down the path to losing half its domestic market (even as it took nearly forty years for U.S. automakers to begin losing market share).

There is much to learn from the rise and fall of U.S. auto, but we want to focus on one key lesson from our analysis: the importance of structure in both guiding human agency and shaping its consequences. First we discuss the interaction of structure and agency in our analysis. Then we apply our insights to a discussion of the prospects for the future of the U.S. auto industry (by which we mean U.S. automakers employing U.S. workers).

The Interaction of Structure and Agency

Although the decision to break the effort bargain and violate the industry moral economy was a key contingent moment in U.S. auto history, its consequences were the result of production structure. First, the moral economy of shared sacrifice and reward was made necessary by the structure of flexible production. To reprise the argument we have laid out in detail in this book:

- Flexible production's just-in-time methods, use of flexible machinery, and incredible rates of innovation require extraordinary commitment from workers to a line whose speed is constantly increasing. The physical and mental toll associated with flexible production, then, leads to acts of individual (and eventually collective) resistance.

- At the same time, the concentration of flexible production in mother plants, along with just-in-time delivery, confers on workers high levels of structural leverage. This leverage can be used in highly disruptive (and thus successful) acts of resistance, even with low levels of collective participation.

- For flexible production to function, then, management must placate workers so that they refrain from constantly disrupting production. This leads to an effort bargain that gives relatively generous benefits in exchange for workers accepting the physical and mental toll of flexible production.

- Given that workers still have high levels of structural leverage at their fingertips, even after accepting the effort bargain, it is plausible that they will use it to constantly sweeten the benefits they receive and eventually force a reduction in the speed of the line or the commitment expected from them. Thus, it is also necessary to establish a moral framework to justify the effort bargain as inherently fair. Specifically, the moral economy is based on two beliefs: that the oppressiveness of flexible production is a necessary sacrifice, shared by management, and that the few benefits workers receive (few in relation to the profits of management) are shared rewards.

Without the specific structure of flexible production, it is unlikely that the auto industry would operate on a moral economy of shared sacrifice and shared reward. (The current U.S. industry does not.) Without that specific moral economy, the decision by the Big Three during the Depression to increase their profits by lowering the benefits of workers would have been considered business as usual under capitalism, rather than a violation of trust that would result in permanent activation of worker structural leverage. Profit through cutting labor costs was the strategy of choice for much of corporate America following the 2008 economic crash, yet workers did not engage in disruptions of business.

The shattered trust between autoworkers and management and the subsequent activation of worker leverage were consequences of the actions of management *because* of the structure of flexible production. Given that the Big Three's postwar decision to abandon flexible production was based in large part on the inability of a new effort bargain to placate workers without ceding some discretion over production methodology to workers, structure can be given indirect credit for the shift to a parallel production system. In this case, however, the structure of flexible production also played a direct role in management's calculus. That is, the real problem was not that attempts to disrupt production were constantly being made; it was that the attempts were so successful. If not for the damage done by the 400 percent turnover at Ford in 1914 and the Toyota strike in 1953, neither company would have tried to placate workers with an effort bargain. Had the Flint strike—and later the wartime wildcats—not crippled production, the Big Three would never have abandoned flexible production. The reason worker direct action was so successful was the high level of structural leverage created by flexible production.

Once the Big Three had decided to reduce labor power by restructuring auto production, it was the structure of flexibility that dictated what the new production system had to be. To elaborate, since the leverage of labor flowed from the lack of buffers created by just-in-time delivery and the concentration of production, the way to reduce worker power was to disperse the production of each part and model into multiple plants and begin carrying large stockpiles of inventory. Thus, although U.S. auto executives exercised their agency in deciding where and how to invest capital in the decades following World War II, the resulting system of parallel production featuring rigid, specialized equipment and large stockpiles of parts was shaped by the structure of flexible production, given their aims. Put differently, had the Japanese automakers decided that they needed to reduce worker power by restructuring production, it is very likely that they would have developed a similar dispersed production system.

The structure of the new dispersed production system, which was shaped both directly and indirectly by the structure of the previous flexible production system, had its own consequences. For instance, as we detailed in chapters 1 and 4, flexible production facilitated innovation, and dispersed parallel production slowed the implementation of innovations. Thus, the structure of production is a determining factor in the rate of innovation. These consequences shaped the actions of future executives.

In the 1970s, as a result of the different rates of innovation produced by parallel and flexible production, U.S. automakers (using dispersed parallel production) faced a competitive disadvantage when the Japanese (using flexible production) entered the American market. This competitive disadvantage motivated a new round of restructuring, but the structure of dispersed parallel production made returning to flexible production prohibitively costly. Instead, the Big Three settled on moving production to less developed countries with easy-to-exploit labor. (Again, Japan also built production centers in less developed countries with cheap labor, but what is key is that those new centers did not replace old production complexes in Japan.) Once assemblers migrated, many suppliers had to either close down or seek out their own cheap labor through industrial migration. The long-term result of this strategy has been the deindustrialization of the American economy. Deindustrialization, then, is the result of capitalist agency interacting with the structure of production.

Finally, closing U.S. plants and outsourcing jobs ensured that the trust between workers and management that was broken during the Great Depression remained broken. This absence of trust—itself the result of the interaction of executive agency and production structure—interacted with the structure of dispersed parallel production (further dispersed globally by industrial migration) to make a return to flexible production all but impossible. Thus, our analysis demonstrates that the decline of the U.S. auto industry was not primarily the result of impersonal natural forces, like markets, or of highly individualistic forces, as suggested by analysts who blame specific CEOs. Rather, it resulted from an interaction between the agency of capitalist elites and the structure of auto production. The decision by capitalists at each contingent moment in U.S. auto history to engage in class warfare is key to understanding the fall of the Big Three. It is impossible to fully grasp how and why history unfolded as it did in the industry, however, without taking into account its production structure.

The Likely Future of U.S. Auto

In 2008, the U.S. auto industry crashed, and only a massive bailout of GM and Chrysler by the Obama administration prevented bankruptcy filings.[1] Only seven years later, in 2015, more automobiles were sold in the United States than in any year in history. The next year the industry broke its previous record.[2] In fact, in 2016, GM earned $9.4 billion in profits, with autoworkers receiving their largest amount of profit-sharing in the history of the UAW.[3]

Also in 2016, Donald Trump successfully ran for president on a platform of preserving, expanding, and repatriating manufacturing jobs—particularly in auto—through improved trade deals, corporate tax cuts, and deregulation. One might view the likely future of the U.S. auto industry—and especially the domestically owned portion of that industry—as bright, with the success of the Obama-era bail-out becoming the foundation for new initiatives of the Trump administration.

This optimism would have been misplaced, and our analysis of the dynamics of the auto industry point to why both the apparently successful Obama rescue and Trump's mostly fulfilled policy initiative were not only misdirected but ultimately contributed to the decline of domestically owned auto companies. Moreover, when the record since 2008 is scrutinized, it reveals the continued decline of domestic market share, an unblemished record of plant closings, and the continued migration of auto manufacturing and assembly to countries with dramatically lower wages. Our analysis predicts further decline in both the near and distant future.

If the insights of this book are applied to the problem of saving the U.S. auto industry, it is clear that the solution is a return to flexible production. To accomplish a return to flexibility, suppliers and assemblers must first be spatially concentrated into geographic production centers. This could be done in two ways: (1) close down plants dispersed across the globe and open new ones in areas where parts suppliers and component manufacturing are concentrated; and/or (2) incentivize suppliers (through long-term sole supplier contracts) to move and cluster around existing assemblers around the globe. Once production is reconcentrated, a return to flexible production becomes possible, including its hallmark features, just-in-time inventories and sole sourcing, which would enable the cost-reducing innovations that would make the domestic industry competitive. As we detailed in chapter 5, however, the dual factors of sunk costs and broken trust with labor have erected insurmountable barriers to the Big Three taking the steps needed to reconcentrate production and therefore reinstitute flexible production. A reconstitution of flexible production would subsequently reinstitute the leverage of workers to demand a restoration of a much larger share of the surplus, which management has relentlessly refused to grant.

Given the rhetoric associated with the Obama rescue—which emphasized the preservation of high-paying jobs in the United States as its major goal—we might expect to discover that the return to prosperity in only seven years would include expanded domestic labor forces with increased wages. We would be wrong. The Obama-era bailouts did not lead to reinstitution of the elements of flexibility or to any new benefits for workers. Instead, the domestic industry sought and achieved further reductions in labor forces and labor costs.

An instructive example was the U.S. government–brokered sale of Chrysler to Fiat.[4] Prior to the sale, the government coerced the UAW into accepting 55 percent of the stock in the essentially bankrupt company in exchange for abandoning any claim to its $10 billion retirement fund and granting Chrysler relief from any obligation to pay for retiree health benefits. This 55 percent stock might have at least conferred leverage over company policy and thus ensured that the return to corporate health, in the next round of management decisions, would also restore lost wages and benefits. But the Obama-brokered rescue delivered to the UAW nonvoting shares.

The denouement of this "rescue" arrived when Fiat purchased the company and the UAW stocks were evaluated at $4.35 billion.[5] The workers had lost more than 50 percent of their (previously valued $10 billion) retirement fund and all of their retiree health benefits. Moreover, in the purchase by Fiat—which constituted the only way that the UAW could turn its (essentially worthless) stock into usable funds—the union also agreed to cutbacks in overtime, reductions in break time, suspension of paid Monday after Easter holidays, elimination of cost-of-living allowances, linking 5 percent of wages to the company's performance, and finally, abandoning the Jobs Bank Program.

After negotiating these devastating givebacks, the Italian company's investment representative from the UBS sought unsuccessfully to shake UAW president Ron Gettelfinger's hand. When the confused banker asked the Treasury Department's Ron Bloom—the Obama administration negotiator—why this untoward moment had occurred, Bloom replied, "That handshake you asked for was the undoing of seventy years of UAW bargaining."[6]

Over at General Motors, the UAW made similar concessions. In addition to contract changes such as eliminating the Jobs Bank, it accepted 17.5 percent of nonvoting GM stock in exchange for the $30 billion GM owed to the VEBA (voluntary employees' benefits association), which was responsible for future benefits costs. When the UAW finally sold its stock back to GM, they received $3.2 billion.[7]

Even with the sacrifices that workers made to help save the companies, Chrysler and GM still had to file for bankruptcy. As part of the court-ordered settlement, Chrysler closed eight factories, eliminating 6,500 employees (20 percent of its workforce), while GM closed fourteen factories and laid off 20,000 employees.[8] These closures might have been less devastating if they had been matched by reinvestment in centralizing production (and/or rehiring laid-off workers at new facilities). But such new investment within the United States never materialized; all new jobs for both companies were located in low-wage countries outside the United States. With the government's auto task force paving the way through the Chrysler and GM bailouts and bankruptcies, Ford took advantage by extracting similar compromises from the UAW: shares to pay VEBA debt, elimination of the Jobs Bank Program, and a rollback of a number of benefits.

The auto bailouts, then, enabled the Big Three, with the support of the Obama administration, to temporarily regain profitability by once again closing factories and slashing employee benefits and thus further immiserating their domestic workers.[9] The neoliberal logic underlying this strategy mandated that the Big Three invest these restored profits in developing a long-term solution to their noncompetitive, inefficient, and stagnant production system. But this is precisely what did not occur. Instead, these profits were delivered to shareholders, invested in overseas facilities, and invested in the soaring stock market.

Although the U.S. auto industry was no longer in crisis as Donald Trump began running for president in 2015, he made bringing auto jobs back to the United States an important part of his campaign. This focus by Trump actually made sense given the ongoing decline in auto jobs during the seven-year "revival" engineered by the Obama administration. Like Obama, Trump recognized that U.S. automakers' problems involved costs of production that were too high to compete with Japanese manufacturers. Unlike the Obama administration response, Trump's policies did not demand that autoworkers directly sacrifice gains they had made in order to lower costs. Nevertheless, the Trump administration applied the same neoliberal logic that the Obama administration followed: increase auto company profits and assume that these will be invested in high-wage manufacturing in the United States. The major Trump administration initiatives—lowering corporate tax rates from 35 percent to 21 percent, relaxing and eliminating clean air standards, and raising tariffs on foreign inputs—did indeed deliver huge profits to the auto industry in 2017 and promised further profits in 2018.

The problem for working families in general and autoworkers in particular is that tax cuts, deregulation, and tariffs on foreign imports did not—and cannot—address the long-term cause of auto manufacturing job loss. The huge profits generated by government rescue programs are not invested in expanded domestic manufacturing because Big Three management understands that their inefficient production system depends on finding and exploiting low-wage workers. Instead, they deliver these profits to their shareholders, stockpile it in the soaring stock market, or invest in low-wage enterprises overseas. In the meantime, both the employed and unemployed domestic workers suffer the double immiseration of declining wages and benefits combined with eroded social programs, increased health problems due to deregulation, and increased prices due to protective tariffs.

Even as the Big Three continued to reap their huge Trump administration profits in 2018, the next round of plant closings and migrations to low-wage countries began in earnest. In late 2018, GM announced that it would cut 14,700 jobs in North America, while Ford introduced an $11 billion "restructuring" that Wall Street investors are predicting will result in the elimination of 25,000 jobs.[10]

The findings we have presented in this book lead to a set of depressing expectations for the future of U.S. autoworkers—and the regions that developed around the auto industry—but it is worth closing on this potentially hopeful note: the story of the rise and fall of the U.S. auto industry is one of an interaction of structure and agency. The past may shape the future, but it is human actions and decisions that will determine how it actually plays out. The latent power of the auto industry remains intact, waiting to be activated by resourceful workers finding the needed unity and targeting the pressure points of the production system.

NOTES

Introduction

1. Taylor 2010.
2. Ingrassia 2011; Taylor 2010.
3. Taylor 2010, 211.
4. Although Ford turned down government assistance, the concessions the government auto task force was able to extract from the UAW on behalf of GM and Chrysler also proved integral to Ford's survival (Ingrassia 2011; Taylor 2010).
5. All data presented on the decline of the region from the 1960s onward was taken from the U.S. Census, the Bureau of Labor Statistics, and the American Community Survey.
6. Detroit's population declined by 65 percent, and Flint's by 51 percent. On the cities' loss of wealth, see Bouffard 2015.
7. Taylor 2010, 218.
8. Ingrassia 2011.
9. Taylor 2010, 171, 226.
10. Taylor 2010, 212.
11. Loomis 2006.
12. In this book, when we refer generally to management, we refer to high-level executives such as the CEO, ownership as embodied by individuals and families such as Henry Ford, and the interests of ownership. Thus, we use "ownership," "management," "automakers," and "capitalists" interchangeably. Our decision to treat these groups as one and the same is based on a long line of research on the problem of agency of top managers. This research shows that while there is legally a separation of ownership and control, the interests of top managers are aligned with the interests of ownership almost all the time (see Domhoff 2014; Mintz and Schwartz 1985; Useem 1984; Zeitlin 1974). When we distinguish between these groups, we make that distinction clear.
13. Vernon 1966.
14. Storper and Walker 1989; Wells 1980.
15. Abernathy, Clark, and Kantrow 1983, 15.
16. Drucker, 1971, 110.
17. On risk-averse management, see Taylor 2010, 2. On arrogant and non-detail-oriented management, see Loomis 2006; Monks and Minow 2008; Ingrassia 2011; Taylor 2010.

18. An example of this is the description by the General Motors historian Arthur Pound (1934, 85–86) of the company motto, not as "shall we change?" but rather as "how and when shall we change?"

19. Examples of this narrative are found in Ingrassia 2011, but any perusal of journalistic accounts of the collapse of the U.S. auto industry easily reveals that this narrative is central to the story.

20. Rubenstein 1992; Sugrue 1996.

21. Langfitt 2010.

22. Parts of this summary appeared previously in Murray and Schwartz 2017a, which is a much less detailed and evidence-laden application of this book's argument to an explanation of the decline of Detroit and the suffering of workers in the city.

23. DiMaggio and Powell 1983.

24. We make no distinction in this book between labor-management conflict and the Marxist view of class conflict in a capitalist society. For Marx, class conflict is a collective struggle between those with power and those over whom power is wielded (what he calls "the oppressor" and "the oppressed"), while the particular form of the struggle is dependent on the modes of production in a given society (Marx 1848/2004, 1852/1978). In a capitalist society, class struggle takes the form of conflict over the distribution of surplus value. That is, when workers use the raw materials, tools, and factories that capitalists own to produce something (in this case an automobile), the worker imbues the product with value that exceeds the cost of the raw materials, the upkeep on the means of production (tools, factories, and so on), and the cost of keeping the worker alive (Marx 1857–1861/1973, 246–52). The capitalist class interest in maximizing profit dictates that the working class in general only be paid what is required for subsistence (Marx 1891/1999). The class interests of workers, then, are to be paid for the surplus labor they contribute above that which is required for them to stay alive. When individual workers act collectively (formally as a union or not) to pursue a larger share of surplus value, they represent the class of workers against the interests of capitalists in profits. The interests of capitalists are already made collective by the publicly traded corporation where many individual capitalists own shares of a company (Roy and Parker-Gwin 1999; Mizruchi 1992, 59–64). Thus, the profits of a single company represent the collective interests of ownership. Management, in seeking to maximize profits, represents the collective interests of capitalists. Thus, the struggles between labor and management that we describe are most definitely class struggle.

Chapter 1: The Japanese Advantage: Flexible Production and Innovation

1. Unless otherwise noted, this discussion of flexible production is based on Abernathy, Clark, and Kantrow 1983; Asanuma 1985a, 1985b; Clark 1989; Cusumano 1985; Fujita and Hill 1995; Helper 1987, 1990, 1991c; Murray and Schwartz 2017a, 2017b; Sheard 1983; Shimokawa 1985; Smitka 1991.

2. Womack, Jones, and Roos 1990, 12–13.

3. See, for example, Abernathy, Clark, and Kantrow 1983; Florida and Kenney 1991; Gerlach 1992; Kearns and Nadler 1992; Keller 1989; Piore and Sabel 1984; Rubenstein 1992; Schwartz 1992; Womack, Jones, and Roos 1990.

4. A partial listing would include Abernathy 1978; Abernathy, Clark, and Kantrow 1983; Altshuler et al. 1984; Clark 1989; Cusumano 1985; Estall 1985; Fujita and Hill 1995; Helper 1990, 1991c; Kenney and Florida 1993; Shimokawa 1985; Smitka 1991. Kenney and Florida place special emphasis on the labor process.

5. Abernathy, Clark, and Kantrow 1983, 73. Michael Cusumano (1985, 270) notes that Taiichi Ono, the architect of Toyota's pioneering system that was later copied by Toyo Kogyo and Nissan, saw this system as a radical expansion of Ford's system, since "only Ford's final assembly line achieved anything resembling a continuous process flow." See also Hall 1981.

6. This account of the creation of the Toyota just-in-time system is taken from Cusumano 1985, 264–84; see also Asanuma 1985a, 1985b. For a detailed description of the day-to-day operation of the system, see Hall 1981. We use Cusumano's spelling of Ono's name. Other scholars have translated the Japanese characters as Ouno or Ohno.

7. *Supply* keiretsu are to be distinguished, as Marie Anchordoguy (1990) notes, from *interbank* keiretsu: the networks of corporations surrounding the dominant money market banks, notably the Mitsubishi, Mitsui, and Matsushita banks.

8. Weber 1929.

9. This account is based on Fujita and Hill 1993. See also Cusumano 1985, chap. 5; Kenney and Florida 1993, chaps. 2 and 7.

10. Abernathy, Clark, and Kantrow 1983; Cusumano 1985.

11. Cusumano 1985, 318.

12. Since many countries (including the United States) put tariffs on imported cars from Japan, Japanese automakers transplanted entire production complexes—assemblers and suppliers—to foreign nations (including the United States) and built the cars domestically.

13. Perrucci 1994, chap. 3, 75.

14. Perrucci 1994, 51–71; Kenney and Florida 1993, 99–102, 140; Estall 1985, 130.

15. Florida and Kenney 1991; Kenney and Florida 1993, chaps. 4 and 5.

16. Kenney and Florida 1993, 154.

17. Fujita and Hill 1995, 23.

18. Kenney and Florida 1993, 102.

19. Howes 1993. "Domestic content" is parts and materials produced in the same country where the car is sold—in this case, the United States.

20. Kenney and Florida 1993, 205–06.

21. Smitka 1991, 261–63.

22. One symptom of this imperative to adopt internal flexibility was its widespread adoption among first-tier suppliers in the industry and its lack of prevalence among second-tier suppliers, who were not constrained to make just-in-time deliveries (Cusumano 1985, 298–99).

23. Asanuma 1985a, 68–70; Hall 1981, 12.

24. Helper 1990, 159.

25. Helper 1990, 154; see also Hirschman 1970.
26. Unless otherwise noted, this version of events regarding the implementation of disc brakes comes from Abernathy 1978, 206–07.
27. Details about the implementation of aluminum engines come from Abernathy 1978, 209–10.
28. By 2006, 85 percent of North American cars had aluminum engines (Murphy 2006).
29. A convincing general argument for this point can be found in Boden and Molotch 1994; see also Romo and Schwartz 1995.
30. Unless otherwise noted, this timeline for unit body construction comes from Abernathy 1978, 193–94.
31. Asanuma 1985b, 43–45. See also Asanuma 1985a, 1985b; Clark 1989; Cusumano 1985, chap. 5; Helper 1990, 154–55; Kenney and Florida 1993, 140–43; Kenney and Florida 1993, chap. 5; Smitka 1990.
32. Helper 1990, 154–55.
33. Holusha 1982.
34. Vlasic 2008. The numbers themselves are taken from a Heritage Foundation study by James Sherk (2008).
35. Chappell 2012; Ford Motor Company 2014.
36. Parts of this analysis of the cost-of-production differential between U.S. and Japanese auto production first appeared in Murray and Schwartz 2017a.
37. Abernathy 1978; Abernathy, Clark, and Kantrow 1983.
38. Geng 2005.
39. Clark 1989.
40. Clark 1989, 1251, 1260.
41. Clark 1989, 1261.
42. Cusumano 1985, 301–03.
43. Hill and Lee 1994.
44. Altshuler et al. 1984, 105, 159.
45. Dertouzos et al. 1989, 180.
46. Dertouzos et al. 1989, 180–81.
47. Abernathy, Clark, and Kantrow 1983; Hall 1981, 46.
48. In many cases these high defect rates were the result of faulty parts delivered from outside suppliers. Michael Cusumano and Akira Takeishi, for example, surveyed both American and Japanese assemblers about defect rates on four outsourced subassemblies. In the early 1980s, 2.6 percent of the assemblies received by the Big Three were defective, while the figure was 0.014 percent for the Japanese. That is, the defect rate was *185 times greater in the American plants* (Cusumano and Takeishi 1991, 574). The specific subassemblies studied were shock absorbers, front seat assemblies, gauge assemblies, and instrument panels. Consequently, the Japanese could dispense with inspection of delivered parts, while the Americans had to devote considerable resources to detecting the faulty subassemblies and replacing them. Even then, they typically failed to identify all the problems (see also Helper and Levine 1992, 563).
49. In Cusumano and Takeishi's study of four outsourced subassemblies, the American firms were much further behind. In the late 1980s, the American assemblers were still

experiencing a defect rate of 1.37 percent, while the Japanese had reduced the rate to a microscopic 0.008 percent (Cusumano and Takeishi 1991, 579; see also Kenney and Florida 1993, 124).

50. Monden 1994, 1. For similar views, see also Abernathy, Clark, and Kantrow 1983; Altshuler et al. 1984; Cusumano 1985; Fujita and Hill 1995; Smitka 1991. A notable exception is Helper (1990, 1991b), whose exit-voice analysis emphasizes the similarities between the Japanese system and the pre–World War II American system.

Chapter 2: Innovation and the Structure of Production in the Early U.S. Auto Industry

1. Unless otherwise noted, this account of early U.S. auto production is based on Abernathy, Clark, and Kantrow 1983; Epstein 1927, 3144–28; Gartman 1986, 166–68; Hounshell 1984, 217–305; Kuhn 1986; Lewchuk 1987, chap. 3; Rubenstein 1992, chaps. 1–5; Sorensen 1956; Womack, Jones, and Roos 1990, chap. 2.

2. Abernathy, Clark, and Kantrow (1983, 45) refer to this period as a "limited phase of de-maturity," although its duration into the late 1930s makes it longer-lasting than the initial phase of industry development, a pattern that itself disconfirms product life cycle theory.

3. Similar examples abound in specific aspects of production. David Hounshell (1984, 247–48) describes the application of assembly line techniques to the engine magneto. This process involved no technological innovation except the movement of the line, but it nevertheless reduced labor time from 13 to 5 minutes per magneto. James Womack, Daniel Jones, and Daniel Roos (1990, 29) report that final assembly labor time was reduced by 88 percent, from 750 to 93 minutes, with little or no technological innovation. For a detailed discussion of the relative roles of technology and production redesign in the development of the assembly line, see Gartman 1986, chaps. 1–5; see also Lewchuk 1987, chap. 3; LaFever 1924.

4. These included Maxwell, Paige, Hudson, Packard, Studebaker, Dodge, Reo, Overland, Chevrolet, Buick, and Saxon (Gartman 1986, 88).

5. Faurote 1927, 194; see also Ford 1926, 80–86.

6. J. Edward Schipper, in *Automotive Industries* (June 1922, 1148), quoted in Gartman 1986, 125.

7. Ford 1926, 186–88; Gartman 1986, 124–27; Hounshell 1984, chap. 6.

8. Hounshell 1984, 292.

9. Sorensen 1956, 145.

10. Faurote 1927, 198.

11. Ford 1926, 86–88.

12. Hounshell 1984, 275.

13. Epstein 1926.

14. The original development of this argument is contained in Baran and Sweezy 1966, chap. 4. See also Mintz and Schwartz 1985, chap. 2; Abernathy, Clark, and Kantrow 1983, 46.

15. Kuhn 1986, 184; Cray 1980, 250.

16. See Hounshell 1984, chap. 7; Sorensen 1956, 204–06.
17. Hounshell 1984, 273–74.
18. Hounshell 1984, 271.
19. Hounshell 1984, 273; see also Ford 1926, 86–88.
20. Hounshell 1984, 276; Kuhn 1986, 280–84.
21. Sorensen 1956, 205.
22. Faurote 1927, 194.
23. Hounshell 1984, 300.
24. Hounshell 1984, 284–85.
25. Sorensen 1956, 169.
26. Faurote 1927, 194.
27. Hounshell 1984, 297–99; Kuhn 1986, 284–85.
28. Barclay 1936, 151–53.
29. Barclay 1936, 61.
30. Barclay 1936, 85–86; Beasley 1947, 50; Durham 1927, 62; Hounshell 1984, 285; Williams et al. 1993, 532.
31. This chronology and analysis of the hand-to-mouth inventory system is based on: Abernathy 1978, 89–90; Abernathy, Clark, and Kantrow 1983, 80; Barclay 1936, 24, 109–15; Chandler 1964, 196; Clark 1928; Durham 1927; Faurote 1927, 202; Flugge 1929, 160–65; Ford 1926, 105–15; Helper 1990, 157; 1991b, 791; Knudsen 1927, 67–68; Kuhn 1986, 9, 71, 178, 200–02, 274–75; Langlois and Robertson 1989, 370; Pound 1934, 196–98; Seltzer 1928, 100, 114–18; Sloan 1963, 195–98; Sorensen 1956, 166, 199–200; Stillman 1927.
32. Ford 1922, 224.
33. Clark 1928.
34. Stillman 1927, 1–2; Clark 1928, 394–95.
35. See, for example, Ford 1926, 105–15; Stillman 1927; Flugge 1929.
36. Nevins and Hill 1957, 155.
37. Kuhn 1986, 264–65; Nevins and Hill 1957, 266–72.
38. Durham 1927.
39. Inventory turnover attempts to measure the number of times a year the company's inventory is sold, or turned over. It is calculated as the value of the average inventory during a year divided into the total supplies purchased during that year.
40. Ford 1926, 114. For other data, see Abernathy, Clark, and Kantrow 1983, 80; Barclay 1936, 24; Ford 1926, 109; Kuhn 1986, 178; Pound 1934, 196–98; Sorensen 1956, 166.
41. See Kuhn 1986, chaps. 3–7, for a comprehensive analysis of the early development of the hand-to-mouth system. See also Hounshell 1984, 264–67. For the details of Knudsen's role, see Beasley 1947.
42. Knudsen 1927, 66.
43. Hounshell 1984, 265–66.
44. Sloan 1941, 183, quoted in Kuhn 1986, 94.
45. Stillman 1927, 4.
46. For discussions of the geographic concentration of auto production and the rise of Detroit, see Epstein 1927, 314–42; Gartman 1986, chaps. 3 and 4; Hounshell 1984, chap.

6; Lewchuk 1987, 36–47; Rubenstein 1992, chap. 3; Sorensen 1956, chaps. 10 and 11; Williams, Haslam, and Williams 1992; Williams et al. 1993, 1994.

47. For an analysis of these patterns and the dynamics that produced them, see Rubenstein 1992, 29–42.

48. Epstein 1928/1972, 317. As early as 1914, 75 percent of Ford workers were foreign-born, 50 percent of them from southern and eastern Europe (Raff and Summer 1987).

49. Clawson 1980.

50. Hounshell 1984, chap. 6; Lewchuk 1987, chap. 3; Sorensen 1956. See chapter 3 of his text for a full discussion.

51. Ford 1926, 63.

52. Storper and Walker 1989, 71.

53. Kuhn (1986, 272–78) mounts a blistering critique of the inefficiency of this extreme version of vertical integration.

54. Sorensen 1956, 145; see also Ford 1926, 94–107.

55. Sorensen 1956, 165.

56. Ford 1926, 64–66.

57. Sorensen 1956, 163–64; Ford 1926, 44–45.

58. Ford 1926, 42; Epstein 1927, 100–23.

59. Abernathy 1978, 141–43; Kuhn 1986, 274–75; Sorensen 1956, 246–48.

60. Sorensen 1956, 247.

61. Ford 1926, 41–42.

62. Sorensen 1956, 198.

63. Sorensen 1956, 199.

64. Sorensen 1956, 212.

65. Sorensen 1956, 200.

66. This account of glass manufacturing at River Rouge is based on Ford 1926, 44–56; Barclay 1936, 36; Sorensen 1956, 163–66.

67. Ford 1926, 44.

68. Sorensen 1956, 164–65.

69. Sorensen 1956, 165.

70. Ford 1926, 109.

71. This account of Ford's branch assembly plant system is drawn from Ford 1926, 110–15, 135–50; Rubenstein 1992, chap. 3; Sorensen 1956, 162–63; Hounshell 1984, chap. 6.

72. Ford 1926, 136; see also Rubenstein 1992, 54–61; Weber 1929; Hoover 1948.

73. Rubenstein 1992, 53–54.

74. Court documents quoted by Rubenstein 1992, 53.

75. Rubenstein 1992, 55–66.

76. Rubenstein 1992, 55.

77. Kraus 1947, 56.

78. Ford 1926, 111–12.

79. Ford 1926, 112.

80. H. D. Doss, quoted in Rubenstein 1992, 65.

81. Ford 1926, 148.

82. Abernathy, Clark, and Kantrow (1983, chap. 7) developed the term "transilience" to describe this disruptive aspect of new innovations. The changes during this period had very high levels of transilience.
83. Rubenstein 1992, 63–77.
84. Rubenstein 1992, 67.
85. Kuhn 1986, chaps. 12 and 13.
86. Edwards 1965, 170–84.
87. Such a system was almost certainly beyond the capability of Ford's management system. See Kuhn 1986, chaps. 1, 12, and 13.
88. Ford 1926, 86–88.
89. Ford 1926, 86.
90. The unwieldiness of the system was very likely implicated in the fact that Ford did not offer a midpriced automobile (Mercury) until the late 1930s and did not begin to fill all the price niches until the 1950s.
91. Virtually all of the many accounts of the origins of General Motors criticize Durant's acquisition strategy. This discussion relies mainly on Cray 1980, part I, esp. 72–85; Rubenstein 1992, chaps. 4 and 5; Pound 1934, 111–92.
92. Hyatt Roller Bearings in Harrison, New Jersey; New Departure (bearings and brakes) in Bristol, Connecticut; Klaxon (horns) in Newark, New Jersey; Harrison Radiator in Lockport, New York; National Plate Glass in Blairsville, Pennsylvania (Pound 1934, passim; Rubenstein 1992, chaps. 3 and 4, passim).
93. Rubenstein 1992, 108; Pound 1934, 489–90.
94. This acquisition had an ironic twist. When Durant tried to acquire Champion Ignition (late Champion Spark Plugs) and move it from Boston to Flint, he discovered that Albert Champion did not own the company that he had created. The owner was willing to sell the firm, but not the name, so Durant changed the name to AC Spark Plugs (see Rubenstein 1992, 106–07; Pound 1934, 456–60).
95. Rubenstein 1992, 109.
96. For accounts of these patterns, see Rubenstein 1992, chaps. 4 and 5; Cray 1986, part I; and Pound 1934, appendix.
97. See, for example, Chandler 1964; Kettering and Orth 1932; Pound 1934; Sloan 1941, 1963.
98. Sloan 1941, 49.
99. This account of the General Motors Research Laboratory is taken from Pound 1934, 269–87; Sloan 1963, 77–89; Beasley 1947, 126–28; Kuhn 1986, chap. 9, esp. 83–85; Cray 1980, 195–97, 209–18.
100. Sloan 1963, 76.
101. Sloan 1963, 78.
102. Sloan 1963, 85.
103. Beasley 1947, 127.
104. Sloan 1963, 89.
105. The discussion of Harley Earl is based on Bayley 1983, 19–47, 116; Cray 1980, 244–57, 275; Kuhn 1986, 88–92.
106. In this same period, for example, the General Motors Institute was organized in Flint

to create uniform training and compatible orientations among new generations of leadership (Pound 1934, 408–11; Kuhn 1986, 169–70).

107. Kuhn 1986, 183.

108. Rubenstein 1992, 29; see also Faurote 1927. Meric Gertler reached similar conclusions about the importance of proximity in the context of the suppliers of machinery for manufacturing in Ontario, Canada, in the early 1990s. His findings can be best summarized by the conclusion that "many problems are not easily described or solved over the phone or fax," and that these sorts of unsolvable problems occurred most often in the context of integrating new machinery into production facilities (Gertler 1994, 11).

109. Lewchuk 1987, chap. 3; Gartman 1986, 214.

110. This discussion of Fleetwood is drawn from Pound 1934, 290–93; Cray 1980, 1; Kuhn 1986, 91–95.

111. Pound 1934, 293–94.

112. Pound 1934, 293–94; Rubenstein 1992, 117.

113. Pound 1934, 483–84; Rubenstein 1992, 111.

114. Helper 1990, 1991a, 1991b.

115. Helper 1990, 158.

116. Seltzer 1928, 19–20.

117. Seltzer 1928, 65–101, 240–41; see also Epstein 1928/1972.

118. Piore and Sabel 1984; Saxenian 1990, 1994.

119. Thompson 1954; Seltzer 1928, 42–45.

120. This chronology is based on Thompson 1954 and Seltzer 1928, chap. 2. See also Adams 1919; Clarkson 1916.

121. Thompson 1954, 5–14; Seltzer 1928, 42–45.

122. Thompson 1954, 6.

123. Thompson 1954, 10.

124. Thompson 1954, 17.

125. General Motors had a particularly vexed relationship to the standardization process. Because it acquired a considerable number of parts suppliers as part of its development, it incorporated a number of important activists for part standardization into its corporate shell. These included Charles Kettering, who served as SAE president in 1918 (one year before Delco was acquired by GM), and Karl W. Zimmerschied, who served as chairman of the committee on standardization while a GM vice president in 1915. This led to a movement within GM that culminated in the firm issuing its own standards, independent of SAE, which it could alter whenever the needs of the company dictated. Later, once relationships between GM and the parts industry began to stabilize, GM joined the SAE, ultimately placing representatives on sixteen of twenty-one committees. General Motors does not, however, seem to have ever given up its autonomy in setting its own standards. Its involvement in SAE appears to have been an attempt to amplify the advantages of internal standardization by getting the parts industry as a whole to adopt GM standards (Kuhn 1986, 72–78; Thompson 1954, 18–19).

126. Thompson 1954, 19.

127. Seltzer 1928, 57–59.

128. Ford 1922, 1926; Ford and Crowther 1930; Sorensen 1956.

129. Faurote 1927, 198–99.

130. Sorensen 1956, 165.

131. Barclay 1936, 36.

132. Barclay 1936, 31–36.

133. Barclay 1936, 31–36.

134. Rubenstein 1992, 106–18.

135. For a detailed discussion of the logic that led Sloan to retain the internal subsidiaries acquired by Durant, and the logic that led him to develop the multidivisional form, see Kuhn 1986, esp. 68–78.

136. This account of Fisher Body is taken from Pound 1934, 288–301; Sloan 1963, 160–63; Kuhn 1986, 70–72; Thomas 1973, 128–29; Klein, Crawford, and Alchian 1978, 308–10; Klein 1988; Langlois and Robertson 1989.

137. Their belief was quickly confirmed. By 1926, Hudson had increased its sales by 1,000 percent (from 21,320 in 1917 to 244,667 in 1926), virtually all on the basis of its closed bodies, and the industry as a whole increased its proportion of closed bodies from less than 10 percent in 1919 to 43 percent in 1924. (Fisher produced 58 percent closed bodies in 1924.) In the meantime, the auto industry as a whole increased production by 150 percent, and virtually all of this increase was accounted for by closed-body cars (Seltzer 1928, 57; Kennedy 1941/1972, 164; Thomas 1973, 128–29; see also Langlois and Robertson 1989, 371–72).

138. Seltzer 1928, 240.

139. See Klein 1988 for an elaborate and convincing argument that absorption was necessary, and that GM could not have accomplished the same ends through contractual arrangements, no matter how carefully the contracts were written. Such a contract could only have protected General Motors if it anticipated the sources of overcharging and the areas in which innovation might occur "and [writing] a pre specified response to each event. . . . By integrating, General Motors [could] wait until future conditions [emerged] before determining what should be done." That is, "the relationship becomes flexible to unanticipated market conditions" (210). Klein's argument is straightforward and reasonable in the GM-Fisher context, but it rests on the assumption that the "primary alternative to vertical integration . . . is some form of economically enforceable long-term contract" (Klein, Crawford, and Alchian 1978, 302). This ignores a third alternative: keiretsu arrangements, which achieve the same level of flexibility without either formal contracts or vertical integration.

140. Asanuma 1985b, 40–50.

141. The 60 percent stock block did not give GM managerial control because the terms of purchase had guaranteed the Fisher brothers a majority of the voting stock (Kuhn 1986, 71).

142. Ten years later, long after this dispute was settled, the Fisher plant in Flint that precipitated this crisis became the site of the Great Flint Strike, the most important strike in American labor history.

143. Kuhn 1986, 71; Sloan 1963, 161–62.

144. Sheard 1983, 56–58.

145. Brown 1927/1979, 8.

146. Raskob 1927, 131–32.
147. Hounshell 1984, 272.
148. Hounshell 1984, 272.
149. See Flugge 1929, 160, n. 23. The actual figures, compiled by the Motor and Accessories Manufacturers' Association, were $923,440,000 of replacement sales and $1,123,648,000 in original equipment sales.
150. Flugge 1929, 160–63.
151. Heldt 1933, 548.
152. The examples of mutual dependence cited here are taken from Barclay 1936, 28; Fine 1969, 97, 127–38, 317; Katz 1977, 265–78; Knudsen 1927, 67; Kraus 1947, 80, 229, 281; Kuhn 1986, 274–75; Nevins and Hill 1963, 298–99; Sorensen 1956, 246–48.
153. For much of the period before World War II, GM had a controlling stock position in Bendix (Kuhn 1986, 222).
154. Kraus 1947, 80.
155. Sorensen 1956, 246–48.
156. The term "Toyotism" was first used to refer to the Japanese production system by Knuth Dohse, Ulrich Jurgens, and Thomas Nailsch (1985). Although these authors do recognize some of the structural advantages of the flexible system (such as just-in-time delivery), they focus on Toyotism as a management style. They state that the "organization of production and the system of labor relations" are inextricably tied, but their article does not fully appreciate the structural aspects of the organization of production under Toyotism (117–118). This is why they also do not recognize that Toyotism is evolved from the early U.S. industry's system of flexible production.
157. *Automotive News* 2013.
158. Toyota Motor Corporation 1967, 327–38, cited in Womack, Jones, and Roos 1990, 43–47.
159. Toyoda 1985, 109.
160. DiMaggio and Powell 1983.
161. Even during the original tour, Toyoda appreciated that the copying process would involve certain adjustments; he wrote back to headquarters during his 1950 trip that "there were some possibilities to improve the production system" at River Rouge (Toyota Motor Corporation 1967, 327–28, quoted in Womack, Jones, and Roos 1990, 99).
162. Even production innovations that decreased the cost of assembly were at least partially susceptible to this logic. If such an innovation diffused though the production culture, the prices were likely to decline and therefore nullify the increased margin that derived from lower costs.

Chapter 3: Class Conflict and the Impetus to Abandon Flexible Production

1. Much of this chapter is based on Murray and Schwartz 2015, Murray and Schwartz 2017a, and Murray and Schwartz 2017b. Although some sections from the articles are reprinted in this chapter, they are also interspersed with new analysis.
2. Murray and Schwartz 2015.

3. On structural leverage, see Schwartz 1976; Murray and Schwartz 2015. On positional power, see Perrone 1983. On workplace bargaining power, see Silver 2003.

4. Schwartz 1976, 172–73 (emphasis in original). For other treatments of the concept of worker structural power, see Silver 2003, chap. 2; Wright 2000; Perrone 1983, 1984; Parkin 1979, 80; Olson 1971, 23–40; Edwards 1979. For a sustained argument that structural leverage achieved through disruption was critical to the success of auto industry organizing in the 1930s, see Piven and Cloward 1977, chap. 3, or Murray and Schwartz 2015. For a pointed and convincing argument that the union successes in the 1930s rested on workplace bargaining power, see Silver 2003, 43–49.

5. Our concept of structural leverage is rooted in the interaction of what Erik Olin Wright (2000, 962) terms "associational power" and "structural power." That is, the structural power of workers can enhance their associational power by reducing the number of workers needed to successfully engage in direct action.

6. Young, Banerjee, and Schwartz 2018.

7. Friedrich Engels (1845/2010) termed the unemployed who can replace workers "the army of reserve labor," and Karl Marx (1867/1977) referred to them as the "industrial reserve army."

8. Kraus 1947, 78.

9. For an excellent entry into this body of work, written in English by a Japanese scholar central to this perspective, see Hayashi 1983, 1989.

10. Berggren's (1992) work is particularly valuable because he included insights and summarized data contained in unpublished documents and manuscripts (for example, Adler 1991) and culled negative evidence from otherwise positive texts. He also performed a special service for English-language researchers, since most of the critical scholarship was European and not otherwise available in English. For a useful precursor to Berggren, see Streeck 1986.

11. For examples of the management-by-stress argument, see Parker 2017 and Parker and Slaughter 1990.

12. Berggren 1992, 30–32, 43–44.

13. Berggren (1992, 44) argues, in fact, that lean production facilities contain considerably fewer skilled jobs per capita than Fordist plants.

14. Klein, quoted in Berggren 1992, 45. Klein 1988, 64.

15. Schonberger 1982, 55–62.

16. Berggren 1992, 52–53.

17. Brown and Reich 1989, 33.

18. Perrucci 1994.

19. Hayashi 1983.

20. Cusumano 1985.

21. Kamata 1983, 157 (the English translation).

22. Cusumano 1985, 305, 306.

23. Satei scores are the grades that a worker receives on his yearly personnel evaluation. The evaluation is conducted by the immediate supervisor and is reviewed by multiple senior-level managers. The evaluation focuses mostly on subjective characteristics of the employee, such as eagerness, collegiality, and potential.

24. Berggren 1992, 34; for a similar argument, see Hayashi 1983, 13.
25. Shimokawa 1994, 38.
26. Berggren 1992, 335–36. The internal quotes are from Lysgaard (1976, 73) and Schonberger (1982, 61). For the Western Electric studies, see Roethlisberger and Dickson 1939; Mayo 1946.
27. Cole 1979, 201.
28. Perrucci 1994, 122.
29. Brown and Reich 1989, 29.
30. Kenney and Florida 1993.
31. Most of this section's content (except where noted) comes directly from either Murray and Schwartz 2015 or Murray and Schwartz 2017a.
32. Behrend 1957, 505.
33. Marx 1867/1977.
34. Behrend 1957, 505–06.
35. Behrend 1957, 510.
36. Roethlisberger and Dickson 1939; Mayo 1946; Zetka 1994; Burawoy 1982.
37. Among myriad accounts of this development, the most cited sources are Sward 1947, Meyer 1981, and Hounshell 1984.
38. Milkman 1997, 24; Murray and Schwartz 2015.
39. Ford 1926, 160. Clearly, Ford was mistaken: the Five Dollar Day was introduced in early 1914, not 1915.
40. Gartman 1986.
41. Raff and Summers 1987.
42. Raff and Summers 1987.
43. Williams et al. 1993.
44. Sorensen 1956.
45. Lewchuk 1987, 64.
46. Thompson 1971.
47. Thompson 1971, 78.
48. This account of the Model A changeover is based mainly on Hounshell 1984, 279–93, and Sward 1947, 194–205.
49. This discussion of benefit packages is taken from Porter 1917, 269; Shower 1918, 541; Raskob 1927, 133–34; Pound 1934, 179, 404–08, passim; Seltzer 1928, 220–22; Sorensen 1956, 139; Fine 1969, 123–26; Gartman 1986, 220–32; Kuhn 1986, 50, 202; Steeves 1987, 112, 127.
50. Ford developed what he called a "Sociology Department" to go along with the Five Dollar Day. Its job was to ensure that workers maintained stable lives. The investigators in the department encouraged workers to be financially responsible, to take care of their homes and kids, and to be married by twenty-two. This department functioned until 1921, but the benefits that the company gave out as part of the entire project spread throughout the industry and lasted nearly another decade, until the Depression. For details on the Sociology Department, see Sward 1947 and Meyer 1981. On the auto industry's housing benefits, see Steeves 1987, 150–59; Sward 1947, 59; Levin 1927, 79; Lee 1916, 302–06; Porter 1917.

51. Gartman 1986, 210–15.
52. Much of this section is derived from Murray and Schwartz 2015.
53. Sward 1947, 218–20.
54. This review of auto industry layoffs and furloughs in the early Depression is taken from Bernstein 1969/2010, 255; Fine 1969, 20–23, 61; Sward 1947, 228; Cray 1980, 272; Rothschild 1973, 36; Kennedy 1941/1972, 241; Barclay 1936, 28.
55. Bernstein 1969/2010, 255.
56. Rothschild 1973, 36; see also Cray 1980, 272.
57. Bernstein 1969/2010, 255.
58. Stepan-Norris and Zeitlin 1996, 9–11; Bonosky 1953; Keeran 1980, 1989; Prickett 1975, 117f.
59. Bonosky 1953; Prickett 1975, 117; Stepan-Norris and Zeitlin 1996, 9–11.
60. Peterson 1981, 213.
61. Fine 1969, 20–21.
62. Fine 1969, 21.
63. Unless otherwise noted, annual income for GM workers and employment numbers for GM come from Fine 1969, 20–23, 60–61.
64. Fine 1969, 61.
65. Kraus 1947.
66. Barclay 1936, 28; Kennedy 1941/1972, 255.
67. Galenson 1960, 129.
68. Prickett 1975, 109–73; Bernstein 1969/2010, 94–98, 181–85, 372–79.
69. Kraus 1947, 266.
70. Kraus 1947, 78.
71. Storper and Walker 1989; Romo and Schwartz 1990; Saxenian 1994.
72. Fine 1969, 25.
73. Fine 1969, 36; see also Bernstein 1969/2010, 515–19; Piven and Cloward 1977; Prickett 1975, 180–210; Walsh 1937, 109.
74. Kraus 1947, 6.
75. Nowak quoted in Stepan-Norris and Zeitlin 1996, 64–65.
76. Bernstein 1969/2010, 520–21; Kraus 1947, 5–6: Prickett 1975, 190.
77. Kraus 1947.
78. Fine 1969.
79. Piven and Cloward 1977, 140; Brecher 1974/1999, 187.
80. Prickett 1975, 180–81; see also Mortimer 1971, 103–22; Bernstein 1969/2010, 520–22.
81. Kraus 1947, 21.
82. Prickett 1975.
83. For examples of this phenomenon in the civil rights movement, see Morris 1981, 1986; McAdam 1982; Robnett 2000. For examples in the 2011 Arab Spring, see Schwartz 2011; Akin et al. 2012.
84. Bernstein 1969/2010; Piven and Cloward 1977, chap. 3.
85. Fine 1969.
86. Kraus 1947.
87. This combination of an effective mobilizing organization, a strategy capable of exer-

cising direct power, and a belief in efficacy by the rank and file has been analyzed from a number of perspectives by social movement theorists for the past thirty years. See, among many others, Piven and Cloward 1977, 4, 130f; Schwartz 1976, chap. 4; Morris 1981, 1986, 2007; Andrews 2004; Fantasia 1988.

88. Fine 1969.

89. Kraus 1947.

90. Silver 2003, 47.

91. Spilerman 1976; Morris 1981; Meyer and Whittier 1994.

92. Brecher 1974/1999.

93. Fine 1969, 123. "Widespread attention" is a reference to media coverage and repressive countermeasures by affected management. This "attention" was itself a consequence of the effectiveness of the tactic.

94. This account is based on Fine 1969, 44–49, 75–79; Bernstein 1969/2010, 518–19.

95. Fine 1963, 387–88.

96. Fine 1963, 393.

97. Beasley 1947, 398.

98. Quoted in Fine 1963, 400.

99. Adamic 1936a, 1936b, 1938; Bernstein 1969/2010, 591–602; Brecher 1974/1999, 193–204; Fine 1969, 122–23; Levinson 1938/1995, 143–46.

100. Quoted in Brecher 1974/1999, 200–01.

101. Brecher 1974/1999, 201.

102. Adamic 1936b, 702.

103. Adamic 1936b.

104. Adamic 1936a, 1936b.

105. Adamic 1936b, 704.

106. Fine 1969, 125.

107. Adamic 1936b; Fine 1969, 121–28; Lescohier 1937, 1; Levinson 1938/1995, 169–71; Tilly and Shorter 1974, 127–37; Torigian 1999, 324–27; Vincent 1937, 524–25.

108. Adamic 1936b, 702.

109. Fine 1969, 128.

110. Quoted in Fine 1969, 128. Fine's source for this quote is Beasley 1947, 165–66.

111. Kraus 1947, 46.

112. Mortimer 1971, 120.

113. Fine 1969, 129–30.

114. Kraus 1947.

115. Fine 1969.

116. Kraus 1947, 79.

117. This account of the conduct of the Flint strike is based, unless otherwise noted, on Bernstein 1969/2010; Brecher 1974/1999; Fine 1969; Kraus 1947; Mortimer 1971; Murray and Schwartz 2015; Piven and Cloward 1977; Prickett 1975.

118. Mortimer 1971, 124.

119. Kraus 1947, 82–83.

120. Fine 1969, 144.

121. Kraus 1947, 88–89.

122. Regular *New York Times* coverage began on December 30, 1936, and continued almost daily thereafter. See, for example, *New York Times* 1937.

123. Perhaps the most dramatic overt expression of this structural leverage had been the 400 percent turnover experienced by Ford during the rise of the assembly line. The profound disruption caused by the constant departure of workers from the line animated Ford's institution of the Five Dollar Day.

124. Levinson 1938/1995, 153.

125. Fine 1969, 180.

126. Kraus 1947, 266.

127. Fine 1969, 304–05.

128. Fine 1969, 327.

129. Fine 1969, 303–12. The Battle of Running Bulls was a confrontation between strikers and their supporters in the community and GM guards and local police. On January 11, 1937, guards tried to block the delivery of supplies to strikers. When the strikers took control of the entrance to the plant from company guards, local police arrived and attempted to physically remove strikers. The police were defeated in a violent battle.

130. Cushman 1998, 237.

131. Fine 1969, 235.

132. Glaberman 1980, 36.

133. Fine 1969, 196.

134. Kraus 1947, 159; Fine 1969, 331.

135. Glaberman 1980, 36.

136. Fine 1969; Glaberman 1980; Silver 2003.

137. For accounts of the final chapter in the long effort to organize Ford, see Galenson 1960, 178–84; Bennett 1951, 138–45.

138. Galenson 1960, 178.

139. Bennett 1951, 139.

140. Jefferys 1986, 91.

141. Compared to 1940, itself a very active strike year, 1941 recorded a 50 percent increase in the number of strikes, a 450 percent rise in the number of strikers, and a 350 percent rise in the number of man-hours lost. It exceeded even 1937 in the number and percentage of workers involved (*Monthly Labor Review* 1946, 720).

142. Lichtenstein 1982, 83.

143. The CIO had adopted the slogan "Victory through Equality of Sacrifice" during the war, but the UAW explicitly complained that the sacrifice of industry was not equal (Lichtenstein 1982, 99).

144. Marx 1845/2000.

145. Sloan 1963, 406.

146. Sayles 1954, 52.

147. Sayles 1954, quoted in Glaberman 1980, 37.

148. Sayles 1954, 50.

149. Scott and Homans 1947.

150. *Monthly Labor Review* 1946, 720; Brooks 1971, 204.

151. Preis 1972, 236.
152. As the auto industry transitioned into war production, it increasingly took up aircraft manufacture. These figures for the "automobile industry" therefore include manufacturers of transportation vehicles, aircraft, and a host of related products.
153. Glaberman 1980, 51–60, 98–119; Lichtenstein 1982, 133–35; Preis 1972, 228.
154. Glaberman 1980, chap. 3; Lichtenstein 1980; Lichtenstein 1982, chap. 6.
155. Sayles 1954, 52.
156. Mangum 1960, 94.
157. Glaberman 1980, 36; Lichtenstein 1982, 133; Zetka 1995, 45. James Zetka reports an average of forty-four strikes per year in auto between 1946 and 1950, with 85 percent of them wildcats. These numbers dropped steadily afterwards: by the end of the 1960s, the average per year was twenty-two, with only 30 percent unauthorized by union management.
158. Although the Big Three produced almost no automobiles during World War II, they used flexible production methods to change over to wartime production and make military vehicles and artillery. The automakers made large profits from government contracts during wartime production; thus, workers' structural leverage under flexible production was very much still an issue during the war.
159. Lichtenstein 1982, 112.
160. All union membership and total employment numbers during World War II come from Mayer 2004.
161. Spilerman 1976, 771–93; Morris 1981; Meyer and Whittier 1994, 277–98.
162. This description of the inequalities in autoworker wages during the war and the UAW response come from Lichtenstein 1982, 114–16.
163. Lichtenstein 1982, 125.
164. Lichtenstein 1982, 126.
165. Lichtenstein 1982, 276, n. 48.
166. See, for example, Jefferys 1986, 121f.
167. Leonard Woodcock, regional director of UAW-Chrysler, quoted in Glaberman 1980, 38.
168. Mangum 1960, 95; Jefferys 1986, 163; Lichtenstein 1980, 339.
169. Jefferys 1986, 113.
170. Jefferys 1986.
171. Jefferys 1986, 124.
172. Jefferys 1986, 113.
173. Glaberman 1980, 38.
174. Mangum 1960, 95; Jefferys 1986, 163; Lichtenstein 1980, 339.

Chapter 4: The Dire Consequences of Abandoning Flexible Production

1. See our description in chapter 3 of the spread from Fisher Body No. 2 to Fisher Body No. 1. For more details on the spread of the sit-down among plants in Flint, see Murray and Schwartz 2015.

2. Robert Michels (1915) famously argued that all organizations, no matter how democratic, will eventually turn into oligarchies. That is, they will become hierarchical in nature, with a small number of individuals at the top of the organization controlling it. Nearly every account of UAW history stresses the process of bureaucratization, whereby the union structure became more hierarchical, with top-down leadership. It is not clear to what extent bureaucratization of the UAW was inevitable and operated independently of the automakers' dispersion of production. It is possible that some of the shift to top-down control was motivated by the effects of dispersal on the functioning of union democracy. It is also likely that other factors, such as efficiency concerns and the need to delegate tasks, contributed to bureaucratization independently of dispersal. At the minimum, however, geographic dispersal is one of the factors that played a role in weakening the organizational democracy of the UAW.

3. Rubenstein 2001, 92.

4. Kuhn 1986, 148–49.

5. Kuhn 1986, 148–49.

6. Rubenstein 1992, 104.

7. Automation is not unique to U.S. automakers. In fact, the Japanese are the leaders in robotization. Automation is not incompatible with flexible production, but it is used differently depending on the production structure. In the dispersed U.S. system, automation is used to replace human workers and lower labor costs. In flexible production, Japanese automakers use robotization to improve the production process and enhance the work of their human labor rather than totally replace it. Automation does increase the productivity of workers in the flexible system, and thus their potential exploitation, but that is qualitatively different from replacing them as workers.

8. Kuhn 1986, 148.

9. Rubenstein 1992, 122.

10. Stepan-Norris and Zeitlin 2003, 95–97.

11. Rubenstein 1992.

12. Sugrue 1996.

13. Abernathy, Clark, and Kantrow 1983, 75.

14. Fine 1969.

15. Glaberman 1980.

16. Zetka 1994, 215.

17. Milkman 1997, 23.

18. Zetka 1994, 45–46.

19. Zetka 1994, 79–89.

20. Data on auto sales come from Ward's Automotive Group. Population data come from the U.S. Census Bureau. The 1951–1955 period was chosen for comparison because foreign market share reached only 1 percent in 1955, so auto sales in the United States during this period represent sales by U.S. automakers.

21. Abernathy and his colleagues created this weighted index by first placing innovations in one of four categories: drivetrain, process and assembly, body and chassis, and miscellaneous. They are then weighted on a seven-point transilience scale

(1 = little to no impact on the production process, 7 = very disruptive to products or processes); for each epoch, the 1-to-7 weight was squared, then summed across the years in the epoch (Abernathy, Clark, and Kantrow 1983, 152–54). Our time periodization is necessarily adopted from Abernathy and his colleagues (1983). This data limitation dictates making comparisons between pre-Flint and post–World War II, as the immediate post-Flint period data are not included in the Abernathy group's analysis. Nevertheless, given that Ford and Chrysler did not disperse production until after the war, the comparison is an apt one for our purposes.

22. Rubenstein 1992, 16.
23. Monks and Minow 2008, quoted in Taylor 2010, 2.
24. Loomis 2006.
25. Taylor 2010, 2.
26. Festinger 1957.
27. By "too costly" we do not mean that the Big Three lacked the resources to make changes. Indeed, they had billions of dollars of revenue. Instead, we mean that the costs associated with implementing the innovation exceeded the short-term benefits of the innovation and threatened to cut into profits, drop stock prices, put management jobs at risk, and result in further losses to the Japanese. Thus, innovation was slow to be adopted because it was too costly in the short term.
28. Pound 1934, 85–86.
29. Freeland 2001.
30. Abernathy, Clark, and Kantrow 1983, 51.
31. Abernathy 1978, 194–207.
32. GM's and Ford's European subsidiaries were embedded in concentrated production structures that used aspects of flexible production. The virtues of stand-alone production complexes, however, were not the primary motivation for their creation. Instead, the original decisions were motivated by European countries' protective tariffs, which could be immediately appreciated by cost-conscious executives. In fact, GM's top executives sought for many years to find a cost-effective way to ship American-made vehicles through European tariff barriers rather than undertake the complexities of overseas production. They only begrudgingly settled on this strategy when all else failed.
33. We say that deindustrialization "accelerated" because Detroit had already lost 145,000 manufacturing jobs by the mid-1960s as part of the dispersal of auto production around the United States.
34. General Motors 2014.
35. Kutscher and Personick 1986. U.S. manufacturing employment as a percentage of the labor force is calculated based on data from the Bureau of Labor Statistics.
36. For thorough documentation of increasing economic inequality, see Piketty 2014 and Saez and Zucman 2016.
37. Japanese manufacturing employment as a percentage of the labor force in 1970 comes from the U.S. Bureau of Labor Statistics series, "International Comparisons of Annual Labor Force." The 2015 numbers come from the Japan Institute for Labor Policy and Training.

38. Silver 2003.
39. This discussion of Toyota City is based on Fujita and Hill 2009.
40. Sugrue 1996; Murray and Schwartz 2017a.
41. Piore and Sabel 1984.

Chapter 5: The Japanese Counterfactual: Maintaining Flexible Production

1. This account of the union movement after World War II is taken from Berggren 1992, 24–26; Fujita and Hill 1993, 23–25; Shimokawa 1994, 31–35; Smitka 1991, 7; Toyoda 1985, 103–05.
2. This account of the 1950s strikes at Toyota, unless otherwise noted, come from Kume 1998.
3. Wimmer 2011.
4. Wimmer 2011.
5. Kume 1998.
6. Kimeldorf 2013, 1055.
7. Kume 1998, 70.
8. Kenney and Florida 1993, 115–16; Perrucci 1994, 120–24.
9. Ouchi 1981, 58.
10. Frank Romo and Michael Schwartz (1990) observed that in Nissan's key truck assembly plant in Tokyo, the computer facility, which controlled production in the robotized core of the facility, employed almost exclusively former assembly-line workers.
11. Fujita and Hill 1993; Armstrong 1985.
12. Brown and Reich 1989, 38–39. In Japan, lifetime employment was not a part of any official arrangement but instead an informal verbal commitment that became credible when the industry suffered setbacks without resorting to layoffs. Among the transplants, the non-union establishments had no formal guarantees, and even the union guarantees contained escape clauses that allowed layoffs in "severe economic conditions"—as the agreement between NUMMI and the UAW worded it (see also Kenney and Florida 1993, 115, 358, n. 112).
13. Simon 1957, 1991.
14. The beginning of this section derives from Murray and Schwartz 2017b.
15. Ford 1926, 109.
16. For a complete discussion of the development of the model A, see chapter 2.
17. Beasley 1947; Toyoda 1985; Toyota Motor Corporation 1967.
18. Abernathy, Clark, and Kantrow 1983, chap. 6; Florida and Kenney 1991; Rubenstein 1992, chaps. 6 and 7.
19. This viewpoint was held by both the core of the economic mainstream (for example, Galbraith 1958) and the most critical Marxists (for example, Baran and Sweezy 1966).
20. This chapter is based on ideas first published in Murray and Schwartz 2017a.
21. For detailed analysis of the failure to reinstitute flexible production, see Murray and Schwartz 2017a, 2017b; Helper 1991b.

22. UAW membership has steadily fallen, from a high of 1.5 million in 1979 to 382,000 in 2013.
23. Rubenstein 1992; Klier and Rubenstein 2008.
24. Keller 1989.
25. Rubenstein 1992, 256.
26. Parker 2017.
27. Romo and Schwartz 1995.
28. Rubenstein 1992, 243–44.
29. The discussion of Lopez is based on Taylor 2010, 128–30.
30. Taylor 2010, 81.
31. Levin 1991.
32. Levin 1992.
33. Taylor 2010, 81–90.
34. Parker 2017.
35. Ingrassia 2011; Taylor 2010.
36. Keenan, Smith, and Lowell 1995.
37. Taylor 2010, 146.
38. Keenan, Smith, and Lowell 1995.
39. Milkman 1997, 98.
40. Milkman 1997, 98–103.

Chapter 6: Conclusion

1. Taylor 2010; Ingrassia 2011.
2. DeBord 2016.
3. Snavely 2017.
4. Details of the Chrysler-Fiat deal come from Taylor 2010 and Ingrassia 2011.
5. Muller 2014.
6. Ingrassia 2011, 252.
7. Klayman 2013.
8. Ingrassia 2011, 256.
9. Although it is beyond the scope of this book to analyze why Obama's auto task force came up with this set of policies, we do want to note that the bailout would have appeared to be a solid solution to those who subscribed to the "greedy union" narrative of auto industry decline, which we dispelled in chapter 1.
10. Eisenstein 2018; Naughton 2018.

REFERENCES

Abernathy, William J. 1978. *The Productivity Dilemma: Roadblock to Innovation in the Automobile Industry*. Baltimore: Johns Hopkins University Press.

Abernathy, William J., Kim B, Clark, and Alan M. Kantrow. 1983. *Industrial Renaissance: Producing a Competitive Future for America*. New York: Basic Books.

Adamic, Louis. 1936a. "Sitdown." *Nation* 143 (December 5): 652–54.

———. 1936b. "Sitdown II." *Nation* 143 (December 12): 702–04.

———. 1938. *My America, 1928–1938*. New York: Harper's.

Adams, C. A. 1919. "Industrial Standardization." *Annals of the American Academy of Political and Social Science* 82: 289–99.

Adler, Paul. 1991. "The 'Learning Bureaucracy': New United Motor Manufacturing, Inc." (typescript). School of Business Administration, University of Southern California, Los Angeles.

Akin, Idil, Carlos Encina, Michael Restivo, Michael Schwartz, and Juhi Tyagi. 2012. "Old Wine in a New Cask? Protest Cycles in the Age of the New Social Media." *Whitehead Journal of Diplomacy and International Relations* 13(1): 89–103.

Altshuler, Alan, Martin Anderson, Daniel Jones, Daniel Roos, and James P. Womack. 1984. *The Future of the Automobile: The Report of MIT's International Automobile Program*. Cambridge, Mass.: MIT Press.

Anchordoguy, Marie. 1990. "An Overview of Japanese Keiretsu and of Japanese Government Efforts to Nurture a Domestic Computer Industry" (two brief essays in a larger article by Charles H. Ferguson, "Computers and the Coming of the U.S. Keiretsu"), *Harvard Business Review* 68(4): 55.

Andrews, Kenneth T. 2004. *Freedom Is a Constant Struggle: The Mississippi Civil Rights Movement and Its Legacy*. Chicago: University of Chicago Press.

Armstrong, L. 1985. "Frugal, Reclusive Commanders of an Industrial Army." *Business Week*, November 4, 45–46.

Asanuma, Banri. 1985a. "The Contractual Framework for Parts Supply in the Japanese Automotive Industry." *Japanese Economic Studies* 13 (Summer): 54–78.

———. 1985b. "The Organization of Parts Purchases in the Japanese Automotive Industry." *Japanese Economic Studies* 13 (Summer): 32–53.

Automotive News. 2013. "Eiji Toyoda's Rouge Trip Changed Auto History." September 23. https://www.autonews.com/article/20130923/OEM02/309239967/eiji -toyoda-s-rouge-trip-changed-auto-history (accessed January 29, 2019).

Baran, Paul A., and Paul Sweezy. 1966. *Monopoly Capital: An Essay on the American Economic and Social Order* . New York: Monthly Review Press.

Barclay, Hartley W. 1936. *Ford Production Methods*. New York: Harper & Brothers.

Bayley, Stephen. 1983. *Harley Earl and the Dream Machine*. New York: Alfred A. Knopf.

Beasley, Norman. 1947. *Knudsen: A Biography*. New York: McGraw-Hill.

Behrend, Hilde. 1957. "The Effort Bargain." *Industrial and Labor Relations Review* (July): 503–15.

Bennett, Harry. 1951. *We Never Called Him Henry*. New York: Fawcett.

Berggren, Christian. 1992. *Alternatives to Lean Production: Work Organization in the Swedish Auto Industry*. Ithaca, N.Y.: ILR Press.

Bernstein, Irving. [1969] 2010. *The Turbulent Years: A History of the American Worker, 1933–1941*. Boston: Houghton Mifflin; new edition, Chicago: Haymarket.

Boden, Deirdre, and Harvey L. Molotch. 1994. "The Compulsion of Proximity." In *NowHere: Space, Time, and Modernity*, edited by Roger Friedland and Deirdre Boden. Berkeley: University of California Press.

Bonosky, Philip. 1953. *Brother Bill McKie: Building the Union at Ford's*. New York: International.

Bouffard, Karen. 2015. "Census Bureau: Detroit Is Poorest Big City in U.S." *Detroit News*, September 16. http://www.detroitnews.com/story/news/local/michigan /2015/09/16/census-us-uninsured-drops-income-stagnates/32499231/ (accessed October 17, 2017).

Brecher, Jeremy. [1974] 1999. *Strike!* Greenwich, Conn.: Fawcett; revised and updated edition, Boston: South End Press.

Brooks, Thomas R. 1971. *Toil and Trouble: A History of American Labor*, 2nd ed. New York: Delta.

Brown, Claire, and Michael Reich. 1989. "When Does Union-Management Cooperation Work? A Look at NUMMI and GM–Van Nuys." *California Management Review* 31 (Summer): 26–44.

Brown, Donaldson. [1927] 1979. "Centralized Control with Decentralized Responsibility." *American Management Association Annual Convention Series: No. 57;* reprinted in *Managerial Innovation at General Motors*, edited by Alfred D. Chandler. New York: Arno.

Burawoy, Michael. 1982. *Manufacturing Consent: Changes in the Labor Process under Monopoly Capitalism*. Chicago: University of Chicago Press.

Chandler, Alfred D., Jr., ed. 1964. *Giant Enterprise: Ford, General Motors, and the Automobile Industry: Sources and Readings*. New York: Harcourt, Brace & World.

Chappell, Lindsay. 2012. "Mexico's Auto Boom Is about Wages." *Automotive News*, February 1, http://www.autonews.com/article/20120201/BLOG06/120209989 /mexico E2%80%99s-auto-boom-is-about-wages (accessed October 10, 2017).

Clark, Fred E. 1928. "An Analysis of the Causes and Results of Hand-to-Mouth Buying." *Harvard Business Review* 6 (April): 394–400.

Clark, Kim. 1989. "Project Scope and Project Performance: The Effect of Parts Strategy and Supplier Involvement on Product Development." *Management Science* 35 (October): 1247–62.

Clarkson, C. F. 1916. "Government Transportation Plans: Great Work of the Society of Automobile Engineers in Standardizing Parts." *Scientific American* 64: 582–92.

Clawson, Dan. 1980. *Bureaucracy and the Labor Process: The Transformation of U.S. Industry, 1860–1920.* New York: Monthly Review Press.

Cole, Robert. 1979. *Work, Mobility, and Participation: A Comparative Study of American and Japanese Industry.* Berkeley: University of California Press.

Cray, Ed. 1980. *Chrome Colossus: General Motors and Its Times.* New York: McGraw-Hill.

Cushman, Barry. 1998. *Rethinking the New Deal Court: The Structure of a Constitutional Revolution.* New York: Oxford University Press.

Cusumano, Michael A. 1985. *The Japanese Automobile Industry.* Cambridge, Mass.: Harvard University Press.

Cusumano, Michael A., and Akira Takeishi. 1991. "Supplier Relations and Management: A Survey of Japanese, Japanese-Transplant, and U.S. Auto Plants." *Strategic Management Journal* 12: 563–88.

DeBord, Matthew. 2016. "The U.S. Auto Market Is on the Verge of Doing Something It's Never Done Before—Again." *Business Insider,* December 2, https://www .businessinsider.com/the-us-auto-market-2016-record-sales-2016-12 (accessed December 10, 2018).

Dertouzos, Michael L., Richard K. Lester, Robert Solow, and MIT Commission on Industrial Productivity. 1989. *Made in America: Regaining the Competitive Edge.* Cambridge, Mass.: MIT Press.

DiMaggio, Paul J., and Walter W. Powell. 1983. "The Iron Cage Revisited: Institutional Isomorphism and Structural Conformity." *American Sociological Review* 48(2): 147–60.

Dohse, Knuth, Ulrich Jurgens, and Thomas Nailsch. 1985. "From 'Fordism' to 'Toyotism'? The Social Organization of the Labor Process in the Japanese Automobile Industry." *Politics and Society* 14(2): 115–46.

Domhoff, G. William. 2014. *Who Rules America? The Triumph of the Corporate Rich,* 7th ed. New York: McGraw-Hill.

Drucker, Peter. 1971. "What We Can Learn from Japanese Management." *Harvard Business Review* (March). https://hbr.org/1971/03/what-we-can-learn-from -japanese-management (accessed December 10, 2018).

Durham, C. B. 1927. "We Make 1,400% More Cars with 10% More Men." *Magazine of Business* 52 (July): 29–31, 56–64.

Edwards, Charles E. 1965. *Dynamics of the United States Automobile Industry.* Columbia: University of South Carolina Press.

Edwards, Richard. 1979. *Contested Terrain: The Transformation of the Workplace in the Twentieth Century.* New York: Basic Books.

Eisenstein, Paul A. 2018. "GM to Slash over 14,000 Jobs from North American Workforce." *NBC News,* November 26, https://www.nbcnews.com/news/us-news/gm

-slash-over-14-000-jobs-north-american-workforce-n940091 (accessed December 10, 2018).

Engels, Friedrich. [1845] 2010. *Condition of the Working Class in England*. Available at Marx/Engels Internet Archive, https://www.marxists.org/archive/marx/works/download/pdf/condition-working-class-england.pdf (accessed January 29, 2019).

Epstein, Ralph C. 1926. "The Rise and Fall of Firms in the Automobile Industry." *Harvard Business Review* 5 (October): 157–74.

———. 1927. "Leadership in the Automobile Industry, 1903–1924." *Harvard Business Review* 5: 281–92.

———. [1928] 1972. *The Automobile Industry: Its Economic and Social Development*. New York: A. W. Shaw; reprint, New York: Arno.

Estall, R. C. 1985. "Stock Control in Manufacturing: The Just-in-Time System and Its Locational Implications." *Area* 17(2): 129–33.

Fantasia, Rick. 1988. *Cultures of Solidarity: Consciousness, Action, and Contemporary American Workers*. Berkeley: University of California Press.

Faurote, Fay L. 1927. "Henry Ford Still on the Job with Renewed Vigor." *Industrial Management: The Engineering Magazine* 74 (October): 193–202.

Festinger, Leon. 1957. *A Theory of Cognitive Dissonance*. Stanford, Calif.: Stanford University Press.

Fine, Sidney. 1963. *The Automobile under the Blue Eagle*. Ann Arbor: University of Michigan Press.

———. 1969. *Sit-Down: The General Motors Strike of 1936–1937*. Ann Arbor: University of Michigan Press.

Florida, Richard, and Martin Kenney. 1991. "Transplanted Organizations: The Transfer of Japanese Industrial Organization to the U.S." *American Sociological Review* 56(3, June): 381–98.

Flugge, Eva. 1929. "Possibilities and Problems of Integration in the Automobile Industry." *Journal of Political Economy* 37 (April): 150–74.

Ford, Henry. 1922. *My Life and Work*, in collaboration with Samuel Crowther. Garden City, N.Y.: Doubleday.

———. 1926. *Today and Tomorrow*, in collaboration with Samuel Crowther. Garden City, N.Y.: Doubleday, Page and Co.

Ford, Henry, and Samuel Crowther. 1930. *Moving Forward*. Garden City, N.Y.: Doubleday.

Ford Motor Company. 2014. *Ford Motor Company 2014 Annual Report*. https://corporate.ford.com/content/dam/corporate/en/investors/reports-and-filings/Annual%20Reports/2014-ford-annual-report.pdf (accessed January 19, 2019).

Freeland, Robert. 2001. *The Struggle for Control of the Modern Corporation: Organizational Change at General Motors, 1924–1970*. New York: Cambridge University Press.

Fujita, Kuniko, and Richard Child Hill. 1993. "Toyota City: Industrial Organization and the Local State in Japan." In *Japanese Cities in the World Economy*, edited by Kuniko Fujita and Richard Child Hill. Philadelphia: Temple University Press.

————. 1995. "Global Toyotism and Local Development." *International Journal of Urban and Regional Research* 19(1, March): 7–22.

————. 2009. *Japanese Cities*. Philadelphia: Temple University Press.

Galbraith, John Kenneth. 1958. *The Affluent Society*. New York: Harcourt Brace.

Galenson, Walter. 1960. *The CIO Challenge to the AFL: A History of the American Labor Movement, 1933–1941*. Cambridge, Mass.: Harvard University Press.

Gartman, David. 1986. *Auto Slavery: The Labor Process in the American Automobile Industry, 1897–1950*. New Brunswick, N.J.: Rutgers University Press.

General Motors. 2014. *General Motors Annual Report 2014*. http://annualreports.com/HostedData/AnnualReportArchive/g/NYSE_GM_2014.pdf (accessed January 29, 2019).

Geng, Diane. 2005. "GM vs. Toyota by the Numbers." *NPR*, December 19, https://www.npr.org/news/specials/gmvstoyota/ (accessed December 11, 2018).

Gerlach, Michael L. 1992. *Alliances and the Social Organization of Japanese Business*. Berkeley: University of California Press.

Gertler, Meric S. 1994. "'Being There': Proximity, Organization, and Culture in the Development and Adoption of Advanced Manufacturing Technologies." *Economic Geography* 18: 1–26.

Glaberman, Martin. 1980. *Wartime Strikes: The Struggle against the No-Strike Pledge in the UAW during World War II*. Detroit: Bewick.

Hall, Robert W. 1981. *Driving the Productivity Machine: Production and Control in Japan*. Falls Church, Va.: American Production and Inventory Control Society.

Hayashi, Masaki. 1983. "The Japanese Style of Small-Group QC Circles—Circle Activity." *Research Papers* 2 (October). Institute of Business Research, Chuo University, Tokyo.

————. 1989. "QC Circles in Japanese Management." *Shogaku Ronsan: The Journal of Management* 30 (March): 225–48.

Heldt, P. 1933. "Parts Makers' Role Gets Bigger as Automotive History Unfolds." *Automotive Industries* (May 6): 546–48, 554f.

Helper, Susan R. 1987. "Supplier Relations and Technical Change: Theory and Application to the U.S. Automobile Industry." PhD diss., Department of Economics, Harvard University, Cambridge, Mass.

————. 1990. "Comparative Supplier Relations in the U.S. and Japanese Auto Industries: An Exit/Voice Approach." *Business and Economic History* 19 (2nd series): 153–62.

————. 1991a. "An Exit-Voice Analysis of Supplier Relations." In *Morality, Rationality, and Efficiency: New Perspectives on Socio-Economics*, edited by Richard M. Coughlin. New York: M. E. Sharpe.

————. 1991b. "Strategy and Irreversibility in Supplier Relations: The Case of the U.S. Automotive Industry." *Business History Review* 65 (Winter): 781–824.

————. 1991c. "How Much Has Really Changed between U.S. Automakers and Their Suppliers?" *Sloan Management Review* 32 (Summer): 15–28.

Helper, Susan R., and David I. Levine. 1992. "Long-Term Supplier Relations and

Product-Market Structure." *Journal of Law, Economics, and Organization* 8(3): 561–81.

Hill, Richard Child, and Yong Joo Lee. 1994. "Japanese Multinationals and East Asian Development: The Case of the Automobile Industry." In *Capitalism and Development*, edited by Leslie Sklair. London: Routledge.

Hirschman, Albert O. 1970. *Exit, Voice, and Loyalty*. Cambridge, Mass.: Harvard University Press.

Holusha, John. 1982. "U.S. Japanese Wage Gap: Dispute over Its Extent." *New York Times*, January 8.

Hoover, Edgar M. 1948. *The Location of Economic Activity*. New York: McGraw-Hill.

Hounshell, David A. 1984. *From the American System to Mass Production, 1800–1932: The Development of Manufacturing Technology in the United States*. Baltimore: Johns Hopkins University Press.

Howes, Candace. 1993. "Are Japanese Transplants Restoring U.S. Competitiveness or Dumping Their Social Problems in the U.S. Market?" Paper presented to the conference on lean production, Wayne State University, Detroit (March).

Ingrassia, Paul. 2011. *Crash Course: The American Automobile Industry's Road to Bankruptcy and Bailout—and Beyond*. New York: Random House.

Jefferys, Steve. 1986. *Management and Managed: Fifty Years of Crisis at Chrysler*. New York: Cambridge University Press.

Kamata, Satoshi. 1983. *Japan in the Passing Lane: An Insider's Account of Life in a Japanese Auto Factory*, translated by T. Akimoto. New York: Pantheon.

Katz, Harold. 1977. *The Decline of Competition in the Automobile Industry, 1920–1940*. New York: Arno Press.

Kearns, David T., and David A. Nadler. 1992. *Prophets in the Dark: How Xerox Reinvented Itself and Beat Back the Japanese*. New York: Harper Business.

Keenan, Tim, David Smith, and Jon Lowell. 1995. "The Story Behind GM's Costly J-Car Launch." *WardsAuto*, April 1. https://www.wardsauto.com/news-analysis/story-behind-gms-costly-j-car-launch (accessed January 29, 2019).

Keeran, Roger. 1980. *The Communist Party and the Auto Workers' Union*. Bloomington: Indiana University Press.

———. 1989. "The International Workers Order and the Origins of the CIO." *Labor History* 30 (Summer): 385–408.

Keller, Maryann. 1989. *Rude Awakening: The Rise, Fall, and Struggle for Recovery of General Motors*. New York: William Morrow.

Kennedy, Edward D. [1941] 1972. *The Automobile Industry: The Coming of Age of Capitalism's Favorite Child*. New York: Reynal & Hitchcock; reprint, Clifton, N.J.: Augustus M. Kelley.

Kenney, Martin, and Richard Florida. 1993. *Beyond Mass Production: The Japanese System and Its Transfer to the U.S.* New York: Oxford University Press.

Kettering, Charles Franklin, and Allen Orth. 1932. *The New Necessity: The Culmination of a Century of Progress in Transportation*. Baltimore: Williams and Wilkins.

Kimeldorf, Howard. 2013. "Worker Replacement Costs and Unionization: Origins of the U.S. Labor Movement." *American Sociological Review* 78(6): 1055.

Klayman, Ben. 2013. "GM to Buy Back Some Preferred Shares from UAW Trust for $3.2 Billion." *Reuters*, September 23, https://www.reuters.com/article/us-autos -gm-buyback/gm-to-buy-back-some-preferred-shares-from-uaw-trust-for-3-2 -billion-idUSBRE98M0KV20130923 (accessed December 10, 2018).

Klein, Benjamin. 1988. "Vertical Integration as Organizational Ownership: The Fisher Body–General Motors Relationship Revisited." *Journal of Law, Economics, and Organization* 4 (Spring): 199–213.

Klein, Benjamin, Robert G. Crawford, and Armen A. Alchian. 1978. "Vertical Integra- tion, Appropriable Rents, and the Competitive Contracting Process." *Journal of Law and Economics* 21 (October): 297–323.

Klier, Thomas H., and James M. Rubenstein. 2008. *Who Really Made Your Car? Re- structuring and Geographic Change in the Auto Industry*. Kalamazoo, Mich.: W. E. Upjohn Institute for Employment Research.

Knudsen, William S. 1927. "For Economical Transportation: How the Chevrolet Mo- tor Company Applies Its Own Slogan to Production." *Industrial Management* 74 (August): 65–68.

Kraus, Henry. 1947. *The Many and the Few: A Chronicle of the Dynamic Auto Workers*. Los Angeles: Plantin Press.

Kuhn, Arthur J. 1986. *GM Passes Ford, 1918–1938: Designing the General Motors Perfor- mance Control System*. University Park: Pennsylvania State University Press.

Kume, Ikuo. 1998. *Disparaged Success: Labor Politics in Postwar Japan*. Ithaca, N.Y.: Cor- nell University Press.

Kutscher, Ronald E., and Valerie A. Personick. 1986. "Deindustrialization and the Shift to Services." *Monthly Labor Review* (June): 3–13.

LaFever, Mortier W. 1924. "Workers, Machinery, and Production in the Automobile Industry." *Monthly Labor Review* (October): 1–26.

Langfitt, Frank. 2010. "The End of the Line for GM-Toyota Joint Venture." National Public Radio, *All Things Considered*, March 26. http://www.npr.org/templates /story/story.php?storyId=125229157 (accessed December 15, 2017).

Langlois, Richard N., and Paul L. Robertson. 1989. "Explaining Vertical Integration: Lessons from the American Automobile Industry." *Journal of Economic History* 49 (June): 361–75.

Lee, John R. 1916. "The So-Called Profit-Sharing System in the Ford Plant." *Annals of the American Academy of Political and Social Science* 65 (May): 297–310.

Lescohier, Don D. 1937. "Sit-Down Strikes: An Invention of Mediaeval Europe Now Adopted in Present-Day America." *The World Today: Encyclopedia Britannica* 4(4, April): 1–3.

Levin, Doron P. 1991. "Ideas and Trends; Saturn: An Outpost of Change in GM's Steadfast Universe." *New York Times*, March 17.

———. 1992. "Company News; GM Parts Plant Struck; Saturn Halt is Seen." *New York Times*, August 28.

Levin, Samuel M. 1927. "Ford Profit Sharing, 1914–1920," and "The End of Ford Profit Sharing." *Personnel Journal* 6 (August): 75–86, 161–70.

Levinson, Edward. [1938] 1995. *Labor on the March*. Ithaca, N.Y.: ILR Press.

Lewchuk, Wayne. 1987. *American Technology and the British Vehicle Industry.* New York: Cambridge University Press.

Lichtenstein, Nelson. 1980. "Auto Worker Militancy and the Structure of Factory Life, 1937–1955." *Journal of American History* 67 (September): 335–53.

———. 1982. *Labor's War at Home: The CIO in World War II.* New York: Cambridge University Press.

Loomis, Carol. 2006. "The Tragedy of General Motors." *Fortune,* February 6. http://archive.fortune.com/magazines/fortune/fortune_archive/2006/02/20/8369111/index.htm (accessed December 10, 2018).

Lysgaard, Sverre. 1976. *Arbejderkollektivet* [The Worker Collective]. Oslo: Universitetsforlaget.

Mangum, Garth L. 1960. "Taming Wildcat Strikes." *Harvard Business Review* 38(2, March/April): 88–96.

Marx, Karl. [1845] 2000. *The German Ideology.* Available at Marx/Engels Internet Archive, https://www.marxists.org/archive/marx/works/1845/german-ideology/ch01a.htm (accessed January 29, 2019).

———. [1848] 2004. *The Communist Manifesto.* Reprinted in *Marx/Engels Selected Works,* vol. 1. Available at Marx/Engels Internet Archive, https://www.marxists.org/archive/marx/works/1848/communist-manifesto (accessed November 20, 2017).

———. [1852] 1978. "Class Struggle and the Mode of Production." In *The Marx/Engels Reader,* edited by Robert C. Tucker. New York: W. W. Norton.

———. [1857–1861] 1973. *The Gundrisse.* New York: Penguin Books/*New Left Review.*

———. [1867] 1977. *Capital,* vol. 1. New York: Vintage Books.

———. [1891] 1999. "By What Are Wages Determined?" In Karl Marx, *Wage and Labor Capital.* Available at Marx/Engels Internet Archive, https://www.marxists.org/archive/marx/works/1847/wage-labour/ch04.htm (accessed December 10, 2018).

Mayer, Gerald. 2004. "Union Membership Trends in the United States." Washington: Congressional Research Service (August 31).

Mayo, Elton. 1946. *The Human Problems of an Industrial Civilization,* 2nd ed. Boston: Graduate School of Business Administration, Harvard University.

McAdam, Doug. 1982. *Political Process and the Development of the Black Insurgency, 1930–1970.* Chicago: University of Chicago Press.

Meyer, David S., and Nancy Whittier. 1994. "Social Movement Spillover." *Social Problems* 41(2): 277–98.

Meyer, Stephen, III. 1981. *The Five Dollar Day: Labor Management and Social Control in the Ford Motor Company, 1908–1921.* New York: State University of New York Press.

Michels, Robert. 1915. *Political Parties: A Sociological Study of the Oligarchical Tendencies of Modern Democracy,* translated by Eden Paul and Cedar Paul. New York: Free Press.

Milkman, Ruth. 1997. *Farewell to the Factory: Auto Workers in the Late Twentieth Century.* Berkeley: University of California Press.

Mintz, Beth A., and Michael Schwartz. 1985. *The Power Structure of American Business.* Chicago: University of Chicago Press.

Mizruchi, Mark. 1992. *The Structure of Corporate Political Action.* Cambridge, Mass.: Harvard University Press.

Monden, Yasuhiro. 1994. "Total Framework of the Toyota Production System." In Monden, *Toyota Production System: An Integrated Approach to Just-in-Time.* Boston: Springer.

Monks, Robert A. G., and Nell Minow. 2008. *Corporate Governance.* New York: Wiley.

Monthly Labor Review. 1946. "Work Stoppages Caused by Labor-Management Disputes." *Monthly Labor Review* (May).

Morris, Aldon. 1981. "Black Southern Student Sit-In Movement: An Analysis of Internal Organization." *American Sociological Review* 46(6): 744–67.

———. 1986. *Origins of the Civil Rights Movement.* New York: Free Press.

———. 2007. "Naked Power and the Civil Sphere." *Sociological Quarterly* 48: 615–28.

Mortimer, Wyndham. 1971. *Organize! My Life as a Union Man,* edited by Leo Fenster. Boston: Beacon Press.

Muller, Joann. 2014. "Fiat Agrees to Buy Rest of Chrysler from UAW Trust for $4.35 Billion." *Forbes,* January 1, https://www.forbes.com/sites/joannmuller/2014/01/01/fiat-agrees-to-buy-rest-of-chrysler-from-uaw-trust-for-4-35-billion/#1390c5cc7b7c (accessed December 10, 2018).

Murphy, Tom. 2006. "Aluminum Claims No. 2 Ranking." *WardsAuto,* March 10. https://www.wardsauto.com/news-analysis/aluminum-claims-no2-ranking (accessed December 8, 2017).

Murray, Joshua, and Michael Schwartz. 2015. "Moral Economy, Structural Leverage, and Organizational Efficacy: Class Formation and the Great Flint Sit-Down Strike, Detroit 1936–7." *Critical Historical Studies* 2(2): 219–59.

———. 2017a. "Collateral Damage: How Capital's War on Labor Killed Detroit." *Catalyst: A Journal of Theory and Strategy* 1(1): 117–50.

———. 2017b. "The Dialectics of Class Conflict in the Auto Industry: Management by Stress and the Activation of Structural Leverage." *Catalyst: A Journal of Theory and Strategy* 1(3): 151–68.

Naughton, Keith. 2018. "Morgan Stanley Predicts Ford to Cut 25,000 Jobs in Overhaul." *Bloomberg,* December 3, https://www.bloomberg.com/news/articles/2018-12-03/morgan-stanley-predicts-ford-to-cut-25-000-jobs-in-restructuring (accessed December 10, 2018).

Nevins, Allan, and Frank Ernest Hill. 1957. *Ford: Expansion and Challenge, 1915–1933.* New York: Scribner's.

———. 1963. *Ford: Decline and Rebirth, 1933–1962.* New York: Scribner's.

New York Times. 1937. "Sit-Down." *New York Times,* January 2.

Olson, Mancur. 1971. *The Logic of Collective Action.* Cambridge, Mass.: Harvard University Press.

Ouchi, William G. 1981. *Theory Z: How American Business Can Meet the Japanese Challenge.* Reading, Mass.: Addison-Wesley.

Parker, Mike. 2017. "Management-by-Stress: A Reply to Joshua Murray and Michael Schwartz." *Catalyst* 1(2): 173–97.

Parker, Mike, and Jane Slaughter. 1990. "Management-by-Stress: The Team Concept in the U.S. Auto Industry." *Science as Culture* 1: 27–58.

Parkin, Frank. 1979. *Marxism and Class Theory: A Bourgeois Critique.* New York: Columbia University Press.

Perrone, Luca. 1983. "Positional Power and the Propensity to Strike." *Politics and Society* 12(2): 231–61.

———. 1984. "Positional Power, Strikes, and Wages," edited by Erik Olin Wright and Larry J. Griffin. *American Sociological Review* 49(3): 412–26.

Perrucci, Robert. 1994. "Japanese Auto Transplants in the Heartland: Corporatism and Community." Berlin: Aldine de Gruyter.

Peterson, Joyce Shaw. 1981. "Auto Workers and Their Work, 1900–1933." *Labor History* 22(2): 213–36.

Piketty, Thomas. 2014. *Capital in the Twenty-First Century.* Cambridge, Mass.: Belknap Press of Harvard University Press.

Piore, Michael, and Charles Sabel. 1984. *The Second Industrial Divide: Possibilities for Prosperity.* New York: Basic Books.

Piven, Frances Fox, and Richard A. Cloward. 1977. *Poor People's Movements: Why They Succeed, How They Fail.* New York: Vintage.

Porter, Harry Franklin. 1917. "Giving the Men a Share: What It's Doing for Ford." *System* 31 (March): 262–70.

Pound, Arthur. 1934. *The Turning Wheel: The Story of General Motors through Twenty-Five Years, 1908–1933.* New York: Doubleday, Doran and Co.

Preis, Art. 1972. *Labor's Giant Step: Twenty Years of the CIO.* New York: Pathfinder.

Prickett, James R. 1975. "Communists and the Communist Issue in the American Labor Movement, 1920–1950." PhD diss., Department of History, University of California, Los Angeles.

Raff, Daniel M. G., and Lawrence H. Summers. 1987. "Did Henry Ford Pay Efficiency Wages?" *Journal of Labor Economics* 5: S57–86.

Raskob, John J. 1927. "Management the Major Factor in All Industry: How It Enables General Motors to Decentralize Operations and Responsibilities under Coordinated Control." *Industrial Management* 75 (September): 129–35.

Robnett, Belinda. 2000. *How Long, How Long: Women in the Civil Rights Movement.* New York: Oxford University Press.

Roethlisberger, Fritz Jules, and William J. Dickson, with the assistance and collaboration of Harold A. Wright. 1939. *Management and the Worker: An Account of a Research Program Conducted by the Western Electric Company, Hawthorne Works, Chicago.* Cambridge, Mass.: Harvard University Press.

Romo, Frank P., and Michael Schwartz. 1990. "Escape from New York." *Challenge* (January/February): 18–25.

———. 1995. "The Structural Embeddedness of Business Decisions: A Sociological Assessment of the Migration Behavior of Manufacturing Plants in New York

State between 1960 and 1985." *American Sociological Review* 60 (December): 874–907.

Rothschild, Emma. 1973. *Paradise Lost: The Decline of the Auto-Industrial Age.* New York: Random House.

Roy, William, and Rachel Parker-Gwin. 1999. "How Many Logics of Collective Action?" *Theory and Society* 28(2): 203–37.

Rubenstein, James M. 1992. *The Changing U.S. Auto Industry: A Geographical Analysis.* New York: Routledge.

———. 2001. *Making and Selling Cars: Innovation and Change in the U.S. Automotive Industry.* Baltimore: Johns Hopkins University Press.

Saez, Emmanuel, and Gabriel Zucman. 2016. "Wealth Inequality in the United States since 1913: Evidence from Capitalized Income Data." *Quarterly Journal of Economics* 131(2): 519–78.

Saxenian, Annalee. 1990. "Regional Networks and the Resurgence of Silicon Valley." *California Management Review* 33 (Fall): 89–112.

———. 1994. *Regional Advantage: Culture and Competition in Silicon Valley and Route 128.* Cambridge, Mass.: Harvard University Press.

Sayles, Leonard R. 1954. "Wildcat Strikes." *Harvard Business Review* 32 (November/December): 42–52.

Schonberger, Richard J. 1982. *Japanese Manufacturing Techniques: Nine Hidden Lessons in Simplicity.* New York: Free Press.

Schwartz, Michael. 1976. *Radical Protest and Social Structure.* New York: Academic.

———. 1992. "Japanese Enterprise Groups: Some American Parallels." *Shoken Keizai* 180: 123–32.

———. 2011. "The Egyptian Uprising: The Mass Strike in the Time of Neoliberal Globalization." *New Labor Forum* 20(3, Fall): 33–43.

Scott, Jerome F., and George C. Homans. 1947. "Reflections on the Wildcat Strikes." *American Sociological Review* 54 (June): 278–87.

Seltzer, Lawrence H. 1928. *Financial History of the American Automobile Industry.* Boston: Houghton Mifflin.

Sheard, Paul. 1983. "Auto-Production Systems in Japan: Organizational and Locational Features." *Australian Geographical Studies* 21 (April): 49–68.

Sherk, James. 2008. "Auto Bailout Ignores Excessive Labor Costs." *Heritage Foundation,* November 19. https://www.heritage.org/jobs-and-labor/report/auto-bailout-ignores-excessive-labor-costs (accessed January 29, 2019).

Shimokawa, Koichi. 1985. "Japan's *Keiretsu* System: The Case of the Automobile Industry." *Japanese Economic Studies* 13(4): 3–31.

———. 1994. *The Japanese Automobile Industry: A Business History.* London: Athlone Press.

Shower, C. J. 1918. "Guiding the Workman's Expenditures." *Automotive Industries* 38 (March 14): 539–41, 547.

Silver, Beverly J. 2003. *Forces of Labor: Workers' Movements and Globalization since 1870.* New York: Cambridge University Press.

Simon, Herbert. 1957. "A Behavioral Model of Rational Choice." In *Models of Man, Social and Rational: Mathematical Essays on Rational Human Behavior in a Social Setting*. New York: Wiley.

————. 1991. "Bounded Rationality and Organizational Learning." *Organization Science* 2(1): 125–34.

Sloan, Alfred P., Jr. 1941. *Adventures of a White-Collar Man*, in collaboration with Boyden Sparkes. New York: Doubleday.

————. 1963. *My Years with General Motors*. Garden City, N.Y.: Doubleday.

Smitka, Michael. 1990. "The Invisible Handshake: The Development of the Japanese Auto Parts Industry." *Business and Economic History* 19: 163–71.

————. 1991. *Competitive Ties: Subcontracting in the Japanese Automotive Industry*. New York: Columbia University Press.

Snavely, Brent. 2017. "GM Earns $9.43 Billion in 2016; UAW Workers Get Record Profit Sharing." *Detroit Free Press*, February 7, https://www.freep.com/story/money/cars/general-motors/2017/02/07/gm-2016-profit-sharing/97572540/ (accessed December 10, 2018).

Sorensen, Charles F. 1956. *My Forty Years with Ford*. New York: W. W. Norton.

Spilerman, Seymour. 1976. "Structural Characteristics of Cities and the Severity of Radical Disorders." *American Sociological Review* 41(5): 771–93.

Steeves, Kathleen. 1987. "Workers and New Technology: The Ford Motor Company Highland Park Plant, 1910–1916." Unpublished diss., George Washington University, Washington, D.C.

Stepan-Norris, Judith, and Maurice Zeitlin. 1996. *Talking Union*. Urbana: University of Illinois Press.

————. 2003. *Left Out: Reds and America's Industrial Unions*. Cambridge: Cambridge University Press.

Stillman, K. W. 1927. "Hand-to-Mouth Buying: What Has It Done—and What Will It Do?" *Automotive Industries* 57 (July 2): 1–4.

Storper, Michael, and Richard Walker. 1989. *The Capitalist Imperative: Territory, Technology, and Industrial Growth*. New York: Basil Blackwell.

Streeck, Wolfgang. 1986 "Industrial Relations and Industrial Change: The Restructuring of the World Automobile Industry in the 1970s and 1980s." *Economic Analysis and Workers' Management* 22: 437–62.

Sugrue, Thomas. 1996. *The Origins of the Urban Crisis: Race and Inequality in Postwar Detroit*. Princeton, N.J.: Princeton University Press.

Sward, Keith. 1947. *The Legend of Henry Ford*. New York: Rinehart & Co.

Taylor, Alex. 2010. *Sixty to Zero: An Inside Look at the Collapse of General Motors—and the Detroit Auto Industry*. New Haven, Conn.: Yale University Press.

Thomas, Robert Paul. 1973. "Style Change and the Automobile Industry during the Roaring Twenties." In *Business Enterprise and Economic Change: Essays in Honor of Harold F. Williams*, edited by Louis P. Cain and Paul J. Uselding. Kent, Ohio: Kent State University Press.

Thompson, E. P. 1971. "The Moral Economy of the English Crowd in the Eighteenth Century." *Past and Present* 50 (February): 76–136.

Thompson, George V. 1954. "Intercompany Technical Standardization in the Early American Automobile Industry." *Journal of Economic History* 14 (Winter): 1–20.

Tilly, Charles, and Edward Shorter. 1974. *Strikes in France.* New York: Cambridge University Press.

Torigian, Michael. 1999. "The Occupation of the Factories: Paris 1936, Flint 1937." *Comparative Studies in Society and History* 41(2): 324–47.

Toyoda, Eiji. 1985. *Toyota: Fifty Years in Motion.* New York: Kodansha International.

Toyota Motor Corporation. 1967. *Toyota: A History of the First 30 Years.* Toyota City: Toyota Motor Corporation (in Japanese).

Useem, Michael. 1984. *The Inner Circle: Large Corporations and the Rise of Business Political Activity in the U.S. and U.K.* New York: Oxford University Press.

Vernon, Raymond T. 1966. "International Investment and International Trade in the Product Life Cycle." *Quarterly Journal of Economics* 80 (May): 190–207.

Vincent, Melvin J. 1937. "The Sit-Down Strike." *Sociology and Social Research* 21 (July/August): 524–33.

Vlasic, Bill. 2008. "UAW Makes Concessions to Help Automakers." *New York Times,* December 3, http://www.nytimes.com/2008/12/04/business/04auto.html?_r=0 (accessed December 11, 2018).

Walsh, J. Raymond. 1937. *CIO: Industrial Unionism in Action.* New York: W. W. Norton & Co.

Weber, Alfred. 1929. *Alfred Weber's Theory of the Location of Industries.* From *Uber den Standort der Industrien* [1909], translated by C. J. Friedrich. Chicago: University of Chicago Press.

Wells, L. T., Jr. 1980. "The International Product Life Cycle and U.S. Regulation of the Auto Industry." In *Government, Technology, and the Future of the Automobile,* edited by Douglas H. Ginsburg and William J. Abernathy. New York: McGraw-Hill.

Wimmer, Englebert. 2011. *Motoring the Future: VW and Toyota Vying for Pole Position.* Basingstoke, U.K.: Palgrave Macmillan.

Williams, Karel, Colin Haslam, and John Williams. 1992. "Ford Versus 'Fordism': The Beginning of Mass Production?" *Work, Employment, and Society* 6(4): 517–55.

Williams, Karel, Colin Haslam, John Williams, Andy Adcroft, and Sukhdev Johal. 1993. "The Myth of the Line: Ford's Production of the Model T at Highland Park, 1909–16." *Business History* 35(3): 66–87.

———. 1994. *Cars: Analysis, History, Cases.* New York: Berghahn Books.

Womack, James P., Daniel T. Jones, and Daniel Roos. 1990. *The Machine That Changed the World.* New York: Maxwell MacMillan International.

Wright, Erik Olin. 2000. "Working-Class Power, Capitalist-Class Interests, and Class-Compromise." *American Journal of Sociology* 105(4): 957–1002.

Young, Kevin A., Tarun Banerjee, and Michael Schwartz. 2018. "Capital Strikes as Corporate Political Strategy: The Structural Power of Business in the Obama Era." *Politics and Society* 46(1): 3–28.

Zeitlin, Maurice. 1974. "Corporate Ownership and Control: The Large Corporation and the Capitalist Class." *American Journal of Sociology* 79: 1073–1119.

Zetka, James R., Jr. 1994. *Militancy, Market Dynamics, and Workplace Authority: The*

Struggle over Labor Process Outcomes in the U.S. Automobile Industry, 1946 to 1973.
Albany: State University of New York Press.

———. 1995. "Union Homogenization and the Organizational Foundations of
Plantwide Militancy in the U.S. Automobile Industry, 1959–1979." *Social Forces*
73(3, March): 789–807.

INDEX

Boldface numbers refer to figures and tables.

Abernathy, William J.: on aluminum engines, 27; on decentralization, 162; on disc brakes, 26; *Industrial Renaissance*, 14–15; on innovation, 34, 165, **166**, 226–227*n*21; on production inefficiency, 4, 32

Adamic, Louis, 130

Addes, George, 125

aircraft manufacture, 225*n*152

Altshuler, Alan, 35

American Federation of Labor (AFL), 128–129, 143, 147

Ananich, John, 135

annual model changes, 53–54, 59, 92

Asanuma, Banri, 22, 89

assembly line system: branch plants for, 185–186; in early U.S. auto industry, 8, 39–47, 51–52, 213*n*3; innovation and, 57; mechanization of, 52; spread of, 83; in steel mill practice, 87; turnover rate of employees and, 8, 201, 224*n*123; V-8 engines and, 48; work pace and, 111–112, 120–121

Association of Licensed Automobile Manufactures, 84

auto design: adapting branch plants to changes in, 70–74; annual model changes, 53–54, 59, 92; body form, 41, 88, 170–171, 218*n*137; body-on-chassis, 27–28; brakes, 26, 45; clutch improvements, 93; early U.S. auto makers and, 40, 44, 60–63, 76–79; engineering hours for, 34–35; fuel efficiency and, 26, 28, 169–170, 189; glass and, 27–28, 60–61, 63–64, 66–67, 94; luxury cars and, 79–81; rustproofing machine, 49–50; size and, 169–170; standardization of parts and, 84–85; worker commitment and, 49–50. *See also* engines

automakers: class conflict and, 147–153, 210*n*24 (*see also* class conflict and flexible production); cultural differences and, 5–6, 167–169; defined, 209*n*12; flexible production, abandonment of, 187–198; Great Depression and, 117–118; labor unions, undermining, 9–11, 123–124, 141–144, 147–153 (*see also* dispersed parallel production); personnel evaluations and, 106–108, 220*n*23; power differentials and, 108–109; supplier relations (*see* supplier relations); trust of workers and, 191–192, 194–197, 201, 203; work process, control of, 111–112, 120–121, 150–153, 192. *See also* Big Three U.S. automakers; *specific automakers*

supply keiretsu: American supplier relations compared, 36–37, 86–90, 93; informal commitments of, 29–30; overview of, 17–19, 211*n*7
Supreme Court, on sit-down strikes, 142–143
suspension systems, 45, 48

Takeishi, Akira, 212–213*nn*48–49
tariffs, 33, 207, 211*n*12, 227*n*33
tax cuts, 203, 207
Taylor, Alex, 167
Thompson, George V., 85
tires, 60–61, 63–66, 129–131
Toyoda, Eiji, 95, 177, 186–187, 219*n*161
Toyo Kogyo. *See* Mazda
Toyota: company culture of, 103–104; effort bargains of, 176–184; flexible production, origins of, 95–97, 186–187, 219*n*156; geographic concentration of production, 18–19, 21; inventory turnover ratios, 56; job security at, 177, 179–181, 228*n*12; just-in-time delivery system of, 15–16, 211*n*6; labor costs and, 32; long-term sole suppliers of, 21–23, 29; strikes at, 176–178; take-over of GM's Fremont factory, 7
Toyota Auto Body, 109
Toyota City, 18–19, 173, 187
Toyotism: accident and suicide rates, 106; benefits of, 181; competition of, 107–108; creation of, 95; explanation of, 219*n*156; power differential in, 108; strikes resulting from, 176
trade, 10, 170, 203. *See also* tariffs
Travis, Bob, 135–136
Treaty of Detroit, 163–164
trial-and-error learning, 25, 47, 50, 198. *See also* innovation
Trump, Donald, 12, 203–204, 206–207

UBS (Unione Sindacale di Base), 205
unemployment, 117–120. *See also* layoffs and furloughs

unit body construction, 27–28
United Auto Workers (UAW): beginning of, 122–123*n*87, 123–126; bureaucratization of, 226*n*2; as cause of decline of auto industry, 6–7, 32, 34; community relations and, 123; concessions gained by government auto task force, 209*n*4; culture of, 6–7; Jobs Bank Program, 197–198, 205–206; no-strike pledge, 143, 147–148, 152, 163; Obama-era bailout of auto companies and, 205–206; sit-down strikes, 126–133; on unequal wages, 148. *See also* Great Flint Strike
United Rubber Workers, 130–131
unskilled labor, 103–104
upholstery, 62–63
upward mobility, 105, 106–107, 181

V-8 engines, 48, 86–87
violence, 139–141, 224*n*129
Vlasic, Bill, 32
Volkswagen, 169–170

wages and benefits: bailout, effect on, 204–205; company profits and, 195; cuts to, 119, 205; death benefits, 116; Five Dollar Day and effort bargains, 8, 111–117, 221*n*39, 224*n*123; Great Depression and, 118–121; housing programs, 115–116; Industrial Mutual Association for, 122–123; inequality in, 148; Japanese auto industry and, 176–179; medical benefits, 115–116; retirement benefits, 205; Sociology Department of Ford, 221*n*50; Toyotism and, 181–182; of union vs. non-union workers, 32. *See also* effort bargains
Wagoner, Richard, 1–2, 196
Wait, E. F., 65
Walker, Richard, 61
welfare services from auto companies, 115–116, 119, 122–123, 221*n*50
Wibel, A. M., 46, 91

wildcat strikes: abandonment of flexible production and, 101, 154–155, 159, 175, 184, 191, 201; causes of, 147; class consciousness and, 149; decline in, 164–165, 225n157; defined, 9; democracy of unions and, 146–147, 152; dispersed parallel production and, 164–165; effectiveness of, 9, 151–153, 163–164; labor contracts and, 163

Williams, Karel, 112

Womack, James, 213n3

Woodcock, Leonard, 153

worker commitment: concession to maintain, 102; in early U.S. auto industry, 49–50; effort levels and, 111; flexible production and, 200; Great

Depression and, 120; just-in-time delivery and, 16; machine flexibility and, 17; stress of, 104–106; trial-and-error learning and, 25. *See also* effort bargains

workers. *See* auto workers

work groups, 105, 106–107, 194

World War II: abandonment of flexible production and, 9, 157–159; auto industry used for war production, 147, 225n152, 225n158; strikes during, 149, 151, 159, 163 (*see also* Great Flint Strike); worker leverage during, 142–147

Wright, Erik Olin, 220n5

Zetka, James, 164, 225n157

Zimmerschied, Karl W., 217n125